I0814478

Louis XIV's Marshals of France

Louis XIV's Marshals of France

Servants of the Sun King

James Falkner

AN IMPRINT OF PEN & SWORD BOOKS LTD.
YORKSHIRE – PHILADELPHIA

First published in Great Britain in 2025 by
Pen & Sword Military
An imprint of
Pen & Sword Books Ltd
Yorkshire - Philadelphia

ISBN 978 1 39906 266 4

A CIP catalogue record for this book is available from the British Library.

Typeset in INDIA by IMPEC eSolutions
Printed and bound in England by CPI (UK) Ltd.

The Publisher's authorised representative in the EU for product safety is Authorised Rep Compliance Ltd., Ground Floor, 71 Lower Baggot Street, Dublin D02 P593, Ireland.

www.arccompliance.com

For a complete list of Pen & Sword titles please contact

PEN & SWORD BOOKS LIMITED
47 Church Street, Barnsley, South Yorkshire, S70 2AS, England
E-mail: enquiries@pen-and-sword.co.uk
Website: www.pen-and-sword.co.uk

or

PEN AND SWORD BOOKS
1950 Lawrence Rd, Havertown, PA 19083, USA
E-mail: uspen-and-sword@casematepublishers.com
Website: www.penandswordbooks.com

Contents

List of Plates

Preface

During the long years of the reign of King Louis XIV of France, 1663–1714, no fewer than sixty-seven Marshals of France were in post at one time or another, although some of these stalwarts were inherited, having been appointed during the reign of his father, Louis XIII (see Appendix 1 for detailed list); the remarkable humbly-born Abraham de Fabert being one such notable. The great ill-fated warrior Viscount Turenne was another, while at the other end of the scale a valiant few soldiered on for many years into the reign of the Sun King's great-grandson, Louis XV, most prominently perhaps the brilliant but wilful Gascon-born Villars, and the English-born Duke of Berwick (himself the son of a king, albeit on the wrong side of the blanket).

To be a Marshal of France was to hold an exalted and highly regarded position to which many aspired and relatively few were admitted, able to be addressed by their king as 'Cousin'. This prestigious French office of state had been instituted in 1185 during the reign of King Philippe III, and to become a marshal was to hold the appointment as such direct from the monarch. Although not, initially at any rate, a specific military rank as such, it being awarded signified long, valued and notable service to the crown. It also signified the possession of considerable talents as a field commander, although, inevitably, some individuals were more gifted in this respect than others.

The first few years of young Louis XIV's reign were bedevilled by open revolt by over-mighty subjects, in the fractious and self-indulgent civil wars known as the 1st and 2nd 'Frondes' (stemming from a nickname for a street-urchin game played in Paris, despite official disapproval). The king's remarkable achievement, once the reins of power were safely in his own hands, was over time to firmly bind to himself the loyalty and energies of the highly ambitious, skilful, but potentially dangerous, men who made up the marshalate at the time. Loyalty to the crown was not, yet, an automatic trait to be taken as read, and it was said that at the outset, 'Within his kingdom lay hidden another more powerful kingdom'.[1] These men were plainly powerful and strong-willed soldiers, with armies at their back who often served for extended periods, loyal principally to their commanders, who might in time become a threat both to centralized authority and the crown itself, although it can be seen in retrospect that this kind of freebooting self-seeking belonged largely to an earlier age than the one into which the astute young Louis XIV was moving. 'Nonetheless, the French army as it stood in the early 1660's lacked discipline and cohesion, [while] provincial governors treated their garrisons and strongholds as though they belonged to them.'[2] The inherent dangers of such a thing were obvious, and the troubles of the Frondes taught the king an unforgettable lesson. In 1653, Louis XIV first accompanied Marshal Turenne at the siege of Sainte-Menhould, and the venture, which sparked a pronounced liking for the military life, was a powerful formative experience, and for many years he would accompany his marshals on their campaigns, often with a large and appropriately glittering retinue.

In the event, the effectiveness of ruthless and firmly established bureaucracy, with able Secretaries of State in place and entrusted with formidable powers, was a highly effective brake on any wayward personal ambitions of army commanders that might, given time, grow beyond acceptable bounds. As an early practical measure, amongst the first acts of Louis XIV on taking power into his own hands was to disband many units whose usefulness or loyalty was in doubt, or which had been inactive for some time, even though often their absent officers had happily continued to draw their pay with punctilious regularity, apparently looking upon this arrangement as a kind of sinecure to which they were entitled.

That the early reforms to administration and discipline instigated by Louis XIV, and especially those overseen by his most formidable Minister for War, François-Michel le Tellier, Marquis de Louvois, were highly effective, can be seen in the opening moves of the unprovoked French attack on the United Provinces of Holland in 1672. The army mustered at Charleroi for the campaign that spring was reported to comprise 8,000 of the elite Maison du Roi, 56,000 infantry of the line, and 25,000 cavalry, all units comprised only of French troops, In addition, there were a further 30,000 soldiers recruited from abroad, notably the Catholic cantons of Switzerland and certain Italian and German states, together with 6,000 English hired from King Charles II in London. There was also formidable train of artillery with ninety-seven guns and mortars. An observer noted that, 'Never had one seen an army so magnificent and at the same time so disciplined'.[3]

Then there were the army indendants, each one an able civilian administrator with wide responsibility and powers, and answerable only to the minister for war, and specifically not to the army commander they accompanied on any particular campaign. Having no outright military responsibility during active operations, but active in ensuring the smooth functioning and well-being of the army and the troops when in quarters or at rest, their presence helped ensure that no one marshal became too mighty a subject, or too ambitious for personal gain other than in pursuit of the wider and over-riding objectives of the king and the state.

> It was the general's prerogative to have the final authority during the campaign. But, when the army had concluded the active phase of fighting and entered into winter quarters

> or the occupation of territory, it was the Intendant who was to have the final disposition of things. He was to consult the general and listen to his advice, but he did not need to have the general's formal consent to things. Civilians gained this power partly because they were more efficient administrators, but also because the government did not trust its military officers to levy impositions, fix rations, distribute pay, or arrange lodgings . . . Moreover, the crown did not want the generals to use occupied territory as a power base where they could control patronage and make themselves independent.[4]

That there was scope for friction between highly opinionated army commanders and their appointed intendants was obvious, but their abilities were put to good use. When Turenne set off on his famous march in mid-winter in late 1674, taking the road that led to battles at Mulhouse and Turkheim, the relevant intendant was tasked to ensure that, even at this late season, the troops had food, fodder and forage, and did so efficiently and at remarkably short notice. In addition, 'Louvois added his considerable administrative skills to the task, commanding intendants of neighbouring provinces to gather oats and dry forage to feed the army's horses'.[5] Nonetheless, a growing and persistent shortage of funds, despite widespread tax-gathering arrangements, was a concern, and this was attributed, at first, to the relative inexperience of Louvois, who underestimated the demands that embarking on a war would present. This was not a problem that could be wished away, or ignored, and during the War of Devolution in 1667, an intendant would write that, 'By not paying the soldiers, it is impossible to keep them in rigorous discipline'.[6]

The activities of the notably headstrong Louis de Bourbon, Prince of Condé, and other nobles during the Fronde civil wars, taught lessons that were clearly not about to be forgotten in Vincennes, Fontainebleau and subsequently Versailles. In this regard, the army intendants were required to report to the minister for war on the actions, and even the trains of thought, as far as that was possible, of the army commanders they accompanied. Louvois once wrote to an intendant in this vein 'You will see by the copy of my letter, what the king ordered me to tell him. Please take care to inform me if he executes those intentions of his majesty that I have made known to him.'[7] The king's own instructions were often no less pointed – a marshal might argue his case, to a degree and with passion but no further – and on a particular occasion Louis XIV wrote to one of the best, Louis-Guillaume de Villars, when he had thought fit to question an order, 'You have my last letter on the subject . . . You must apply yourself'.[8]

It is clear that the king chose his servants well, and treated and rewarded them equally well, and this was fully reciprocated in all but a scant handful of cases, yet there was always an element of steel in the relationship, no matter how senior and favoured a marshal might become. This can be seen when Louis XIV wrote to one of his principal army commanders after a particularly stormy meeting, at which the king's decision on a certain issue had been challenged, 'I was master of myself, the day before yesterday, to conceal from you the sorrow I felt at hearing a man whom I have overwhelmed with benefits talk to me in the fashion you did . . . Profit thereby, and do not risk vexing me again.'[9]

With so many marshals in place over a span of Louis XIV's 71-year reign, to attempt to describe the careers and characters of them all would be an overly monumental task, risking fragmentation, a lack of focus, and potential fatigue to the reader. Accordingly, I have chosen a select few, just twelve, to concentrate on their careers, ambitions and achievements, together with a quiet look into their private lives, each one so intriguing and yet so different from the other. In the process of this selection some notable names, such as Ferté-Sennetière, Bellefonds, d'Humieres and Tessé, will be found to be largely absent, other than for occasional passing references, for this selection was certainly a subjective exercise. Nonetheless, the picture presented is undeniably vivid, covering an extraordinarily wide span of years of military campaigning. There will also be noticed a bias towards the later years of the reign, and this is deliberate and surely appropriate. Those years of armed conflict over whether a French prince or an Austrian archduke should occupy the throne of Spain were ones of acute peril and potential catastrophe to France, which left an ageing king in his wonderful palace at Versailles, declaring on his deathbed that he had loved war too much. This struggle, which saw the then current Marshals of France perform remarkable feats when under the greatest pressure, while fighting John Churchill, 1st Duke of Marlborough, and Prince Eugene of Savoy, opponents who could themselves justly lay claim to be true masters of the field, constitutes a quite unique and lengthy passage of arms that rightly continues to attract wide attention and admiration.

I have included as an Introduction, a brief account of the wars in which the Sun King was involved, both to set the scene and to add detail for a proper consideration of the careers and impact of those marshals that I have chosen to discuss and portray. A certain element of repetition may therefore be detected, as the campaigns and the careers involved inevitably overlapped to a degree, but I hope that this is not excessive. Each chapter is by its nature biographical and focussed, and so can stand alone, so that it is hoped that the exploits of these great men will, accordingly, be able to be seen clearly and in their proper context.

Chronology of the Reign of King Louis XIV

(Principal events only)

1638 Louis born in Fontainebleau.

1643 Louis XIII dies, Louis XIV succeeds, with his mother, Queen Anne, and Cardinal Mazarin heading a regency.

1648 Treaty of Westphalia brings the Thirty Years War to an end. Fronde civil wars begin against the regency and centralized authority. Spain gets involved.

1653 Fronde civil wars cease, but Franco-Spanish hostilities continue.

1659 The Treaty of the Pyrenees ends war between France and Spain. Louis XIV's marriage to the Infanta of Spain, Maria-Thérèse.

1661 Louis XIV begins personal reign on death of Cardinal Mazarin.

1667 The War of Devolution (the Queen's Rights) begins, France invades Spanish Netherlands, and Lille captured.

1668 The Triple Alliance formed by Holland, Sweden and England, to counter French aggression. The Treaty of Aix-la-Chapelle ends the war between France and Spain.

1670 The Treaty of Dover signed between Louis XIV and Charles II of England. French occupation of Lorraine.

1672 The Anglo-Dutch war begins, with Louis XIV subsequently declaring war on Holland. Inundation of much of the Dutch countryside.

1673 French troops capture Dutch-held Maastricht. The naval battle of the Texel.

1674 The Treaty of Westminster brings Anglo-Dutch War to a close.
Turenne and Condé victorious against Dutch and allies at Sinzheim, Seneffe and Ensheim. Occupation of the Franche-Comte.

1675 Turenne succeeds at Turkheim, subsequently mortally wounded. French seizure of Kehl. Revolt in Brittany.

1676 Willliam of Orange fails to re-take Maastricht. Battles of Stromboli and Palermo.
Sieges of Phillipsburg and Valenciennes.

1677 French capture Valenciennes, St Ghislain, St Omer, Bouchain, Cambrai and Freiburg, successful in battle at Mont Cassel and Kockersberg.

1678 Ghent and Ypres captured by the French. William of Orange defeated at St Denis. 1st Treaty of Nijmegen ends France's war with Holland. 2nd Treaty of Nijmegen ends the war with Spain.

1679 'Chamber [War] of Reunions' created, to regularise the borders of north and eastern France, by obliging major cities to acknowledge Louis XIV.

1681 French blockade of Luxembourg. Dragonnades against Huguenots. The French seize Strasbourg, and Louis XIV purchases Casale in northern Italy from the Duke of Mantua.

1683 Louis XIV threatens to invade Spanish Netherlands, Spain declares war on France.
Ottoman siege of Vienna defeated.

1684 French capture Luxembourg. The Truce of Ratisbon ends the war.

1685 Revocation of the Edict of Nantes, so that many Huguenots flee France.

1686 The League of Augsburg formed between Austria, Sweden and German states.
Capture of Buda (Ofen) from the Ottomans by Austria. Campaign against Vaudois rebels in Savoy-Piedmont.

1687 Ottomans defeated by Austria at Battle of 2nd Mohacs (Berg Hazan).

1688 The French capture Phillipsburg and Mannheim. Holland declares war on France; the Nine Years War begins. William of Orange arrives in England to take the throne.

1689 The Grand Alliance formed between England, Holland, Austria and Savoy. Devastation of much of the Palatinate by French forces. Mainz and Bonn seized by Imperial troops.

1690 Marshal Luxembourg victorious at Fleurus. Duke Victor-Amadeus II of Savoy defeated by the French at Staffarda.

1691 French troops capture Mons, Liège and Nice. Luxembourg successful at Leuze engagement.

1692 Seizure of Namur by French troops. Naval battles of Barfleur-La Hogue.
Largely inconclusive Battle of Steinkirk between William III and Luxembourg.

1693 Heidelberg, Huy and Charleroi taken by the French. William III defeated at Landen by Luxembourg. Catinat defeats Duke Victor-Amadeus of Savoy at Marsaglia.

1694 The Spanish beaten at Battle of the Ter, and Gerona seized by the French.
Allied landing at Camaret Bay defeated. William III captures Dixmuide, Deynse, and Huy.

1695 Casale taken by Savoyard troops. The Allies re-capture Namur. Brussels bombarded.

1696 The Treaty of Turin ends war between France and Savoy.

1697 The French capture Ath, and Barcelona. The Treaty of Ryswick ends the Nine Years War. Defeat of the Ottomans at Zenta in Hungary.

1698 The 1st Partition Treaty agreed on the impending succession to the throne in Spain.

1699 Death of Prince Joseph-Ferdinand of Bavaria.

1700 2nd Partition Treaty agreed between France, Holland and England.

King Carlos II of Spain dies having named the Duc d'Anjou as his successor.

1701 The French defeated in Italy at Carpi and Chiari by Prince Eugene. Louis XIV sends French troops to occupy key barrier towns in the Spanish Netherlands.

A Treaty of Grand Alliance agreed between Austria, England and Holland.

1702 The Battle of Cremona, death of William III, declaration of war on France by the Grand Alliance. Marlborough to command of Anglo-Dutch forces. Bavaria allies to France. Anglo-Dutch troops take Kaiserwerth and Liège, siege of Landau. Camisard uprising in France. Battles of Luzzara, Cadiz, and Vigo Bay. Villars successful at Friedlingen.

1703 Anglo-Portuguese Treaty signed. The Allies take Bonn and Huy. Dutch defeated at Eckeren. French capture Kehl. Austrian defeat at Höchstädt, French gain Speyerbach and Landau. Siege of Limburg. Savoy joins the Grand Alliance. Rebellion in Hungary.

1704 Seizure of Gibraltar by the Allies. Allied victories at the Schellenberg and Blenheim, and subsequent capture of Landau and Trarbach. Villars quells Camisard rebellion.

1705 Death of Leopold I, Joseph becomes emperor. Allied loss and recapture of Huy. French beaten at Elixheim. Narrow French success in Battle at Cassano, sieges of Barcelona and Badajoz.

1706 Berwick captures Nice, French success in battle at Calcinato, but defeats at Ramillies and Turin. Allied sieges of Menin, Antwerp, Ostend and Dendermonde.

1707 Treaty (Convention) of Milan between Austria, Savoy and France enables Louis XIV to withdraw garrisons from Italy. Marshal Villars raids central Germany, failure of Allied attack on Toulon. French victory at Almanza. British capture Minorca.

1708 The French capture Ghent and Bruges but suffer defeat at Oudenarde. Allied siege of Lille. Sardinia captured by the Allies. Ghent and Bruges retaken. The Great Frost strikes northern Europe.

1709 Swedish defeat at Poltava. Siege of Tournai, Battle of Malplaquet, loss of Mons by the French.

1710 Capture of Douai, Bethune, St Venant and Aire by Marlborough. Allied successes in Spain at Almenara and Saragossa, but French and Spanish victories at Brihuega and Villaviciosa.

1711 Capture of Bouchain by Marlborough. Archduke Charles succeeds his brother Joseph on Imperial throne. Marlborough dismissed by Queen Anne.

1712 Villars' victory at Denain over Prince Eugene. French recapture Marchiennes, Douai, Le Quesnoy and Bouchain. British troops withdrawn from campaign.

1713 The French retake Landau. Treaty of Utrecht agreed between Great Britain, Holland, Portugal, Savoy and France. Siege of Freiburg.

1714 The Treaty of Rastadt agreed between France and Austria. Treaty of Baden agreed between France and Austria. Franco-Dutch Treaty agreed.

1715 The French capture Minorca. Death of Louis XIV, succeeded by his great-grandson, Louis XV. Regency begins under Philippe, Duc d'Orleans, subsequent period of uncertainty with near national bankruptcy.

1717 Austrian capture of Belgrade from the Ottomans.
1719 War of the Quadruple Alliance, Spain defeated.
1730 Outbreak of the War of the Polish Succession.
1736 Prince Eugene dies in Vienna. Berwick killed at siege of Phillipsburg.

Notes on dating, spelling and grammar

In the seventeenth and early eighteenth century the Julian Calendar was in use in the British Isles, while on the Continent the newer Gregorian Calendar was used. From 1700 onwards the new system (N.S.) was 11 days ahead of the old system (O.S.). As most of the events described in this book took place on mainland Europe, (N.S.) has been used throughout for dating, unless stated otherwise. The often idiosyncratic and erratic spelling and grammar used in many contemporary accounts quoted in this book have been corrected for greater clarity, sensitively it is hoped, with additional explanatory comments, where these seem to be needed, inserted in square brackets.

Ranks terminology

The term 'Marechal de Camp' will be found mentioned on several occasions. This rank was akin to that of a major-general in the British Army; subordinate to a lieutenant-general, but superior to a brigadier (not in itself regarded a general rank as such). The less prestigious appointment of 'Mestre de Camp' was approximate to that of a British full colonel.

Maps

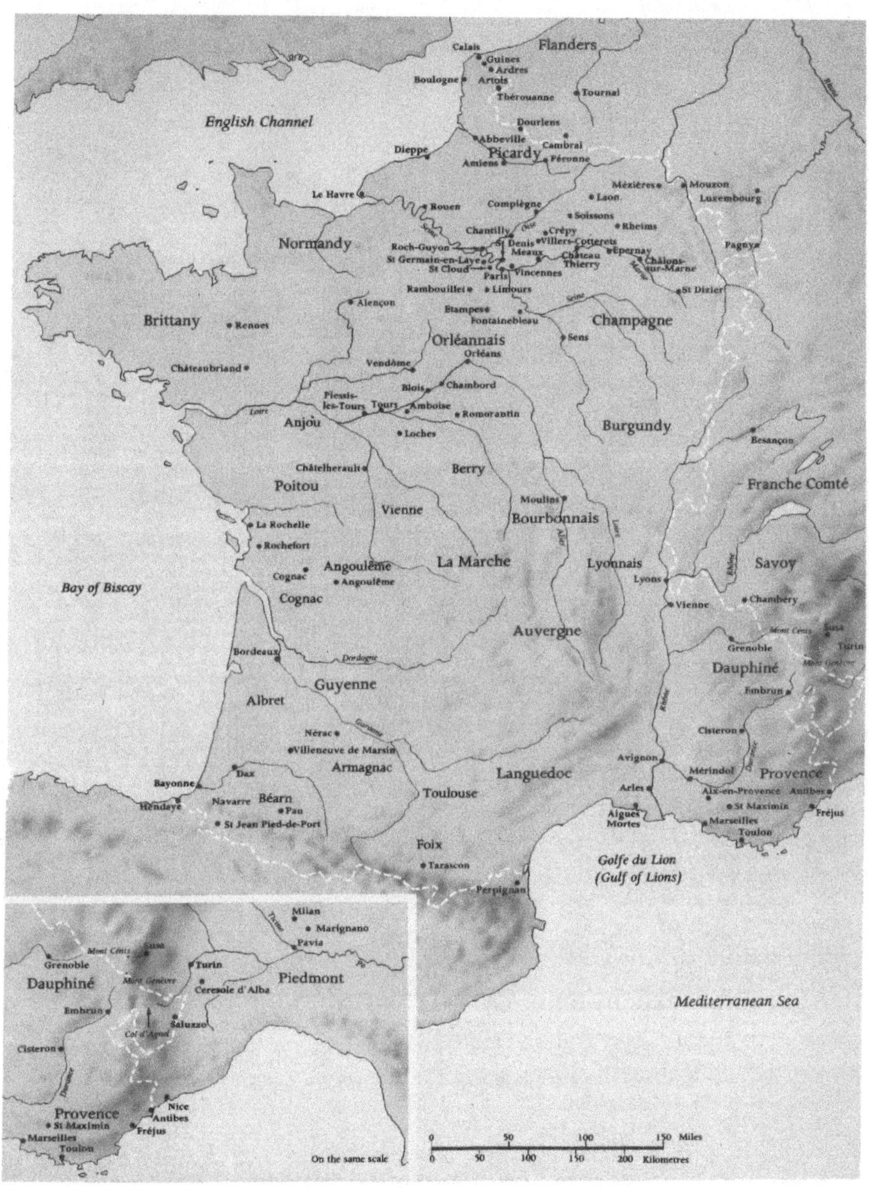

Map 1: France in the seventeenth century.

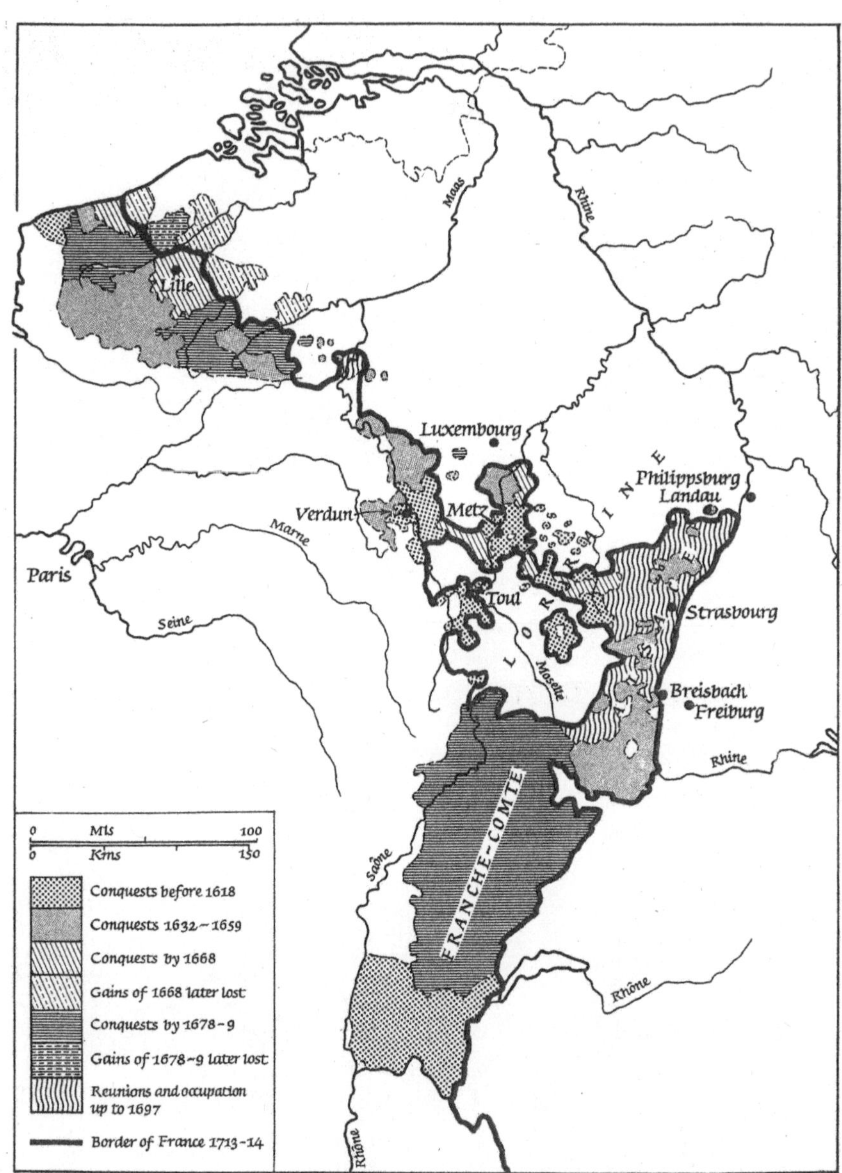

Map 2: French expansion in the seventeenth century.

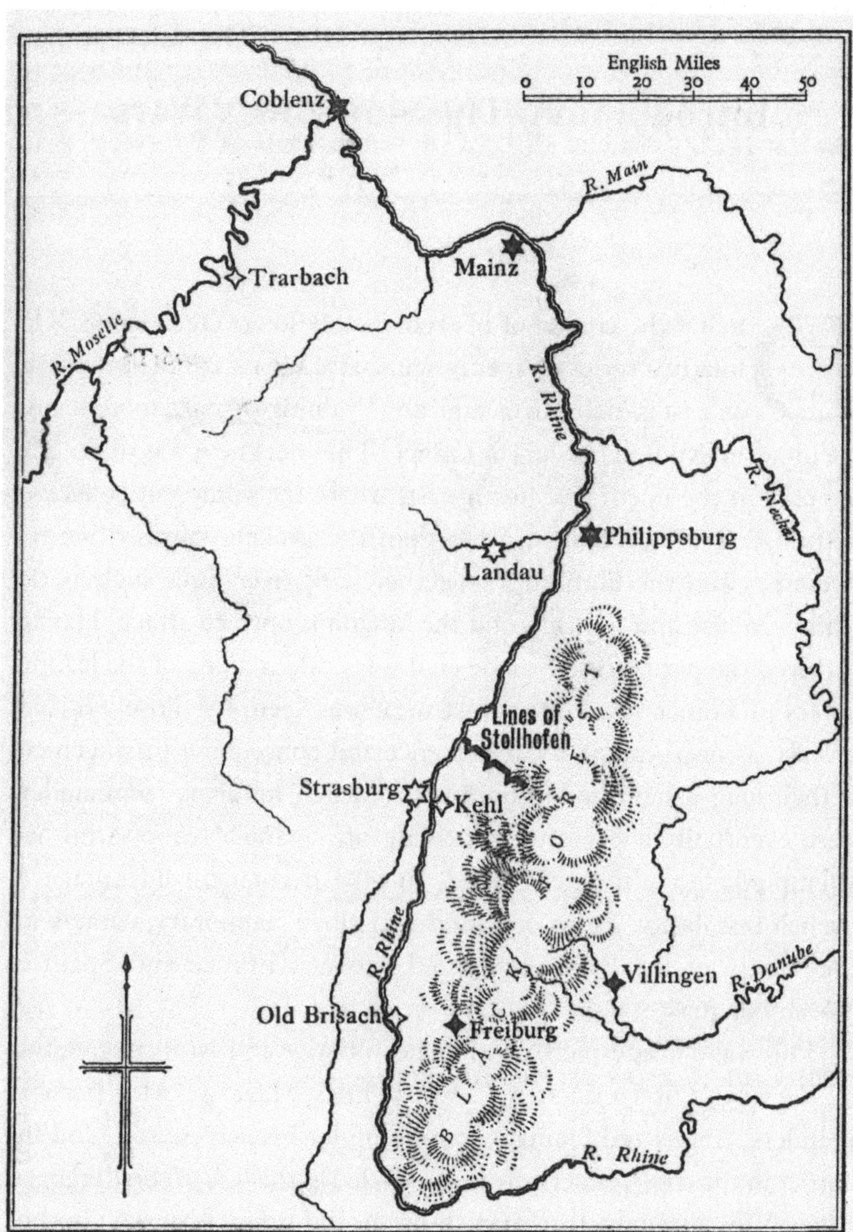

Map 3: The Rhine frontier.

Introduction: The Sun King's Wars

During the course of his remarkably long reign, Louis XIV fought a series of openly aggressive wars with the intention, at least initially, to expand and by doing so make more secure the hitherto exposed borders of France. This weakness was noticeably the case in the north and north-east, where the comparative lack of natural defensive features, other than the broken country like the Ardennes and the Hunsrück, together with river lines such as the Rhine, Meuse and Scheldt, laid the kingdom open to attack. Having survived the peril of the Fronde civil wars, when many of the leading nobles of France revolted against what was seen, by those worthies at least, as overbearing royal influence and consequent infringement of their long-established rights and privileges, his army commanders were eventually successful in driving off Spanish troops who had attempted, but ultimately failed, to take permanent advantage of French instability. Peace of a kind and albeit temporary, came with the Treaty of the Pyrenees agreed between France and Spain in November 1659.

This was a masterpiece of strategic initiative and astute negotiation by the king's first minister, Cardinal Jules Mazarin, with parts of Flanders, Artois and Hainaut coming under French control, and the border in the south effectively being settled at the line of the Pyrenees. Louis XIV also gained a Spanish bride, the Infanta Maria-Thérèse, and when her father (as was widely anticipated) failed to pay over her enormous agreed dowry, Louis used this as a pretext to 'enforce the Queen's rights' and embarked in 1667 upon the first of his own aggressive wars, the War of Devolution,[1] sending his marshals with their troops marching into the Spanish (Southern) Netherlands. This was a highly successful campaign fought against ill-prepared opponents, and amongst the prizes gained were Tournai, Courtrai, and most notably the great city of Lille, where the king had the gratification of having the keys of the place presented to him by the magistrates. Also taken was the Franche-Comte region, the heart of the old, now defunct, Burgundian empire which would from then on, with brief interludes, be a part of France and provide an effective additional bulwark on the Rhine.

It was noted that, 'The years between 1668 and 1672 were years of [military] preparation' for the young king.[2] Acting as he did, Louis XIV was undoubtedly cynically using perceived weakness in Madrid for his own benefit, although he was, while behaving openly as the aggressor, adopting a strategically defensive strategy, in seeking actively to make his realm more stable. The aim, to make the borders of France set securely on the ocean, the mountains, and the Rhine, with neighbouring states so enfeebled or overawed as to pose no viable threat, was both rational, from the French point of view, and far-sighted. With the Treaty of Aix-la-Chapelle in May 1668, although the Franche-Comte was reluctantly given up for the time being, much of Artois and southern Flanders remained in French hands. Near neighbours such as the dukes of Lorraine and of Savoy-Piedmont in the south, had increasingly come under Louis XIV's influence, both as potential allies although, in due course, proving over time to be persistently troublesome client states. The Dutch, to no great surprise, viewed this French advance appreciably closer to their own southern border with concern, while French diplomacy almost triumphantly managed to detach England and Sweden from their recently constructed alliance with the States-General of Holland.[3] French money persuaded the German electors of the Holy Roman Empire to remain neutral or even to lend support to the king, and

Emperor Leopold in Vienna, distracted by the Ottomans and their long-standing ambitions in greater Hungary and along the course of the Danube valley, chose not to become involved, so long as he felt his own interests not to be directly threatened. This would have to change in time, but at first the exception in all such tacit acceptance of French ambition was the Elector of Brandenburg (Prussia), who stoutly maintained his continued support for the Dutch when they were threatened and then invaded by France.

Absolute power, of the kind enjoyed by the young monarch, had inherent dangers, one such being *folie de grandeur*, a sense that everything that was desired was possible, in particular when seeking to overawe, or failing in that to overpower his neighbours. This was most marked in the gratuitous attack made on Holland which came early in April 1672, in large part a contrived dispute over trading rights, import duties and taxes. Louis XIV's chief minister, Jean-Baptiste Colbert, was looking to curb the burgeoning Dutch overseas trade, and the king wrote, in patently flimsy self-justification for going to war, of the need to 'Protect our subjects from the aggression which threatened them owing to the extraordinary levies of infantry and cavalry you [the States-General of Holland] raised, and the fleet you stationed off our coasts . . . By doing this we have obeyed the laws of prudence, and provided the protection that we owe our people.'[4]

After a formal review of the army at Charleroi by the king and his elegant entourage, and without bothering just yet with the niceties of any formal declaration of war, the French advance against the Dutch was swift, taking the route through the theoretically neutral Bishopric of Liège. The powerful Dutch-held fortress of Maastricht on the river Meuse was screened, but left alone for the time being, as, Louis XIV wrote, 'It has appeared to me, so important for the reputation of my armies only to begin my campaign by some brilliant feat, that I have not considered an attack on Maastricht as sufficient for the purpose'.[5] The now-forgiven Prince of Condé joined forces with Marshal Turenne to swiftly cross the lower Rhine at Tollhuis on 12 June, but the senior officers present at the crossing of the river attracted some criticism from the king for allowing this impetuous dash across the water, when casualties were suffered that might well have been avoided with a little less verve and a touch more finesse. The king wrote:

> With a little patience we would not have lost one of these men. The Comte de Guiche could have enveloped [the Dutch] from one side, and from the other we could have pushed them with the other squadrons and with infantry, in place of this wild-eyed action that cost us so dearly.[6]

French progress was swift and impressive, seeing dramatic initial successes against flimsy and poorly co-ordinated Dutch resistance, with Turenne taking Arnhem and outflanking his opponents' positions along the river Ijssel, and Utrecht was also seized. Amsterdam looked bound to fall and Condé wanted to mount a *coup de main* assault on the city with his cavalry, but Turenne was for once more cautious. The king agreed with his marshal-general's assessment of the benefit in maintaining what had become a steady pace to the campaign, but by doing so, the Dutch were allowed time to prepare a more robust and yet patently more desperate defence.

The remarkable tactic of breaching their sea-dykes, opening the sluices, and flooding much of the land saved the burghers of Holland from utter defeat and future French domination. That this was highly unpopular with many of the common people is perhaps not surprising, but it was nonetheless very effective in stopping the French offensive. It ought not to have been a great surprise really, as the same desperate course had been adopted during the Dutch war of independence from Madrid. Still, the States-General, urgently looking for a peace settlement, offered to give up Maastricht and other key towns which would perhaps satisfy Louis XIV's ambitions, and enable him, when and if he wished, to more effectively mount a further advance into what remnant remained of the Spanish Netherlands. The king, unwisely, demanded much more, and quite remarkably that he also be fully compensated for the costs of having to go to war in the first place. In large part this was due to pressing financial concerns, for some nine million livres was now being spent each year simply servicing the interest due on the royal debts. The French demands were rather predictably refused, and in July William, the doughty Prince of Orange, took the field as the appointed commander of the Dutch troops, an undoubted turning point in the course of the war.

The Elector of Brandenburg approached to threaten the flank of the French forces, and Louis XIV had no option but to divide his forces and in doing so dilute the strength of the attack on the Dutch heartland. French strategy rapidly unravelled, and although the bold elector was eventually forced away by Turenne and had to seek terms, for the time being at least, by the end of the year William of Orange felt strong enough to threaten the French lines of supply and communication leading south to Charleroi. This endeavour did not succeed, but the French commanders were shocked at the prince's new-found confidence and apparent audacity, at a time when a large part of their own army was frustratingly stuck fast in the flooded polders of Holland, with little ability to manoeuvre and few prospects of making significant advances against a visibly strengthening Dutch resistance.

The campaign in 1673 saw Turenne on the Rhine and the Moselle, engaged in driving off the elector and his Brandenburgers, while Condé had command of the faltering French operations in Holland. Louis XIV occupied himself in laying siege to the formidable fortress of Maastricht, with the invaluable assistance of his gifted military engineer, Sebastien le Prestre de Vauban; matters can hardly have been helped, though, by the presence with the army of much of the royal court, including the queen who was accompanied by, amongst others, several of the king's mistresses. All this remarkable excursion added complexity and posed a burden on the provision of supplies for the fighting troops, but it is only fair to say that the royal attendance on campaign was no sybaritic excursion undertaken purely for pleasure. 'Even in this terrible weather,' one of his officers wrote, 'the king rode on horseback at the head of the army . . . the same as a simple officer.'[7] The Dutch garrison in Maastricht had to submit on 1 July, very much to Louis XIV's satisfaction.[8] But French problems mounted, their fleet having been savaged by the Dutch in a naval battle off Zeeland the previous month, and on 7 September William of Orange's troops retook the key Dutch town of Naarden. The prince now had other allies, as the Spanish had been outraged that Louis XIV had crossed their territory when moving to attack Maastricht, and the incursions Turenne made into German territory, regarded as Imperial lands in fact, inevitably offended Leopold in Vienna.[9] By November Dutch troops were operating very effectively together with Imperial units in the territory of the Elector of Cologne, an ally of the French King, while Condé could no longer viably maintain his stance in Holland, and had to withdraw from an advanced position that was rapidly becoming untenable and vulnerable.

The looming failure of this campaign, the first real major tangible setback for Louis XIV, was a sobering moment, but he wrote in grudging admiration of the determination shown by his opponents, 'What would one not do to save oneself from foreign domination?'[10] The irony of the sentiment, given his unwarranted and opportunistic attack in the first place on a country that had so recently been allies of the French against the Spanish, seems to have been missed. The venture also had the unintended consequence of uniting the Protestant powers, England and Sweden, with the Dutch, and pushing the United Provinces closer to both the emperor in Vienna, and to the German electors, most notably of course that of Brandenburg. French over-ambition and aggression had alarmed many, and Louis XIV would face increasingly effective coalitions in the future, something that was not foreseen or had been catered for. France's ability to isolate and pick off opponents at will, was at an end.

The French under Turenne were successful in battle at Sinzheim near to Heidelburg in July 1674, while a month later Condé won a particularly expensive victory over William of Orange at Seneffe, but the scale of the casualties suffered in the affair caused consternation at court when they became known. Although the king's field commanders would gain further successes, taking Besançon in the Franche-Comte, and in battle at Enzheim and at Turkheim on the Rhine in the following January, the war ambled aimlessly on now, with little strategic gain for Louis XIV in sight. Turenne was killed by a stray round-shot in July 1675 while preparing for a battle, while Condé could now hardly mount his horse, having become increasingly frail and gouty; these were hard men to replace. Marshal de Créquy was beaten by an Imperial army at Consar-Brucke east of the Rhine, and after a rather feeble defence the fortress of Trier on the Moselle fell shortly afterwards. Alsace was necessarily evacuated by French troops, but the next year, William of Orange tried but failed to take back Maastricht. In the meantime, the French engaged in siege operation against Bouchain and Aire-sur-la-Lys in Flanders, but both sides avoided a major clash in open battle, although an Imperial army pounced on and captured the fortress of Phillipsburg on the Rhine in September.

The king's campaigns of easy conquest were at an end, and 'by 1677 the expansionist dreams of 1672 had faded into the mists of Dutch resistance'.[11] Faced with increasingly effective coalitions, he would write that, 'The efforts of my enemies leagued against me, obliged me to take great precautions. I resolved after finishing the campaign of 1677 to employ my forces only in those places where they would be necessary.'[12] Well, the coalitions he faced only existed because of his own aggressive actions so it is always best to be careful what you wish for. Once the French had captured Valenciennes, a bloody battle was fought at Mont Cassel in April 1677, with the king's brother, known to all as 'Monsieur', in nominal command of the successful troops, and Cambrai was secured soon afterwards. Freiburg on the approaches to the Black Forest was neatly seized by a rehabilitated Marshal de Créquy that winter, but by now everyone was war-weary, significant strategic gains were elusive, costs were high, and Louis XIV looked earnestly towards a good negotiated peace.

Ypres and Ghent duly fell to the French, but the 1st Treaty of Nijmegen, agreed between France and Holland in August 1678, and subsequent treaties with Spain and Austria in following months, eventually brought hostilities to a tired end. Maastricht, Courtrai, Oudenarde, Ath, Charleroi, Ghent and Limburg were given up by France, but St Omer, Cassel, Ypres, Cambrai, Bouchain, Valenciennes, Condé sur Escaut and Mauberge were retained, while Emperor Leopold astutely relinquished his hold on Phillipsburg in exchange for the return of Freiburg. After much effort, cost and blood, it could just about be held that Louis XIV had gone some way to making the rather porous north-eastern border of France more secure, but in addition, by attacking Holland in the first place, the king had earned the lifelong enmity of the Dutch Stadtholder William of Orange (King William III from 1688 onwards). This was undoubtedly a bad thing, with long-term consequences. Economic distress in France, just as much as a lack of many clear successes on the battlefield, had taken its inevitable toll, but for all that the king could count as a gain a rather more regular border with the Spanish Netherlands, in addition to the Franche-Comte region, together with tacit control of the Duchy of Lorraine which had been occupied by French troops in 1670.

The uneasy peace brought about by the 1678–9 treaties would only calm things for a while, and the policy in Versailles of inviting 'reunions' from cities and minor states to the eastwards which might, with varying degrees of veracity, be thought to be within the orbit of French influence, was not a hopeful sign for lasting peace in the future. Chambers of Reunion had been established at Metz, Besançon, Briesach and Tournai to look into French claims of outright sovereignty in the Franche-Comte, Alsace and Flanders. As these chambers were stacked with French judges and jurists, the outcome was hardly ever in doubt, and the simple fact that Louis XIV kept 140,000 troops under arms, despite the ending of obvious open hostilities and the enormous associated cost, had a powerful effect on the deliberations. By 1680 the only independent city-state unaffected was largely Protestant Strasbourg, autonomous and not under Imperial or German influence, having been an ally of France in the later stages of the Thirty Years War, but remaining neutral in the French war with the Dutch. Imperial troops had briefly occupied the city but were removed in August 1679, when Louis XIV objected. The Chamber of Reunions at Breisach eventually ruled that Strasbourg did come within the French orbit, but this was not technically correct and merely a simple legal device by which the king could act to move and take the place when he was ready.

Louis XIV did not wait long before acting, and French troops isolated Strasbourg, and prevented the rebuilding of the bridge over the Rhine by which the city had maintained contact with the neighbouring German states. A deputation of the magistrates of the city went to Versailles to ask for relief from the military pressure, and they were courteously received, but got nothing more. Furthermore, they were told that if Imperial forces were admitted into Strasbourg, this would be regarded as an act of war against France, so that events took a predictable course, and in September 1681 over 35,000 French troops formally invested the city, and on the 30th of that month the magistrates gave in. Three days later Louis XIV heard a *Te Deum* sung in the cathedral, while, coincidentally, on that same day French troops took possession of Casale in northern Italy, purchased from the Duke of Mantua on payment to that impecunious nobleman of a huge sum, in addition to an annual pension. Occupation of that Italian fortress, a forward outpost in effect, would enable France to maintain and when necessary, increase pressure on an occasionally recalcitrant Duchy of Savoy-Piedmont.

The attention of Emperor Leopold had been fixed in the meantime by the Ottoman advance on Vienna, which was only turned back late in 1683 from the very walls of the city where the depleted garrison under Field Marshal Gundaker von Starhemberg had been on the point of having to submit. Temporarily unhindered by concerns of active Imperial intervention, Louis XIV again pushed forward with renewed energy and a little daring his strategic campaign to expand and make more robust his borders, a project which was firmly encouraged by Vauban. With the commencement of fresh hostilities between France and Spain, a blockade of the fortress of Luxembourg had begun in July 1681, although the eventual seizure of the place only took place three years later, after a six-week siege. Before this, French troops ravaged the area around Brussels and Bruges, and seized Diksmuide and Courtrai. Following the fall of Luxembourg in June 1684, an uneasy peace returned to western Europe, with the conclusion of the Treaty (Truce) of Ratisbon in August that year, and by the terms agreed, Louis XIV formally secured Strasbourg, Luxembourg and most of Alsace, together with strengthened French influence over the Duchy of Lorraine.

Dragonnades – punitive campaigns against French Protestant communities – had been underway for some time, and to exacerbate matters the almost inexplicable Revocation of the Edict of Nantes, proclaimed in 1685, constituting perhaps Louis XIV's grossest strategic mistake, forced many otherwise loyal French Huguenot Protestants to flee, coincidentally swelling the ranks of veteran soldiers who would face the Sun King's troops in the years to come. The wryly observant Duc de St Simon recalled that:

> The Revocation of the Edict of Nantes, decided upon without the least excuse or any need, and the many proscriptions as well as declarations that followed it constituted a terrible plot which depopulated one-quarter of the Kingdom, destroyed its commerce, enfeebled all parties, caused widespread pillage . . . ruined a numerous people, tore families to pieces, set relatives against one another, in a fight for food and property, caused our manufacturers to move abroad, where they flourished.[13]

The true effects, and the debility that these expulsions would cause France, together with the reaction in other countries that such a brutal, apparently pointless, and self-harming measure could seemingly take place at will, were yet to be fully seen.

Louis XIV had formally agreed terms for a treaty with the Duke of Savoy, but in the meantime the League of Augsburg, formed in 1686 by Austria, Sweden and German states, was a fresh attempt to more robustly deter the king and his seemingly endless ambitions being enacted at the expense of his neighbours. Two years later, finding that bribes, threats and blandishments were no longer having the desired effect that they once had, Louis XIV was again at war with Emperor Leopold and his German electors, so that the French marshals took the field once more, moving to occupy the Palatinate. The king's reasoning was pre-emptive, as significant Habsburg successes against the Ottomans in Hungary, including the dramatic capture of the city of Buda (Ofen), meant that Imperial attention would almost certainly be once again directed to events along the Rhine, rather than to the troubles in the east. The optimum course seemed to Louis XIV to be to strike first and strike surely, without waiting for Imperial strength to be built up and deployed.

Following the French seizure of Liège, Phillipsburg on the Rhine, and then Mannheim, which fell in the second week of November 1688, came the devastation of the Palatinate that winter and the burning of much of Heidelberg, a wantonly pointless act which seemed to take even the king by some surprise. Not that the damage inflicted on the Palatinate, severe as it was, was as widespread as is sometimes stated as plain fact. 'The French army was commanded by noblemen who had their own ideas about their obligations to people who had surrendered without fighting, together with considerable feeling about the fate of [those] people left without shelter.'[14] Marshals of France, by virtue of their calling, had to be men with a ruthless streak, but this quality was evidently not utterly blind, and one general wrote to Minister for War Louvois (who was to die in July 1691), 'I must represent to his majesty the bad effect which such a desolation would make upon the world in respect to his glory and reputation'.[15] True enough, and newly alarmed at such a demonstration of ruthlessness, German states that had hitherto been on fairly good terms with Versailles backed away, Bavaria and Saxony in particular, while the Elector of Brandenburg again prepared to despatch troops to the Rhine. Holland had formally entered the war, and Mainz and Bonn were re-occupied by Imperial troops, while the region around Tournai on the river Scheldt was ravaged by Allied cavalry. A Grand Alliance was formed in May 1689 between William III (now newly the king in London) and Emperor Leopold, with the Dutch of course following suit. Duke Victor-Amadeus II of Savoy also joined in, despite earnest French diplomatic efforts to have him maintain his allegiance to Versailles. In this way the resources and energies of England, Holland and the largely German Holy Roman Empire, were combined for the first time to confront the French and their king.

Louis XIV could put three major armies in the field in 1690; in Alsace Marshal de Lorge had command, General Catinat (not yet a Marshal of France) commanded in northern Italy, while Marshal Luxembourg led the army in Flanders, perhaps the area most under threat, and where he achieved a very neat victory over the Dutch and their allies at Fleurus in July. The following month Catinat soundly defeated Duke Victor-Amadeus of Savoy at Staffarda, but renewed Ottoman activity inconveniently diverted the emperor's attention for the time being towards events unfolding in Hungary The next year the fortress of Nice was taken by the French in April, as was Mons with the king and his retinue in attendance to receive the submission in person, while Luxembourg pulled off a small but skilful victory in a cavalry action at Leuze in Flanders. In late May and early June 1692, the French Channel fleet was beached and burned at Barfleur and La Hogue by English and Dutch ships, and any plans that had been laid for an invasion of southern England in support of a restoration of King James II fell to pieces in the process. Namur was taken by the French the next month after a stout defence, and in August a bloody and somewhat indecisive battle was fought at Steinkirk, where William III surprised Marshal Luxembourg in camp, and came close, but not close enough, to carrying the day before being smartly driven off. The hard-fought battle at Landen in late July 1693 saw another significant French victory, but at a heavy cost, although an initially hesitant Luxembourg was able to go on, when urged to do so by the king, to take Charleroi in the second week of October. In that same month Catinat was again successful against Victor-Amadeus, in battle at Marsaglia in Italy.

The successes of 1693 saw the apex of French achievement in this war, with a raft of new marshals being created, and the inauguration of the Order of St Louis by the king. The cost of the war was from the onset onerous, all the same, and France's treasury was under renewed strain. Louis XIV tentatively sought peace, but this was not to be had as both he and William III made inflated demands of the other, terms which were bound to be unacceptable. An attempted landing in Brittany by English troops and their allies in the summer of 1694 was poorly organized and an abject failure, while the fortress of Huy on the river Meuse was seized by French troops late in September. French-held Casale was under siege by Imperial and Savoyard troops for much of the summer of 1695, while King William succeeded in taking back Namur that September, after conducting, with the able assistance of the Dutch engineer maestro Meinheer van Coehorn, an epic siege, despite a valiant defence put up by the garrison under Marshal Boufflers. This was a notable achievement for the Allies, and pretty well the first major setback of its kind experienced by French arms since Louis XIV had come to the throne. In the summer of 1696 Victor-Amadeus agreed matters with Versailles under the terms of the Treaty of Turin, and accordingly the duke left the Grand Alliance. The Imperial position in northern Italy was thereby put in jeopardy, and the emperor in Vienna reluctantly agreed to a cessation of hostilities there, very much to the irritation of his allies, William III and the Dutch.

The French took Ath after a very well-handled siege in June 1697, but the Nine Years War (War of the League of Augsburg), had produced few clear results and much frustration for the combatants on either side. Although the occasional French victories, on land at least, were notably absent for their Allied opponents, a limit had been set on the previous seemingly indomitable ambitions of Louis XIV. Having adroitly ruptured the alliance by persuading Savoy back into the fold, and yet with an all but exhausted treasury, the king was wearily content to agree a peace with the Treaty of Ryswick in September 1697, with Vienna belatedly agreeing terms with Versailles the following month. This was only a pause, however, for along with French recognition of William III as King of England as a key part of the treaty, it was agreed that the Spanish throne, when it became vacant (as was confidently and widely expected to happen at any moment), should be awarded to the young son of the Elector of Bavaria, Joseph-Ferdinand Wittelsbach, a neutral choice broadly acceptable to both France and Austria, and coincidentally also to the Maritime Powers (England and Holland). The Spanish nobility had not, however, been consulted, and the provision that their wide empire would in effect be divided at the pleasure of Versailles and Vienna, would be highly unacceptable. In any case the young Bavarian died in Brussels suddenly and unexpectedly and the plan fell to pieces.[16] Another partition treaty to address the problem, without the necessity of going to yet another war, was agreed between France, Holland and England, although the emperor was unimpressed, but when the ailing King Carlos II died early in November 1700, the offer of the vacant throne, together with the whole and undivided Spanish empire, was made Philippe Duc d'Anjou, the second grandson of Louis XIV.

Although aware of the trouble that would certainly be caused, the king felt unable to resist the offer when it was made to his grandson, but to the neighbours of the French this appeared to raise the unacceptable probability of the danger of the combined power, wealth and energies of France and Spain with the resources of its empire, perhaps even (although a little unlikely, surely) that the two nations might even be brought together under one crown. Such a potentially powerful combination in the hands of the French king was not to be borne, and fresh war on an almost worldwide scale was the result, despite a general lack of enthusiasm on all sides for renewed hostilities. Louis XIV could count the Elector of Bavaria as a key ally, although Spanish military power had faded and the need to campaign energetically in the Iberian Peninsula, to make the French claimant secure on the throne, was a lasting drain upon the attention, strength and resources of France. However, this was also true of the effect on their opponents' energies in almost equal measure. The Grand Alliance was reformed in September 1701 between England (Great Britain from 1707 onwards), Holland, Austria and eventually Portugal, together with Savoy once more being a member, off and on. The stated aim of the Allies was originally to secure a division of the Spanish empire between the French claimant, and the Austrian Archduke Charles (younger son of Emperor Leopold), and not at that point intended to require that the archduke must have the throne no matter what; that fatal and flawed demand would emerge in time, when a string of unexpected Allied successes bred over-confidence and arrogance.

France had the advantage of holding a central position when facing her opponents at the formal outbreak of war in May 1702, but hostilities had already broken out in northern Italy, with pitched battles between French, Savoyard and Imperial forces at Carpi, Chiari and Cremona. William III had died after falling from his horse, but the Allied cause was pushed forward vigorously by his successor, his doughty sister-in-law Queen Anne. An early effort to drive Holland out of the war before the full strength of the alliance could be deployed failed, and French efforts there faltered while the borders of Holland were, after a few early scares, held secure. Meanwhile, operations in Italy dragged rather with a series of tactical missteps on both sides, Austrian efforts were diverted to dealing with renewed rebellion in Hungary (a distraction actively fostered by the French king), and the key Imperial-held fortress of Landau on the Rhine was captured by the Duc de Tallard late in 1703. A grand plan for the French to attack Vienna in conjunction with the Elector of Bavaria came to grief in the high summer of 1704 when Tallard, by now a marshal, was beaten at the Battle of Blenheim in southern Germany, The French war effort never fully recovered from this disaster, for the loss of an entire field army in this dramatic way could not readily be made good, and this was compounded two years later with the Duke of Marlborough's utter defeat of Marshal Villeroi at Ramillies to the south of Brussels. The Allied occupation of the Southern Netherlands followed quickly, and the division of the Spanish empire could be said to be taking shape; that same summer also, the French siege of Turin was dramatically foiled by the Imperial commander, Prince Eugene of Savoy. However, these were the very successes that made the Allies greedy, and the explicit demand now became that the Archduke Charles must have the throne in Madrid, and accordingly the French claimant removed

– 'No Peace without Spain' became the fatal cry. Emperor Leopold having died in May 1705, his eldest son, Joseph, took the Imperial throne in Vienna (dying in 1712 and to be succeeded by his brother, Charles, who had of course hoped to be king in Madrid).

This Allied demand of the throne in Madrid was an absurdity, as d'Anjou (King Philip V) was making himself quite popular with the Spanish nobility and people, and largely due to the skill displayed by Marshal Berwick and Marshal Vendôme, Allied military operations in Spain were mostly abject failures, with a scarce few notable exceptions, such as the seizure of Gibraltar and Barcelona in 1704 and 1705 respectively. An Allied attempt to seize the port of Toulon in southern France was a dismal failure in 1707, a year which also saw a decisive Allied calamity in battle at Almanza in Spain. In Flanders, France suffered a heavy defeat at Oudenarde on the river Scheldt the next year, followed by the loss of the important city of Lille in December, albeit only after an epic French defence. The Allied commanders, Marlborough and Eugene, were increasingly drawn into lengthy siege operations in the extensive French fortress belt, although fighting (with heavily qualified success) at the expensive Battle of Malplaquet in September 1709. The Allied effort in Spain saw brief revival during the summer of 1710 with successful actions at Almenara and Saragossa, but their commanders could not hold on to Madrid, and a small British army was defeated at Brihuega early in December, although the French and their Spanish allies were held to a hard-fought draw by Guido von Starhemberg, the Imperial commander in Spain, the following day at Villa-Viciosa. Soon, though, the Allied hold in Spain (Gibraltar excepted) comprised just the city of Barcelona and its environs.

Louis XIV had once more earnestly sought terms for an equitable peace, but the excessive demands made by the Allies meant that the war had to stumble on, although the British reached a covert understanding with Versailles and withdrew their troops from active campaigning in 1712. The alliance was ruptured and French efforts re-invigorated, and Eugene was badly beaten by Marshal Villars at Denain in that same year. Eventually, and after lengthy negotiations, the treaties agreed at Utrecht, Rastädt and Baden in 1713–14 brought the tired war to an end at last. The French claimant remained secure, more or less, on the throne of Spain, but in the process France had been brought almost to the edge of ruin, and that this catastrophe was averted, only narrowly, was due primarily to the skill and energy when on campaign of the Marshals of France, whether in the Low Countries, along the course of the Rhine, on the upper Danube, in Italy, and on the plains of the Spanish peninsula. All the same, it was noted that the agreed settlement was almost exactly what could have been achieved in 1701 with some astute negotiation, before the commencement of a ruinous war no one really relished.

Summary

In each case of four major wars, those of Devolution, that against the Dutch, the Nine Years, and for the Spanish Succession, together with the more minor campaign of Reunions, Louis XIV had initially envisaged a brief contest, looking to overwhelm his smaller and relatively isolated opponents. This was clearly a significant miscalculation, and the ability of his neighbours to form lasting alliances to address what were widely acknowledged to be overbearing French threats to their common good was both remarkable and effective. France, for all its central strategic position, numerous population, admirable tax-gathering capabilities and martial prowess, had in the end proved unable to impose its will on near neighbours, other than in certain very specific and quite narrow instances. This is not to say that Louis XIV failed in his initial endeavour to make his borders more secure and militarily coherent, for in this he was successful, but this was true only in a limited sense, for the financial stress on the economy and people of France was significant. In this, the king may be said to have weakened the long-term position of the crown, for burdensome and inequitable taxation of the common people was highly resented and ultimately unsustainable. The seeds for trouble in the future had been sown, while efforts to make the tax system more equitable were brushed aside.

Moreover, the successes which were to be counted were in effect internal, making borders more regular where they had previously been porous and irregular, and not to any great degree impinging on the territory and interests of others. Regions such as the Palatinate, Franche-Comte, Alsace and Lorraine were *de facto* already firmly in the French sphere of influence at the outset, and no one would go to war over the fact. It is arguable that the loss to Spain of the Southern Netherlands was perhaps less significant than that of their Italian territories which passed, in large part, to Vienna in the early 1700s. However, in a curious and even wandering way, by the time of the king's death at a good old age in 1715, with the relative lack of wide-ranging French success, a kind of balance of power had been achieved in Europe, with no one state able easily to dominate all the others, and that would have to wait for Emperor Napoleon with his brilliant but dangerous abilities some ninety years later.

Warfare under Louis XIV

Given the timespan in which these wars were fought, it is not at all surprising that the nature of warfare, and the tactics, weapons and techniques employed should evolve and mature. With a commendable wish to put the murderous horrors of the Thirty Years War behind them, there was certain sense of restraint, and a real desire to make more civil what was inherently an uncivilized business. Instances such as the French campaign of destruction in the Palatinate and the razing to the ground of much of Heidelberg in the 1680s can be cited, but so too can the devastation of Bavaria by the Duke of Marlborough before the Battle of Blenheim in 1704, the massacre of prisoners by Marshal Vendôme after the Battle of Calcinato in 1706, and the maltreatment of British captives after defeat at Brihuega in 1710, but by and large these were exceptions to the general rule, seen as objectionable and wasteful, and attracted much criticism both inside France and across Europe. With just a hint of sugar-coating, given the brutality inherent in warfare, it could be said that:

> After the fury of battle was spent, both sides laboured to rescue the wounded instead of leaving them to perish inch by inch in agony. Although the great causes in dispute were stated with robust vigour and precision no hatred, apart from military antagonism, was countenanced amongst the troops. All was governed by strict rules of war, into which bad temper was not often permitted to enter, mob violence and mechanical propaganda had not yet been admitted.[17]

In the 1640s, when Louis XIV came to the throne, at the tender age of 4, the 18ft-long pike was still the 'Queen of the weapons on the Battlefield'. Massed pikemen in close order had the ability to fend off the attentions of fast-moving hostile cavalry, accompanied as these foot soldiers were by the firepower of increasing numbers of musketeers, even when having to use the rather cumbersome and slow-firing matchlock pieces of the day, weapons tending to be particularly unreliable in wet weather. A certain stately progress was the result as these massed phalanxes wielding pike and matchlock manoeuvred around the battlefield, but that is not to suggest that the contests were not in themselves fiercely fought, for they certainly were and the casualty toll was often significant; this kind of loss was generally regretted, good soldiers being hard to come by and not to be wasted. The cavalry, often the cuirassiers clad still in half-armour and helmet, had in western Europe largely put away the lance to employ instead the long horse pistol or carbine, in a tactic known as the caracole. The troopers rode forward to discharge their pieces, whether at opposing horsemen or the ranks of pikemen, before turning about and making for the rear of the troop or squadron to reload their weapon and make ready to go forward once again when the moment came. Such stately and rather cumbersome tactics in time gave way, under such innovative commanders as the Swedish King Gustavus Adolphus, to the massed attack sword in hand, potentially a battle-winning method if properly handled, but again of limited effectiveness if the massed pikemen and their matchlock-wielding comrades were well trained, maintained formation and stood their ground.

As time went on more efficient and lighter muskets were available, and the tactics of the foot soldier evolved accordingly, with the requirement to deploy greater firepower and the proportion of musketeers to pikemen increasing dramatically, By the early 1700s the pike had, as a direct result, all but disappeared from the European battlefield, this process having been accelerated by the introduction of the bayonet, first a dagger-like plug, and then a socket device which enabled foot soldiers to better fend off cavalry even when their pieces had been discharged and not yet reloaded. Over time expensively trained and mounted cavalry troopers became less valued than previously when compared to the humbler foot soldier, whose own tactics evolved to take advantage of the lighter musket which, from 1700 onwards, was increasingly likely to have a flintlock mechanism rather than that of the less reliable matchlock. The employment of cavalry *en masse*, with which commanders like Marshal Turenne were very familiar, was also less simple to manage in close country, often cut through with waterways and hedges more typically to be found in Flanders or the Rhine valley, than on the more open plains of Germany.

To astute observers it was increasingly seen that the progress of a battle would be dictated by the steady and disciplined firepower of the foot soldiers, rather than the dash of the cavalry. This process was accelerated by the adoption in most armies in western Europe of an innovative 'platoon firing' practice, whereby selected sub-units would discharge the muskets in set order while others reserved their fire while waiting for their turn. In this way, an opponent could be kept under a continual lash of musketry, which was also better able to be controlled than the previous technique of whole ranks of soldiers discharging their pieces all at the same time. By the early 1700s this new practice was commonplace, although the French were rather slower in its adoption than the Dutch and English. Although light infantry tactics seem to belong to a later period, not everything was done in neat ranks, and in 1706 Tom Kitcher, an English soldier born in Hampshire, remembered having to clear out hostile 'skirmishers' (his term) from the thickets as he and his comrades advanced across marshy ground in the opening stages of the Battle of Ramillies.[18]

Artillery pieces were still heavy and cumbersome, despite the innovative attempts by the Swedish king to improve their design, and once in place they tended to be fought from that position throughout the course of an action, although the Duke of Marlborough managed to drag his heavy pieces, including some massive 24-pounders, forward across soft ground at Ramillies in 1706. Increasingly, enterprising commanders were seeking to move their guns once the fighting began, but this was always a difficult and arduous business, while the development of what became horse artillery was yet to show itself to any great degree. Round shot was the usual missile employed by artillerymen, although canister, bags of musket balls fired like a giant shotgun at close ranges, was also employed. Explosive shell, expensive and difficult to manufacture, was also employed, alongside round-shot, against the defences of fortresses in order to create a breach.

Pitched battles, the exciting chance in a single day to outwit, outfight and overwhelm an opponent in open conflict, were not that common. This was not simply to do with opposing commanders being averse to combat, although some might answer to that charge, but the proliferation of first-class fortresses in those relatively few regions agriculturally rich enough to provide the vast amounts of fodder and forage necessary to maintain armies on campaign meant that the reduction of those fortresses were not only a well-regarded military imperative, but also as a matter of acute polity in provided good bargaining counters for use in the eventual negotiations for peace that sooner or later were bound to come about. The utter destruction of an opponent, or the demand for an unconditional and abject surrender, was in fact a rare thing, at least in western Europe, which is why the huge Allied victory at Blenheim in 1704 was regarded as the wonder of the age. Even in south-eastern Europe, Imperial clashes with Ottoman forces would often be centred on the reduction of key fortresses, and matters were quite often resolved by bargaining and astute negotiation.

Siege warfare, with all its rituals and well understood phases, was accordingly a major part of military campaigns at this time, and a good reputation could be built by a commander around these sorts of operations; such events were not necessarily the invitingly easy option. The fierceness of the fighting, with the fortress commander doing his best to slow the progress of the besieger, was often of the highest order, with attack and counter-attack coming hard upon the heels of the other. Casualties could be high, and the great military engineer Vauban cautioned against wasting good soldiers in ill-prepared and premature attacks, but with campaign seasons limited to the warm months from spring to late summer and early autumn (the poor state of the roads often permitted little else), the imperative was often to just get on with things; heavy losses were often the consequence. Inevitably, some thrusting souls thought the gifted engineer to be too cautious and pressed on with attacks which had scant chance of ready success. Not that this was a uniquely French failing, as the Imperial commander, Prince Eugene, conducted several such rash enterprises at the siege if Lille in 1708, the last of which saw him concussed by a musket ball strike to the forehead, that had it been a half an inch lower would have almost certainly killed him. The essential preliminary for any successful attack was always the artillery bombardment to create a breach in the defensive works, and these siege guns were mighty pieces, often firing shot of 24lbs weight and more, in addition to the heavy mortars and stone-firing perriers, whose steep elevation and trajectory enabled an attacker to search into dead ground and strike opponents sheltering behind defensive works with fearful effectiveness.

In an age when roads were almost all un-paved and would be swirling in dust in dry weather and resembling little more than muddy tracks, if not actual ditches, when it was wet, the ability of an army to move efficiently was of the greatest importance. The efforts of the engineers to maintain mobility, by improving these roads, building or repairing bridges, and laying pontoons across otherwise impassable water obstacles was of prime interest to any army commander. Hence the absolute value of the pontoon bridging train that accompanied all armies, together with the usefulness of the waterways themselves, the canals, streams and rivers of a region, when moving stores and materiel, the loss of which was a serious blow. The other side of the coin was that those same engineer skills could be used to deny mobility to an opponent, by cratering the roads, pulling down bridges, diverting streams and felling trees to impede easy movement. Inevitably, army commanders would be striving to maintain mobility for their own troops and ensuring counter-mobility to hamper their opponents, and if a campaign appeared to move at, to modern eyes, a rather sedate pace, more often than not it was the essential requirements of just how to move large numbers of troops, horses, guns and the essential impedimenta of an army on the move, that held things up.[19] Nonetheless, that armies did often move at this time with surprising speed was an undoubted fact.

An army on campaign in the seventeenth and eighteenth centuries would be accompanied by a train of smiths, farriers, bakers, laundresses, sutlers, and other purveyors of stores, spirits and necessities ready for sale to the eager soldiers, in addition in many cases to their own families, faithfully as they were 'following the drum'. Although the French army benefited from the establishment of numerous well-stocked depots and magazines, arranged by Minister for War Louvois (remembered as being a 'rude, hard man, attached to the King and the state but presumptuous')[20] commanders, to a large degree, were expected to live off the land, and foraged, seized or purchased what more was needed from the unfortunate populace of the region being fought over. When operating in what might be regarded as enemy territory there would be fewer constraints or qualms about what was taken, but in all cases the presence of a campaigning army would rarely be welcome to the locals whose herds, flocks, crops and storerooms would be open to pillage or sequestration, the offer of prompt payment for what was being taken being a regrettably unusual event, and when offered, seldom performed subsequently. It would also be a prudent farmer who kept his daughters, and female servants, out of the way at the same time, although licentious conduct by soldiers was punished severely. Once again, the attempt to avoid the horrors of the Thirty Years War were having an effect.

Louis XIV's commanders were particularly robust in this practice of gathering supplies, and for all the ad-hoc nature of the practice, large armies did subsist themselves for considerable periods, although, again, this could only be done in a region sufficiently rich in agriculture to provide the forage and provisions necessary. There was also even the ruthless added strategic practice of occasionally 'eating up' a country so that no opposing army could hope to operate there. The impact upon the local people can well be imagined, especially if they failed to provide a commander what were known euphemistically as 'contributions' in cash or goods, the lack of which would incur reprisals to set an appropriate example to others. The inevitable result, unsurprisingly, was that cautious soldiers commonly did not stray too far, or alone, from their camps, lest they fall into the vengeful hands of the local much put-upon peasantry.[21]

Throughout this period, it is evident that the French army, which in the 1660s had been a very mixed bag of patchily trained, ill-disciplined, sometimes mutinous and often disaffected collection of regiments answering to their immediate commander and few others, came firmly under royal control. One of Louis XIV's first acts, on taking over affairs, was to dramatically reduce the numbers of regiments in being, for their loyalty noticeably lay, not really with the crown, but with the powerful nobles and worthies who recruited and occasionally paid them, 'Within his kingdom', it was said 'lay hidden another more powerful kingdom'.[22] The young king, by employing the bureaucratic skills of his formidable ministers for war, saw that methods of recruitment, terms of service, uniforms and equipment, pay, training and equipment were improved and made standard. This was necessary, as French soldiers, and those foreign troops recruited for the king's service from Switzerland, Scotland and elsewhere, were almost all volunteers, although periodic agricultural depression and rural poverty played a distinct part in encouraging recruitment (enlistment by destitution was a common fact, and not just in France) for, after all, soldiers had at least to be fed and clothed.[23] The Army Intendants accompanying field commanders were also crucial in this endeavour.

Crucially, Louis XIV, with the firmly-established idea of what his kingship represented, provided the mainspring for this transformation, in which loyalty to the crown, the embodiment of the state and what it was, became the key factor above all other considerations. Most significantly, his Marshals of France, all ambitious and eminent soldiers certainly, but no longer men permitted the dangerous luxury of their own active agendas, were expected to become and remain the devoted servants of the Sun King. Without exception, although inevitably enjoying varying degrees of success or failure, they did so and did so very well.

Chapter 1

Marshal Turenne

Henri de la Tour d'Auvergne, Vicomte de Turenne, was born in Sedan on 11 September 1611, into a Protestant Huguenot family, the son of Henri de la Tour d'Auvergne, Comte de Bouillon and Sovereign of Sedan, and his redoubtable second wife, Elizabeth. She was the daughter of William the Silent, the Dutch Stadtholder (and Prince of Orange) and his wife Charlotte de Bourbon Montpensier. With an older brother, Frederic Maurice, known as the Prince of Sedan, and five sisters, the young Henri was at first a frail child, with what was reported to be of a 'tender constitution',[1] and apparently rather given to laziness; accordingly, he seemed to have been an unlikely candidate to become a successful soldier. All the same, at the age of 14, after completing an education which was overseen by a Calvinist minister, Daniel Tilenus, he joined his uncle Maurice of Nassau, who by then had become Prince of Orange, serving alongside his older brother in the ranks and shouldering a musket in the prince's bodyguard. With this unit he was on campaign against the Spanish General Spinola in the latter stages of the ruinous Thirty Years War, which blighted so much of central Europe. By 1626, and despite his youth, Turenne had shown sufficient promise to be granted a commission as a captain by Fredrick-Henry of Nassau, who had just succeeded his brother as Prince of Orange. Although young and still relatively inexperienced, he proved to be a firm disciplinarian, but was nonetheless both efficient and moderate in manner, having a great distaste for dishonesty. He was also much liked by the soldiers in his company, who were noted as having 'made the finest appearance and [were] the best disciplined in the army'.[2] The youthful captain served with distinction at the sieges of Klundert, Williamstadt and Groll, and in 1629 at the renowned capture of 'The Maid of Brabant',[3] although in the process impetuously risking not only himself, but also the safety of his own company. He also accompanied his brother on a cavalry raid to intercept Spanish reinforcements coming from Breda to augment the garrison in Bois le Duc, but the place submitted on good terms in mid-September.

The 'Sovereign States' of Sedan and Bouillon, in effect the Turenne family home, were not at this time regarded as an integral part of France, and friction between the family and King Louis XIII and his first minister, Cardinal Richelieu, was a persistent irritation and distraction. Henri's father, the Comte, having died in 1623, his older brother, Frederic, unwisely picked an argument with Richelieu and was suspected of actively scheming against the interests of the crown. The Turenne family did not, however, acknowledge any royal authority over them other than that which they chose to grant; but the cardinal saw things differently. Still, Turenne's prudent mother, Elizabeth, thought it best to demonstrate her family's attachment to France, while coincidentally seeking to advance her own younger son's career. As a result, in 1630 Henri Turenne entered French service, receiving at the age of just 19 a commission as a colonel with command of an infantry regiment. In the same breath he continued to campaign with the Prince of Orange for the time being, as Holland and France were in alliance against Spain, so that his first action with the French troops was in 1634 at the siege of La Mothe in the Duchy of Lorraine. He was under the command of Marshal Jacques de Caumont, Duc de la Force, and his valiant conduct during the siege, when he successfully attacked a key bastion in the face of fierce resistance, earned him promotion to Marechal de Camp (in effect, major-general). In August of the following year Turenne served at the raising of the Imperial siege of Mainz, and then conducted with considerable skill a major part of the subsequent French withdrawal from an exposed position, brought about primarily by a lack of supplies, to gain the safety of the fortress of Metz.

Turenne was shot and wounded in the arm at the storming of Zabern in 1636, such was the severity of the injury, and the difficulty in extracting the musket ball which had split on entry, that he only narrowly escaped the limb's amputation. He was back in Flanders the following year taking part in the capture of Landrecies and subsequent defence of Mauberge, but perhaps his most notable exploit at this period was serving under the Duke of Weimar at the storm on 17 December 1638 of the powerful fortress of (Alt) Breisach on the Rhine, after a lengthy and complex siege.

Recognized as a most promising young campaigner, Turenne was employed in Italy under Henri, Comte d'Harcourt, during the 1639 campaign, and his innovative moves and driving energy during the battle at Casale-Monferrato in 1640, an action fought to relieve the fortress of Casale (held at that time by France's ally, the Duke of Mantua), secured victory against a much stronger Spanish/Italian force. D'Harcourt had been all but surrounded at one point, but Turenne managed to charge and rout the powerful opposing cavalry in a fine display of tactical brilliance, and then drove the enemy squadrons off in confusion. After this success, and another at Moncaliere where he forded a swiftly flowing river on foot to encourage his wavering troops, Turenne served at the French siege of Turin. The place was held at the time by Prince Thomas-Carignan of Savoy, until d'Harcourt forced a submission from the garrison on 17 September 1640; the citadel of the fortress was actually still in French hands, but the prince had held out in the city itself. 'Nothing could be more complicated than this.'[4] The circumstances were not that unusual, as a citadel could hold out even though the town had been obliged to submit, as was the case with Turin on this occasion. Turenne was once more wounded by a musket ball during the operations but was able to remain active in the siege trenches. After this, he was appointed to be lieutenant-general, a rank not in common use by the French at this time, and when an overtired d'Harcourt returned to France to rest and recuperate, Turenne took over the command of the campaign, his first experience of leading an army on his own account. In fact, he had benefited considerably from the experience of working with the veteran soldier. 'He never forgot the valuable practical experience of serving with his gifted superior at this time, from whom he learned that diligence and activity are the greatest sources of success in the affairs of war.'[5]

Early in 1641, Turenne took Montecalvo after a siege that lasted just ten days, but he was all the while concerned at the headstrong conduct of his brother, now established as the Duc de Bouillon, who persisted in his quarrel with Richelieu, and thereby at one remove, with the king and the court party. Matters soon came to a head, and 'Never in my life,' Turenne wrote, 'have I had any news that moved me so deeply as that my brother had been arrested by the king's order'.[6] Bouillon eventually gained a royal pardon, but in the process had to submit to the dictation of humiliating terms, with what had hitherto been the sovereign principality of Sedan, French inclined but not a part of France, being garrisoned by Louis XIII's troops. Implicit in all this was that the king's authority had been firmly acknowledged at last in Sedan.

Meanwhile, in northern Italy, Turenne still held his independent command while d'Harcourt remained in France, and in the following year he smartly captured a string of fortified Spanish-held posts including Coni, Mondovi and Ceva, before being ordered to go and campaign in the Roussillion region. In 1643 he again had command of the French troops back in the valley of the river Po, campaigning now alongside Prince Thomas-Carignan[7] who had recently forged an alliance with Louis XIII. Cardinal Richelieu was now dead, and the old king died on 14 May. His son, Louis, an infant was not yet 5 years old, and a period of regency under the control of his mother, the widowed Queen Anne of Austria, and her principal adviser, the Italian-born Cardinal Jules Mazarin, began. Although Turenne had suspected that his adherence to the Protestant religion would hamper his career from prospering as much as it might otherwise do, and despite his headstrong older brother's unwise escapades, he was shortly appointed to be a Marshal of France, a sure enough recognition of recognition of his continued successes against the Spanish/Italian forces in Italy.

A severe setback for France took place in the same year of 1643, at the Battle of Tuttlingen on the Rhine. Baron Franz von Mercy with an Imperial army surprised the French in camp and drove them off in confusion, allowing him to then relieve the besieged fortress of Rottweil. Turenne was entrusted by the cardinal with rebuilding the army, but he found to his dismay that he had to purchase many of the required remounts for the cavalry from his own pocket. 'Mazarin hastily collected reinforcements and appointed Turenne to redeem France's reputation.'[8] Previously fragile discipline amongst the troops was restored, and the soldiers were re-equipped and, most importantly, paid their overdue wages. In June 1644 he crossed the Rhine at Breisach and the following month inflicted a heavy defeat on von Mercy who had recently seized Freiburg. Turenne had been joined on campaign by the Duc d'Enghien (the Grand Condé) who took over the command of the combined army by virtue of his superior rank as a prince of the blood. There was apparently no ill feeling over this, and 'If M. d'Enghien is to command the reinforced army,' Turenne wrote to Mazarin, 'I shall deem myself highly honoured to serve under him'.[9] A hard fought and confused battle at Freiburg began on 3 August, lasting intermittently until the 9th, with Turenne neatly turning the flank of Mercy's Bavarians to secure victory, taking guns and the opposing baggage train in the process. He then went on to recover the fortress itself, but Mercy had defended his position with great obstinacy, and the French losses that day were severe.

Condé returned to France, and campaigning in the following year saw a rather unpromising start. Turenne crossed the Rhine and the river Neckar, before going into an entrenched camp at Marienthal. He had failed to concentrate his forces in good time, and was surprised and soundly beaten by Bavarian general Johann von Werth in an action at Mergentheim. The mortifying reverse was in part due to a subordinate ignoring orders, but Turenne lost all his guns and baggage, and had to withdraw towards the Rhine, enlisting the support of the Landgrave of Hesse, before he was rejoined by Condé along with substantial reinforcements. In the wake of this reverse, Turenne offered to resign the command, but Mazarin refused to see any need to replace him. With this welcome augmentation of fresh strength, the two French commanders advanced into Bavaria once again, achieved a concentration of forces with Swedish troops, and on 3 August 1645 attacked Franz von Mercy in a strongly entrenched position at Allerheim just to the south-west of Nordlingen in the Reiss district. Numbers were even, at about 17,000 in each of the opposing armies, the Swedes having been called away to operate elsewhere. Mercy had the advantage of position, and Condé could make little progress against the stoutly-held Bavarian centre, until he sent Turenne to seize the prominent Weinberg feature, which turned their opponent's right flank. As night came on, Mercy fell mortally wounded and his army withdrew from the field in some disarray, leaving some 2,500 prisoners behind, along with a large battery of twelve guns. Condé's report contained a glowing account of Turenne's valour that hard day, 'Marechal de Turenne did incredible things in this affair, and but for his extraordinary courage and military skill, the battle would have been lost'.[10] Nonetheless, the casualties suffered by the French were once again severe, and the troops were too exhausted to pursue their beaten opponents very far on the road leading to the small town of Donauwörth at the junction of the river Wörnitz and the Danube.

Condé was unwell, and left the army shortly afterwards, and when faced with an Imperial army in superior numbers, which had recently joined forces with the Bavarians, Turenne had to withdraw to the Rhine, and prudently re-crossed the river at Philippsburg. A move was then swiftly made to occupy the Moselle valley, which had been in Imperial hands for some time, and the city of Triers was taken, before the marshal returned to Paris with the close of the campaigning season for the year. In May 1646, Turenne rejoined his troops at Mayence, but was under strict orders not to venture across the Rhine, as negotiations were under way for a peace settlement, and such an advance would be sure to antagonize the German states, the Bavarians in particular. However, on learning that they and their Imperial allies were taking the field again, Turenne left a scratch force in Mayence and on his own initiative advanced to Wesel where he once more joined forces with the Swedish troops under the command of Charles Gustavus Wrangel. Meanwhile Turenne had found time for a little gallant dalliance with the beautiful Anne-Geneviève de Bourbon, Duchess de Longueville. He wrote that 'It was impossible to see her without loving her'.[11] So smitten was he that his troops passed in review before the lady 'banners displayed and drums beating', as she was about to leave to rejoin her husband. The whole force it was remembered 'fired a volley and made a deuce of a noise'.[12]

Turning from such agreeable diversions, Turenne crossed the river Main, and with some 17,000 troops, including allies, approached the Danube, entered Bavaria, and reached the river Lech at Augsburg without great difficulty. The stores gathered there for the Imperial army were seized in the process, obliging Archduke Leopold[13] to abandon the field and fall back down the line of the Danube into Lower Austria. In a dazzling campaign of speedy marches, Turenne had isolated his main opponent, Elector Maximilian of Bavaria, who was forced to sue for peace. The campaign in the following year was, however, less successful, with many of Turenne's troops being restive over arrears of pay, and some stern measures were necessary to restore order. Even so, many of the German-recruited units in the marshal's army refused orders to march for Flanders, and having in all but name mutinied, the units concerned were disbanded instead. Matters were complicated further when the Elector of Bavaria resumed hostilities, but the season was by then so late that little could be done for the time being about this open act of bad faith. However, with a refitted and strengthened army, Turenne was able in 1648 to once again cross the Rhine to combine forces with the Swedes, moving on to severely maul the Imperial rearguard under the renowned General Montecuccoli at Susmarshausen, killing their army commander Count Pieter Melander in the process, going on to force the line of both the rivers Isar and the Inn. Such a rapid advance obliged the elector's family and entire court to abandon Munich for the moment. 'Turenne was the first French general to plant the national colours [of France] on the banks of the (river) Inn. In this campaign he overran Germany in all directions, with a mobility and daring in strong contrast to the way in which war has been waged since.'[14] It was only partly coincidental that, together with victories obtained elsewhere by Condé, this string of sparkling French successes in southern Germany put a final end to the ruinous tragedy for Europe that had been the Thirty Years War, which was wearily concluded with the Treaty of Westphalia that same year.

However, peace had not come to France, for the during the minority of the young King Louis XIV, a band of powerful nobles, envious and resentful of the influence enjoyed by Cardinal Mazarin and the 'court party', sought to plant themselves firmly at the helm of public affairs. In this they were encouraged by the Spanish, who saw that French weakness would be their gain and opportunity, particularly in strengthening Madrid's hold on the Southern Netherlands and Flanders, and the still porous and ill-defended northern and eastern borders of France, with Lorraine, Alsace, the Palatinate and the

Franche-Comte, and even Bouillon and Sedan, being regions where suzerainty was in some dispute. The resulting civil wars, known as the 1st and 2nd 'Frondes', saw Spanish troops approach the walls of Paris at one point, with prominent French notables able to summon large numbers of their own retainers for service, resentful at what were seen as infringements on inalienable rights, actively striving to in effect bring the crown to heel. Turenne was not one such, although his older brother had other inclinations and was the cause of renewed trouble for the marshal with both the regent, Queen Anne and Mazarin who for a while, and perhaps with quite good reason, suspected him of doubtful faithfulness to himself and loyalty to the young king.

Matters, and loyalties, were in a state of flux, and Turenne protested in 1650 when the Prince of Condé and the Prince of Conti, both suspected of being in open rebellion, were ordered to be arrested and detained in Vincennes. Refusing the command of the army in Flanders, Turenne rode instead to Stenay, where he was joined by the still much-admired Duchesse de Longueville, who had fled Normandy on an English ship after unsuccessfully attempting to raise the region in revolt against Mazarin. Her husband was, meanwhile, detained at Vincennes along with Condé and Conti, all at risk of attainder, and perhaps even fearing for their lives.

Civil wars are often remarkable and unpredictable events, and this was no exception, for in what to later generations would be seen as his own act of rebellion and even treachery, Turenne concluded an agreement with Madrid to accept money to raise an army to march and free the princes and the other nobles detained at Vincennes. At the head of 5,000 troops, paid for with Spanish gold, Turenne approached Vincennes but found that the detainees had been removed to a place of safer keeping, and in consequence the whole venture was a failure. Nonetheless, Mazarin's position had become so uncertain that in 1651 he ordered that Condé, Conti and the others be freed, and took himself off for the time being to lie low in Cologne, while things calmed down in Paris. Turenne now found that Madrid was openly intent on further weakening the French strategic position, and as a result he broke contact with them, but significantly he also refused an invitation from Condé to actively join a fresh campaign against the court party. That his family's long-standing claim to the Duchies of Evreux and Chateau-Thierry were belatedly confirmed in March 1651 certainly did a great deal to ease troubled feelings and went some way to clear the air for Turenne with the crown. Louis XIV attained his majority shortly afterwards, but Mazarin was already anxious to make even more sure of this renowned soldier's continued loyalty, and there was a clear sense that it was recognized that bygones were best to be left as bygones. He wrote to the secretary for war, Michel le Tellier, on the need to make sure of Turenne's future services, 'I am convinced that nothing in the world would be more to our advantage'.[15]

While all this was unfolding, Turenne found time to marry, the lady in question being the Protestant Charlotte de Caumont, granddaughter of the Duc de la Force and daughter of Marshal de la Force. However, events moved on with ever greater rapidity, and in 1652 the ever-troublesome Condé, by now in Guyenne, raised once more the standard of revolt, and renewed his alliance with Spain. Faced also with the hostility of the Parlement in Paris, the court were soon obliged to remove to Bruges, and then to Poitiers. Turenne joined them there and was appointed to command the troops still loyal to the king, in co-operation with another stalwart, Marshal d'Hocquincourt. After inconclusive actions at Jargeau on 28 March 1652, and Gien a week or so later, Turenne roundly defeated the Frondeurs and their Spanish allies at the Battle of Faubourg St Antoine on 2 July. Paris was re-occupied by royalist troops early in October, but the civil wars were not yet at an end, as Condé re-grouped, and in June 1653 Turenne and Marshal de la Ferté confronted the prince's army at Rethel. Although significantly outnumbered, Turenne was able to manoeuvre to prevent a fresh advance by the rebellious prince on Paris, and he went on to retake both Mouzon and then Sainte-Menehould where the young King Louis was present to watch from a safe distance the progress of the siege operations.

To avoid tedious arguments over who took precedence in the field, Louis XIV would in time order that when two marshals were together on campaign, the one who had been made lieutenant-general first should hold the overall command. This decree caused a fair amount of resentment, with some marshals declaring that they would only accept orders direct from the king, not from another marshal, as that would be regarded as an affront to their dignity. This difficulty became acute in the summer of 1654, when Turenne had to share the command of the royal army at the capture of Stenay, and then at the relief of Arras, together with Marshals de la Ferté-Imberty and d'Hocquincourt, in addition it should be added to James, the exiled English Duke of York. Such a divided command caused predictable friction and delay, although the operations were eventually successful with Condé's diminished and increasingly disheartened troops driven away in late August. He lost sixty-three guns, and eventually had to take shelter near to Le Cateau de Cambrésis. The next year Turenne captured Landrecies close to the Forest of Mormal, and promptly moved on to take the fortresses of Condé sur Escaut and St Ghislain. D'Hocquincourt had been obliged to give up both Ham and Peronne to the Spanish, but in June 1656 Turenne invested Valenciennes, but de la Ferté-Imberty negligently allowed his lines to be overrun by Condé and the marshal was taken prisoner along with over 4,000 of his troops. Turenne attracted some criticism for having allowed the army to have been split by the Escaut river, and in effect open to be defeated in detail, but he made a well-ordered withdrawal, showing a bold front, although having to abandon many of his guns and stores, while both the fortresses of Condé sur Escaut and Le Quesnoy had to be given up to the Frondists. Nonetheless, Turenne's hold on St Ghislain remained firm, and in 1657 he was appointed colonel-general of cavalry, a prestigious role with duties that included counter-signing all the king's orders on matters relating to the cavalry. He also had received the colonelcy of the Colonel-General's Regiment, which took precedence on the march over all other units.

With Cromwell's England now a declared ally of the French crown, Turenne successfully fought the Spanish and their allies at the Battle of the Dunes near to Dunkirk in June 1658, the army being reinforced with a substantial contingent of veteran Ironsides provided by the Lord Protector. A weary peace between Spain and France came with the agreement known as the Treaty of the Pyrenees late in the following year, during which Louis XIV both found a Spanish bride and managed to confirm almost all the French gains made in the recent campaigns. The 'Fronde', and its attendant tribulations, was fading gradually away, but Louis XIV had learned a hard lesson, in particular the danger of having powerful and wilful nobles who commanded larger forces than the crown could readily summon. This was a situation he would not tolerate; France could have only one master, as it would soon learn.

In 1660 the Prince of Condé at last acknowledged that his cause was lost, and submitted to the king, in the process returning to a cautious kind of royal favour, and looking 'To buy back with the best part of his blood, all the trouble he had caused'.[16] Louis XIV now acknowledged Turenne's significant part in the recent defeat of both the rebels and the Spanish, with his appointment to be Marshal-General, enabling him to exercise effective seniority over all the other marshals and general officers. Had Turenne consented to convert to Catholicism at this time, it is likely that Louis XIV would have revived the ancient title for him of Constable of France, but he would not do so, stoutly acting still as the *de facto* leader of French Protestants. In March 1661, Cardinal Mazarin died at Vincennes, and the young king soon took into his own hands all the reins of power. 'It seemed to me then that I was really a King and born to be one.'[17]

With the onset of peace, albeit a temporary respite, Turenne was active in urging the necessity that the army be maintained at an effective strength. The king needed little urging, and would write to his marshal-general that, 'We find ourselves obliged, to the conservation of the state as much as for its glory and our reputation, to maintain in peace as well as war, a great number of troops, both infantry and cavalry, which will always be ready and in good condition'.[18] Turenne arranged and attended frequent reviews of the troops, at which the king was often present, and by 1666 two powerful active army corps had been established near to Compiègne. It was made sure that the soldiers, hitherto wearing a wide range of assorted garb, were clad and equipped to a set standard pattern, and most importantly were promptly paid – something of an innovation. Firm but fair discipline was imposed, but this was simply good practice and Turenne was forgiving of those who at first did not meet his own high standards, 'He reckoned all his [own] misfortunes as blunders; indulgent to those who had fallen short, he treated their blunders as misfortunes'.[19] This was undoubtedly astute, and Turenne's popularity as a highly competent commander, both with officers and the rank and file, was notable. Steps were also taken to ensure that officers were not absent from their troops without express leave, or good reason.

Using his wife's unpaid dowry from Madrid as a rather flimsy excuse, on 24 May 1667 Louis XIV sent his army marching into the Southern (Spanish) Netherlands, in what became known as the War of Devolution (the Queen's Rights). Turenne accompanied the king with the main body of troops, while Marshal d'Aumont manoeuvred to one side and Marshal de Créquy on the other. That Louis XIV, who had the queen and two of his mistresses along for company, was as yet an inexperienced campaigner and relied heavily upon the marshal-general is clear, and he wrote rather naively, 'I have applied myself more earnestly to learning the profession of arms under him, and to give proofs of my courage'.[20] In the event only modest and ill-prepared resistance was met, with Tournai falling on 25 June, after which Douai was taken, and d'Aumont going on to capture Bergues, Furnes and Courtrai without much difficulty. The greatest prize in the campaign, however, was the siege and capture of the great city of Lille, which was invested late in August with the assistance of the troops under the command of de Créquy. Despite a very well-handled sortie by the garrison, the fortress was yielded up on good terms at the end of September, and the king accepted the keys of the city from the magistrates with appropriate good grace. Alost was also captured before the onset of cold weather brought matters to a close for the year. What had been something akin to a triumphal progress, a military 'promenade' as it was called, was not entirely to Turenne's taste, as the magnificence of the numerous and elegant party accompanying the king had been astonishing, but expensive and troublesome to maintain and administer on campaign. One highly-impressed observer wrote that, 'All that you have heard of the magnificence of Solomon and of the pomp of the King of Persia, is not to be compared to the luxury that attends the king on his journeys'.[21] Perhaps so, but military efficiency did not stem from such display, and added not one jot to the fighting strength of the army. It could be argued, of course, that the presence of the king on campaign would encourage the soldiers to perform great feats but might also encourage rash and ill-prepared ventures in an effort to impress. Ironically, Louis XIV subsequently accepted a suggestion that, in the interests of military efficiency, no officer should attend a campaign with more than two personal servants, but even this modest and perhaps rather impractical proposal aroused a fair degree of resentment and perhaps inevitable wide evasion by senior commanders.

The Dutch were understandably concerned at this fresh French venture, bringing as it did the ambitious young king's armies appreciably closer to their own borders. Louis XIV was aware of this and had no wish to offer needless offence, having in the meantime ordered Condé, now restored to favour after a fashion, to lead French troops in the occupation of the Spanish-held Franche-Comte region around Besançon. On 2 February 1668, the king joined Condé with his troops, and within three weeks the campaign was successfully concluded. However, Holland, England and Sweden had now formed an alliance to put pressure on France to cease hostilities, and while Turenne was amongst those who advocated a pre-emptive strike against the Dutch, the state of French finances was not too good, and Louis XIV instead chose peace, at least for the time being. This came with the Treaty of Aix-la-Chapelle signed on 2 May, by which the Franche-Comte was given up, although now irrevocably in the French sphere of influence, and some of the recently captured towns were returned to Spain. Significantly the key fortresses of Lille, Tournai and Oudenarde remained in French hands (in the case of Lille, of course, for ever).

In October that same year Turenne at last converted to Catholicism, to general surprise as his own close family and late wife (died 1666) were all staunchly Protestants in their devotions. It cannot be said that the change was intended to increase his standing and influence, for as a leading Protestant he stood out when seen to be in command of the king's main army, and yet as a Catholic he would be just one of many such. It seems all the same that his motives were good, principally concerned with matters of conscience, and the decision was arrived at only after much thought and, no doubt, prayer. 'M. de Turenne's conversion was the more honourable to himself, and to the church in that it cannot be suspected of any human interest.'[22]

All the while, the marshal-general was less appreciative over letters of advice and instruction he regularly received from the king's ministers, seeking as they did to try to put restraints on their most senior military commander, and he wrote that he saw, 'The direction of armies in the hands of those who better merit the title of valet than that of captain [and] that the king had resolved to gather for himself alone the gloire of all the victories and that there would remain to the Generals only the disgrace of their defeats'.[23] In fact, this was rather ungenerous, for Louis XIV repeatedly turned to Turenne for advice on military matters, but just as with the activities of the army intendants who were required to monitor and report on what he and his colleagues were doing, the message was clear; the king never forgot the trials of the 'Fronde', and the potential risk attached to having powerful and ambitious men at the head of large armies. He was, also, not at all averse to gaining a degree of glory by his presence, sometimes helpful but at other times less so, by being with his armies when in the field, and in this there might be no great surprise, for he obviously enjoyed doing so. Still, Turenne would on more than one occasion openly ignore the directives that came from those bureaucrats he deemed unfit to comment on such matters, and to a large degree Louis XIV went along with what he did, so obvious was the value of his services.

With the commencement of the war with the Dutch in May 1672, Louis XIV had Turenne, at that time in Charleroi, in overall command of the 50,000-strong main force to be employed in the fresh campaign of aggression. At the same stroke he removed from active duty three marshals, de Bellefondes, d'Humières and dé Créquy, who at first refused to accept Turenne's authority over them, even though he was now well established with the authority of being the marshal-general. Louis XIV was not at all amused, and had to order the three of them each to serve under him as lieutenant-generals for at least 15 days, and to do so with good grace. As the campaign gathered pace, things went well at first, and with great panache Condé got his own troops across the Rhine in June at Tollhuis, although not without sustaining casualties that might have been avoided with a little care. Nijmegen fell to Turenne in early July after a short siege, with the taking of Creve-Coeur, in an action lasting just two days, soon afterwards. The outnumbered Dutch were driven back towards Amsterdam, but in their desperation, they opened their sea dykes and sluices and flooded large tracts of land, so that the French army became all but stranded in a watery wasteland of dismal polders.

Spanish troops were soon also involved, and the Elector of Brandenburg (Prussia) entered the hostilities on the Dutch side, so that from autumn 1672 to early in 1673 Turenne was on campaign in Germany at the head of 43,000 troops. Urged by Versailles to be cautious, he wrote with some firmness:

> I think it very important for the King's service that I cross the Rhine in sufficient force to prevent the Germans [Brandenburgers] from spreading to Westphalia, and even to drive them back across the river Weser, if possible. I think that nothing is of more importance for the King's service than to try not to give the Germans any rest . . . I shall act on the lines I have laid down, being persuaded that it is the King's desire to try so to conduct affairs that his arms shall retain their reputation, which, in my opinion, will not happen without some decisive action . . . The King will see that we cannot make war by halves.[24]

The cool response from the minister for war, was that, 'Having explained to you His Majesty's thoughts, he leaves it to you to do whatever you consider most advantageous for his service'.[25] Turenne had won his point, and while generally ignoring the directions he regularly received from Louvois, forced the elector back across the river and to seek terms, abandoning his involvement in the hostilities for the moment; the Imperial forces under Raimondo Montecuccoli, facing isolation, hastily withdrew into Franconia as a result. Turenne had, however, been denied reinforcements, although this was not that surprising as he had a formidable force already to hand, while the Treaty of Vassem, signed on 6 June 1673, formalised the Brandenburgers' withdrawal from the field. The campaign had been marked by a considerable degree of pillaging and destruction, not in itself that unusual with armies out on campaign at the time, but in this case an act of deliberate French policy to prevent opposing armies from quartering themselves over the winter in the region. Nonetheless, the diversion of Turenne to deal with the threat from the elector's forces had significantly diluted French efforts in Holland, although it may be doubted whether this made a great deal of difference in the face of the inundations across much of the Dutch countryside which so hampered offensive operations by either side. When Turenne returned to Versailles at the end of the year, he complained to Louis XIV at the unhelpful and contradictory orders he often received, most particularly from the minister for war, and 'Laid before the king the blunders of M. de Louvois, the lack of definiteness in the orders he had received . . . Louvois was excellent in matters of detail but lacked entirely the knowledge and experience necessary for the conduct of a campaign.'[26] Still, the king was unwilling to lose the services of so accomplished and effective an administrator, so that while lending a sympathetic ear to his marshal-general and his complaints, he did little more.

In 1673 Turenne held firm the French strategic position in the Moselle valley and upper Rhine, while Condé, accompanied by the king and his entourage, maintained pressure on the Dutch and their allies. The marshal-general's strength was much diluted by having to detach a substantial force to assist in the costly siege operations against the formidable Dutch-held fortress of Maastricht and, accordingly, Turenne had to mark time for the moment. He was able, however, by astute manoeuvring, to prevent Montecuccoli with his larger army from moving to link up with the Dutch, while simultaneously taking care to shield Alsace from any major hostile incursion from across the Rhine. Nonetheless, in the end it was not possible to prevent the highly-capable Imperial commander from joining forces with William of Orange, and to then seize the strategically important town of Bonn on the Rhine on 12 November, despite urgent appeals from the king to Turenne to save the place. There was little more he could do but to put his troops into winter quarters, mostly in Alsace, for the time being. During the year, Vienna, Madrid and Holland had concluded terms to operate together against the French king and his ambitions, and with his forces significantly overstretched, Louis XIV began to look towards a peace that would be as advantageous as possible in what had become less than promising circumstances. Before long, the actively aggressive war he had so far pursued was gradually replaced by a distinctly defensive strategic operation, to concentrate and conserve strength, and retain hold of what territory was of most importance.

This did not deter Louis XIV from mounting a rapid campaign to take back the Franche-Comte, with both Besançon and Dole falling to his troops in the early summer of 1674. In that same season, Turenne with a slim detachment of just 8,000 troops, comprised mostly of cavalry, moved quickly to try and take Philippsburg on the Rhine, but on 16 June he was blocked at Sinzheim in the Palatinate by an Imperial force under Count Aeneus Caprara, who had command of a similar number of troops. Turenne charged with his horsemen, and after a hard fight won a notable victory, inflicting 2,500 casualties against a loss of his own of fewer than 1,500 killed and wounded. Reinforced, he went on to approach Heidelberg, before resting and re-grouping his troops, and moved back across the Rhine once more on 3 July. The Imperial forces fell back, although they had also been reinforced since the defeat in June, and the Palatinate was, in consequence exposed to French attention. 'Repeated successes by the French were having an impact on his opponents, and 'There was in their troops,' Turenne noted, 'a terror not to be believed'.[27]

Resisting pointed suggestions from Louvois that he should withdraw from the Palatinate, to avoid alarming the German states too much, Turenne subsisted his troops on the rich region throughout the summer, and in this he was a true commander in the old tradition akin to that of the Thirty Years War, keen to ensure the well-being of his soldiers, but mostly heedless of the sufferings of the civilian population amongst whom they operated. If a village was slow to provide what Turenne's roving commissaries demanded, it was burnt, that was the simple way of things, while the inhabitants would prudently flee to the hills and forests. Early that autumn the French governor of Philippsburg wrote that, 'In the last two weeks I have burned thirteen towns and villages', and that, 'there was not a soul left in them'.[28] The wider success of this ruthless policy, that of 'eating up a country', was demonstrated when an Imperial army approached to challenge Turenne, who had taken up a defensive posture between Landau and Weissenberg. Louvois urged the marshal-general to fall back further, but he refused, saying that his opponents' troops would find nothing to eat in a region so recently devastated. He was soon proved right, and on 20 September the Imperial army re-crossed the Rhine, moving instead towards Strasbourg, at that time a 'Free' neutral city. Taking uncontested possession of the place, the Imperial commander, the Duc de Bournonville, was well placed to threaten a major incursion into Alsace, something that greatly concerned Louis XIV. Turenne moved swiftly to forestall such a move, especially as the Elector of Brandenburg, having imprudently re-entered the fray, was reported to be marching to combine forces with de Bournonville. On 4 October Turenne reached Molsheim, thus threatening the link between the Imperial field army in camp and the garrison in Strasbourg, and in showers of heavy rain he advanced to close with de Bournonville's troops, emplaced as they were at Ensheim with their left flank secure in wooded ground. A fierce and evenly balanced battle ensued which was, in effect, a draw, although the Imperial army had to leave the field at the close of the day, with the reported loss of almost 3,500 killed and wounded. Turenne's casualties were slightly less, but his troops were exhausted after marching and fighting in foul weather for several days at a stretch and could not pursue their opponents with much vigour.

The elector had now joined forces with de Bournonville, and faced with superior odds, Turenne prudently fell back to cover the approaches to Hagenau. There he was joined by a 6,000-strong detachment of the *Arrière-Ban*, a local militia of highly doubtful quantity. Turenne only tolerated them for a week or two before sending them away to be disbanded, so unreliable were they on campaign. 'It is a corps,' he wrote, 'incapable of action and more proper to provoke disorders than to remedy accidents.'[29]

With the Brandenburgers and their Imperial allies moving securely into winter quarters around Colmar, Turenne ignored the normal practice of not campaigning in the cold months and set out on a rapid march through the difficult country of the Vosges in the deep snow of December. He surprised and overwhelmed an Imperial cavalry detachment at Mulhouse on 29 December, and went on to Colmar itself, where the elector was hurriedly trying to pull his army together to re-commence a campaign he had thought to be well concluded for the time being. On 5 January 1675 Turenne drove the Imperial forces away from Turkheim, although only after hard fighting, and this success was followed by a thorough and brutal sack of the town. The French were left in uncontested possession of Alsace once more, because of the highly innovative campaign. Turenne could at last put his hard-marching soldiers into their own winter quarters, and in the meantime the elector went back to northern Germany to deal with a growing threat from Sweden, so that when Montecuccoli took the field again in the late spring he had no real advantage in numbers over his French opponent. Turenne crossed the Rhine on pontoon bridges at Ottenheim so that he could cover the approaches to the French-held fortress of Kehl, but both commanders were suffering from a lack of forage and supplies, in part due to the severe depredations of the previous campaign. The weather was unseasonably foul, so that neither could find a way to out-wit or out-manoeuvre the other, with Montecuccoli eventually taking up a position with his army about ten miles downstream from Strasbourg.

On 22 July Turenne began a turning movement intended to pin his opponent against the Rhine, but a series of preliminary clashes alerted Montecuccoli to the danger, and he began a withdrawal towards the east, and while on that march he was overtaken on 27 July and confronted by the French at Salzbach. Turenne typically went forward on a close reconnaissance with his artillery commander, the Marquis de St Hilaire, and during the expedition he was struck on the chest by a stray round-shot and killed on the spot. St Hilaire was gravely wounded by the same projectile, and General Guy de Durfort, Duc de Lorge (soon to be made a marshal) had to take over the command of the army.[30] Dismayed at the sudden loss of their renowned commander, the French lost heart, and withdrew the next day, pursued by their Imperial opponents who forced a fierce fight at the crossing of the river Schutter, during which the commander of the French rearguard was killed. With de Lorge's troops in some disarray, Montecuccoli quickly followed up and took possession of Strasbourg once more, before moving on into Alsace.

The reaction of Louis XIV to the news of the death of Turenne was marked, and he wrote, 'I have just heard with a sorrow that you can well imagine of the news of the unexpected death of our cousin the Vicomte de Turenne who has been killed by a cannon shot'.[31] The king sent Condé to restore matters in Alsace, which he did with commendable efficiency, and meanwhile it was ordered that Turenne be buried in St Denis, a most unusual honour for someone not of royal blood. In the sombre days following the death of arguably his greatest field commander, Louis XIV created a whole raft of new marshals, as if to assuage the grief at the bitter loss recently sustained, a move that was rather derisively described as 'getting small change in return for a Turenne'.[32] True enough, he was a commander who would be hard to replace, and a measure of the lasting respect in which the old campaigner was thereafter held in France, may be glimpsed in the fact that when St Denis was ransacked by the mob during the French Revolution, his tomb was the only one left untouched. Instead, Turenne's remains were carefully moved to the Jardin des Plantes, but in November 1800 Emperor Napoleon had them taken to the chapel at Les Invalides where they remain.

Gifted, brave and wilful, aware of his own standing and that of his noble lineage, the old marshal-general often chafed at the repeated instructions that came to him from the king and his strident minister for war, together with having to bear the irritating oversight of the army intendants. Turenne was, arguably, the last of the old breed, a nobleman in his own right, a sovereign prince no less, who chose to serve, but was not subservient to, his king. That his robust independence was tolerated by Louis XIV indicates very well the recognition of his abilities and the worth of what service he provided to the crown. 'Turenne was one of the best of the old-style marshals – a member of a great family of counts and peers, sovereign lords in their own names [but] like the great noblemen of earlier times, he rallied to the support of the king on his own terms.'[33]

Chapter 2

Marshal de Fabert

Born in Metz on 11 October 1599, Abraham de Fabert, who became the Marquis d'Esternay, was the second son of Abraham Fabert, Seigneur de Moulins, who had given valuable service to both King Henry IV and his son, Louis XIII, as a highly regarded court printer. One of ten children, of whom only three survived to adulthood, very much against his father's wishes the younger Abraham enlisted as a foot soldier in the Gardes Françaises in 1613 and showed such promise that he was then appointed as an ensign in the Piedmont Régiment, one of the highly regarded old corps in the army. France was beset with religious strife at the time, and Fabert was actively involved in the campaigns against the rebellious Protestants, particularly at the lengthy and hard-fought siege of La Rochelle.

Fabert established for himself a firm reputation as a capable young officer, and the meticulous care he took when scouting the positions taken up by his opponents was noticed. His close study of the siege techniques involved at La Rochelle also paid handsome dividends and he developed a number of ways to minimize casualties, while deploring rash, ill-prepared and costly attacks made by thrusting officers keen to make a name for themselves. In this way, he foreshadowed much of what Sebastien Le Prestre de Vauban would take on later in the century. Transferring to the Rambures Régiment, he served as sergeant-major (not a warrant officer role, but effectively carrying out the combined duties of quartermaster and adjutant). He also took part in a duel with a brother officer, not an uncommon thing at the time although officially frowned on, and was seriously wounded in the throat during the encounter. The prompt care he received, to stem the flow of blood, saved him but it was a narrow escape.

In 1629 the regiment was with the army sent to campaign in northern Italy in support of the Duke of Mantua against the Spanish and Savoyard forces, under Duke Charles-Emmanuel. The route the French took was blocked by the duke's forces, but Fabert went forward and quickly found an exposed flank, which obliged the Savoyard troops to retire and leave the road open. Louis XIII was lavish in his praise on hearing of the exploit, commenting to Cardinal Richelieu that 'There is the brave [Sergeant] Major of whom I have spoken to you, and to who I owe the success of the day',[1] Fabert was subsequently wounded in the thigh by a musket ball at the storm of the fortress of Privas, but on his recovery, the king offered him a captaincy in the regiment. This he declined, apparently considering it to be an irregular gesture that more properly should have come from his regimental colonel. Louis XIII was not too amused at what could almost be regarded as a snub, and Fabert fell from favour for a while. This all blew over before long, and he was again active on campaign to save the French-held fortress of Casale, and after leading his troops in an attack at Saluzzo, he came off the field unharmed but with two musket ball holes in his hat.

Fabert's father continued to try to persuade him to give up soldiering, and for a time, while on leave, the young man was involved in running an iron forge near Metz, but the enterprise did not hold his attention for long. In 1631 he was promoted to the command of a company of musketeers in the Ramboures, although he had to find the 7,000 livres with which to pay for the commission. Louis XIII permitted him to concurrently retain the post of sergeant-major, an unusual concession. He also found the time to marry, the lady being Claude de Crevant, a near neighbour of the family. It was apparently a love match, although there was a dispute over the payment of the agreed dowry. The bride's grandfather, who was to provide most of the money, seemed not to approve of Fabert's chosen profession, and only on the old man's death was the sum belatedly forthcoming. When the French took possession of Nancy in the Lorraine region in August 1633, Fabert was appointed to oversee the policing of the disgruntled population, a task that he undertook with both firmness and fairness, so that the city remained calm. Present at the subsequent taking of the fortress of Bitche, Fabert became embroiled in an argument with the army commander, Marshal de la Force, over the disciplining of some of his soldiers who had misbehaved (in all probability by engaging in looting). Fabert considered this to be a regimental matter, to be settled by himself, and when the marshal insisted on taking things into his own hands, he offered to resign his commission rather than comply. Louis XIII refused Fabert permission to do so, but he was however permitted to go on leave while tempers cooled.

Shortly afterwards, Fabert was taken captive while scouting the defences of Spanish-held Thionville and kept in uncomfortable circumstances in Luxembourg and then Brussels for over two months. He was only able to communicate with his family by means of covert letters smuggled out with the aid of a sympathetic gaoler. Suspected, quite correctly, of having in effect been spying, Fabert's life was at some risk, but Louis XIII intervened and protested at his treatment to the governor of the Spanish Netherlands, the Cardinal-Infanta Prince Ferdinand (brother of King Philip IV), and as a direct result he was then soon released, in an exchange for a Spanish officer, who had been found to be spying on French defences in the south.[2] The high regard in which Fabert was held, with the king evidently keen to obtain his release, is evident and late in 1633 he was appointed military governor of his home town, Metz, where he immediately set to work to improve the rather dilapidated defences.

In mid-May 1635 Louis XIII formally declared war on Spain, the *causus belli* being the Spanish seizure of Trier together with the archbishop, who enjoyed the tacit protection of France. In fact, active hostilities had already broken out, so the declaration was largely a matter of form more than anything else. Amongst the disruption and damage that resulted, Fabert's iron-foundry, situated at Moyoeuvre, was destroyed by Spanish raiders. French fortunes in the war were largely elusive, but Fabert was appointed to be a staff officer under the Comte Antoine de Guiche (subsequently Marshal Grammont). The role was then reduced to that of aide-de-camp to Cardinal Louis La Valette,[3] apparently because the king's principal adviser, Richelieu, felt that, for a man of such humble origins, he was advancing too far and too fast. His ability to speak German, however, proved useful when he was sent to find out whether the rulers of Franconia and Swabia would change sides, abandon their allegiance to the emperor in Vienna, and ally themselves to France. They were both understandably cautious, particularly as the French grip on Lorraine was still tenuous and declined to do so. To be entrusted with such a delicate mission, while still a relatively junior officer, was a good indication of the confidence reposed by the crown in Fabert at the time.

Late that September, while serving alongside Turenne, Fabert took part with the Ramboures in a sharp engagement against Imperialist troops at Odernheim, where a complete success was had with the capture of sixteen guns. These pieces eventually had to be abandoned, however, as the French were obliged to withdraw due to a lack of supplies in a war-ravaged region. The all-but exhausted army regrouped behind the river Nahe close to Birkenfeld, before falling back again, under heavy pressure, to the Saar and only narrowly escaping after a successful rearguard action had been fought. Fabert was then sent to Metz to bring forward fresh provisions, and so ragged and dirty was he, when calling at his own home while on this errand, that his wife did not at first recognize him. Having subsequently overseen the re-provisioning of the magazines and stores in Metz, Fabert resumed his role as company commander in the regiment. When the Imperialist troops withdrew on the approach of winter, he was sent forward with a detachment to ascertain whether they had indeed gone. All that were found were the sick and wounded who had been left behind, and as Fabert refused to permit his troops to ill treat them, and even had them tended to, many were grateful enough to subsequently enter French service once they had recovered.

At this time Fabert put two proposals forward to re-organize the army; and once again that he could do so, and be listened to, indicates the high regard in which he was held. The first suggestion was that the French cavalry, hitherto mustered and deployed in independent companies, with varying training, weapons and tactics according to the wishes of their commander, should be grouped into squadrons and regiments, along the lines of the Swedish practice, together with the introduction of standard drills. This suggestion was approved, although not overly welcomed by the strong-willed officers concerned, but only coming into effect two years later. The second proposal, that a corps of engineers, sappers and miners, in effect, be formed was too radical however, and would have to wait for the urging of Vauban during the reign of Louis XIV. It should be noted, however, that despite the good reputation he had established, and favourable notice gained, at age 38 Fabert was still only a company commander in a line regiment, while others around him had enjoyed advancement at a faster pace.

When La Valette advanced through the Vosges in the spring of 1636 to raise the Imperial blockade of Hagenau, Fabert was active in ensuring the proper re-supplying of the army, and coincidentally showed himself an adept light cavalryman on more than one occasion. He was active in the siege of Saverne, taking part in a particularly bloody and ultimately unsuccessful storm, during which he was struck by five spent musket balls; the Imperial garrison submitted on good terms on 14 July 1636. In early November, Duke Charles of Lorraine advanced with Imperial troops to threaten Alsace, and Fabert accompanied a Colonel Rantzau in a forced march to strengthen the invested garrison of St Jean on the river Saone, lying between Auxonne and Seurre. The suddenness of their appearance on the road from Auxonne so alarmed the Imperial troops that they hastily raised the intended siege and withdrew in scarcely decent haste. It is apparent from this and other incidents that Fabert, while nominally still only a junior company officer in a somewhat unfashionable regiment (although the Ramboures would belatedly, and rather grudgingly, come to be regarded as one of the 'old corps'), was often employed on detached duties of a highly significant nature within the army, usually at the request of Cardinal La Valette. In this he may not have been that unusual, as others would have been called on in the same way, but his continued lack of promotion persisted, and surely reflected an inbuilt prejudice against him on account of his birth.

After a brief visit to Paris in December, taking a report to Louis XIII on the recent operations, Fabert was back with the army in February 1637 at the capture of both St Avold and Créange. He then undertook a tour of the fortified places in Picardy, many of which had been neglected and left in disrepair. The appropriate reward for his efforts and long service eventually came from the king, when he was appointed to command a company in the Picardy Régiment, the most senior of the 'old corps', and a such this was undoubtedly seen as a prestigious appointment and worthy promotion. To augment his pay, he was also given the revenues of three small estates in Lorraine. The pace of his career accelerated noticeably, and when La Valette went to take command of the army in Flanders in mid-summer, he specifically asked for Fabert to accompany him in the role of a 'confidential adviser', or perhaps what would be regarded today as chief of staff. It is notable that amongst those accompanying the cardinal was Turenne, then still holding the rank of lieutenant-general, and the Duc d'Enghien (Condé). A siege was begun of Landrecies, lying close to the Forest of Mormal and Fabert was active in laying out the lines of circumvallation and contravallation. He also had command of one of the three 'attacks' on the defences, the digging of the trenches for which began on 10 July, and eleven days later Fabert blew a mine under the main defences, with the governor of the fortress duly alarmed and submitting the following day on good terms.

Louis XIII went to his grave on 16 May 1643, and his son succeeded to the throne with a lengthy period of regency necessary due to his youth. Fabert was sent to campaign in Catalonia, where he was taken prisoner by Spanish troops, and briefly held in Rosas before being exchanged. Louis XIV was crowned at Rheims on 7 June 1654, and shortly afterward, Fabert (who had been present at the coronation) was sent to lay siege to Stenay, held for the rebellious Condé. The siege operations were pushed forward vigorously, while the king and his adviser Cardinal Mazarin watched matters unfold from a place of safety nearby. Fabert's use of parallels and zigzag communication trenches attracted notice as being effective by the young Vauban who was present in the trenches. The place capitulated on 5 August, and the garrison (a mix of French and Spanish/Flemish troops) were permitted to march out and go to Montmédy without molestation. The cardinal wrote approvingly of Fabert's conduct to the king's mother, the regent Queen Anne, that 'For three days M. de Fabert has not taken an hour's rest, and it is miraculous that he has escaped a wound, since he would not quit the mines and most dangerous spots. Despite the orders of the king and our constant prayers.'[4] His troops having been sent to support Turenne in Picardy, Fabert then returned to take up his duties as governor of Sedan.

The troubles of the Fronde civil war rumbled on, with Mazarin at one point so unpopular that he felt it necessary to live abroad. His three charming young nieces, the 'Mazarinettes', adorning the court and captivating all and sundry, also went into semi-retirement and Fabert arranged an escort for them while on the road.[5] He was active in securing Mézières and Charleville, visited Metz to encourage the loyal garrison there, and firmly suppressed, with judicious fairness, a mutiny amongst the garrison in Thionville. In this capable way the royal position on the north-eastern borders was held more securely than might otherwise have been the case. In 1656, Fabert received from the crown some long-overdue repayments of debts incurred while on campaign, and he purchased an estate at Epernay in the Champagne region. As Vauban would also do in time, he tried to urge that the complex taxation prevalent throughout France, which bore most heavily upon the common people, be simplified and made more equitable, but he was not attended to, the hunger for tax revenue at court and to finance war being ever formidable. Nonetheless, that Fabert, being almost an echo of a bygone age, was still much in favour was evident, for when his eldest daughter, Anne, was wed to the Marquis de Vervins, both Louis XIV and his mother, Queen Anne, were present at the ceremony in Metz and signed the marriage document.

In the summer of 1658, for the extensive service he had rendered over many years, Fabert received his true reward; Louis XIV created three new Marshals of France, and Fabert was one of them.[6] How high the son of a court printer had risen may be judged, even though some thought that the award was long overdue (Fabert was almost certainly amongst their number). 'It was the first grant of the dignity of a marshal to anyone who had not been born a gentleman, and who had begun his long and faithful service in the ranks. The promotion of Fabert [was] a landmark in French history.'[7] Active hostilities came to an end with the Treaty of the Pyrenees when the king gained as his bride the Spanish Infanta, and it could be seen that the eastern border of France, in large part due to the diligence and energy of Fabert in key places like Metz and Sedan, possession of which Louis XIV was careful to retain under treaty arrangements, had been made firm. Aged now, and increasingly unwell, Fabert was present in Paris for the formal entry of the young infanta, Marie-Thérèse.

Fabert's much-cherished wife, Claude, died in February 1661, and he found it difficult to deal with his grief. That November, he was offered enrolment as a Knight of the Order of St Esprit, but the marshal refused the honour, as he would not invent or fabricate the required noble lineage that holders of the order were required to have. When it was indicated to him the king would not enquire too closely into the credentials that he might provide, Fabert refused to become a liar and forger even at Louis XIV's suggestion. It was not deemed politic to set aside the requirement of showing a noble background, just to make Fabert eligible for the honour, but the king was saddened all the same, and wrote on 29 December 1661:

> My Cousin, I cannot tell you whether it is with more esteem than sorrow that I have seen from your letter of the 7th of this month how you exclude yourself from the Cordon Bleu [insignia of the Order of St Esprit] with which I had resolved to honour you. This rare example of probity appears to me to be so admirable that I confess I regard it as an ornament of my reign. But I regret extremely to see a man who by his valour and fidelity has attained so worthily to the first offices of my kingdom and crown, deprive himself of this new mark of honour by an obstacle which binds my hands . . . I pray God, that he may have you in his Holy and worthy keeping. Louis.[8]

The sovereign council of Sedan had been abolished and made dependant on the overbearing Parlement in Metz, and Fabert protested at this diminution in the powers and privileges of the citizens. He was particularly concerned to protect the rights of the substantial and influential Protestant minority in the city, and the king relented a little, so that the marshal was appointed to be the Grand Seneschal of the city, with wide civic powers, instead.

On 10 May 1662 Fabert took to his bed with a fever, and rapidly weakened. He bade farewell to the many friends and admirers who came and clustered, some weeping without restraint, at the bedside.

The old soldier rallied a little, but died at 5pm on 17 May, and was buried beside his wife in the Church of the Irish Capuchins in Sedan. 'A hard working, ingenious, valiant and honest man . . . who became a Marshal of France, the first of his class who attained that splendid and coveted dignity.'[9] Today, a fine statue of the marshal stands appropriately in the main square in Sedan.

This was all very well, but it might be recalled that for nine years he served without pay or pension, and the arrears were never fully made up by the crown.[10] Fabert and his wife had two sons, one of whom died in infancy, and the other was killed fighting the Ottomans in Crete. Their three daughters all married well; the eldest, Anne, was wed to the Marquis de Vervins, and then on his early demise to the Marquis de Trelon. The second girl, Claude, married the Marquis de Caylus, and the third, Angelique, the Marquis de Genlis and on his death the Marquis de Beuvron.[11]

Chapter 3

Marshal de Créquy

Born in Poix de Picardie on 2 October 1629, François de Blanchefort de Créquy was the youngest of the three sons of Charles de Blanchefort and his wife Anne Grimoard de Roure. His grandfather, Charles I de Blanchefort, had in his time been a renowned Marshal of France, a close adviser to Louis XIII, and notable for ably commanding the French troops and their allies at the hard-fought Battle of Tornavento in Italy in June 1636.[1] Although the de Créquy family had its origins in Artois, at that time still a part of the Spanish (Southern) Netherlands, their loyalty was clearly directed towards the French crown, despite members of the extended family having served in the armies of both the King of Sweden and of the Dutch Republic during the ruinous turmoil of the Thirty Years War. François' eldest brother, Charles, became in turn a trusted adviser to Louis XIV, and his sister-in-law, Charles' wife, was made the chief lady-in-waiting to his queen, Marie-Thérèse, when young. Entering French service as a cadet at age 16, François de Créquy fought for the king in the fractious civil wars of the Fronde, and quickly established for himself a sound reputation as a capable and enterprising commander.

François married in 1657 Catherine de Rougé, and they had three sons, two of whom would die while on campaign serving the French crown.[2] A third son survived to become a noted commander with, just like his father, a fine reputation as being a safe and capable pair of hands. Two years after the marriage, de Créquy purchased the title and estates of Marines in Val de'Oise, and so could style himself the

Marquis de Marines. He had been made lieutenant-general in 1658 and commanded the right wing of the French army under Turenne at the Battle of the Dunes in June of the year, attracting particularly favourable attention for his calm and competent handling of his troops when under heavy pressure.

Campaigning in the Low Countries during the War of Devolution in 1667, de Créquy was present at the capture of Lille, and together with Bernard, Marquis de Bellefonds, and Louis de Crevant, Duc d'Humieres, was tasked by Turenne to intercept a strong Spanish force which was marching to attempt to relieve the beleaguered garrison. This blocking movement was carried out very capably, and some 2,000 casualties were inflicted by de Créquy and his colleagues before their opponents withdrew. The operation was so well handled that Louis XIV, in a rare rush of enthusiasm, promptly made all three men Marshals of France in consequence of their success. However, de Créquy subsequently had difficulty maintaining control over his troops, as their arrears of pay mounted, a complaint made by the army intendants more than once, and the threat of outright mutiny was high for some time. Discipline faltered and desertion became rife, and Etienne Carlier, the highly capable intendant accompanying the army, wrote to Louvois, the minister for war, that, 'As we are in a forested area, it is very difficult to prevent this disorder. Moreover, idleness corrupts the soldier as much as the lack of payment sours him. I assure you that a little money and activity are the appropriate remedies for this evil.'[3] In time order and discipline were restored, and de Créquy's calm handling of what almost became an outright mutiny, with leniency shown towards the recalcitrant (but still unpaid) troops, was noticed with much approval.

Three years later, de Créquy was sent to command the army which took possession of the Duchy of Lorraine, a task which was accomplished without great difficulty. However, in April 1672, at the onset of the punitive war forced on the Dutch Republic, he rashly refused to serve under Turenne, as in theory at least and maintained rather wilfully as a point of honour, no marshal could issue commands to another. Bellefonds and d'Humieres took the same high-handed line as de Créquy, but this was a mistake, as Turenne had been appointed by the king to be marshal-general and accordingly had all the necessary authority to command the others as occasion demanded. Not only that, but the three newly elevated marshals had all served quite happily under Turenne with conspicuous success during the operations to seize Lille, and their obdurate attitude indicated that they were getting a little above themselves. Even more serious was that Louis XIV was highly displeased at this apparent open display of insubordination, which in earlier and more turbulent years a strong-willed marshal might, just about, have got away with. Those days were now past, and the king would not tolerate such behaviour, so that he ordered all three men to serve under Turenne, each in the role of lieutenant-general, for at least two weeks, and furthermore to do so with good grace. This they did, somewhat reluctantly, but de Créquy was deprived of his command, and sent, still simmering with ill-concealed resentment, to live quietly at Marines, openly sulking but having to accept a form of what was almost internal exile, while the king considered what next to do with him.

Almost inevitably, tempers calmed, and skilled commanders clearly were not to be left idle. In 1673 de Créquy was called back into active service, as the war with the Dutch and their staunch ally, the Elector of Brandenburg, and latterly the Spanish troops in the Southern Netherlands, continued to gather pace. He neatly secured Liège, where anti-French riots had recently taken place, so enforcing that city's neutrality, and was then employed to muster almost 6,000 of the *Arrière-Ban* at Nancy to support Turenne's campaign in Alsace. It was soon found that these ill-disciplined militia troops were too troublesome and militarily ineffective and were sent home. 'I ardently hope,' the marshal wrote ruefully, 'that the king will never again have any need to assemble his nobles; because it is a corps incapable of action.'[4] In May 1675 de Créquy moved with 10,000 troops to Givet, to levy 'contributions' in the area, and then on to invest Dinant on the river Meuse, opening the siege trenches on the 22nd of the month. Two mines were blown by French engineers under the defences, and the garrison commander (who in fairness could only muster a meagre and ill-trained force some 250 strong) submitted a week later; de Créquy then went forward to observe the Imperial commander, Duke Charles V of Lorraine, who had taken up a strong position at Metz.

Before long, the marshal was summoned by Louis XIV to put his infantry into Trier on the Moselle, and having left them in place, to then take his cavalry to assist in the difficult operations being undertaken against the fortress of Limburg. That fortress only fell on 21 June, and he then was tasked with returning to relieve Trier, where the Duke of Lorraine had in the meantime begun besieging the French garrison left in place there. De Créquy was impetuous and clearly misread the situation and the duke's dispositions, and while being plainly over-confident, he stumbled into a well-laid trap. He was soundly beaten in battle at Konz-Saarbrück on 11 August 1675, where the French, 14,000 strong, were out-manoeuvred by superior numbers of Imperial troops, and their flank was neatly turned by the Spanish cavalry commander, the Marquis Otto Caretto de Grana. After what had initially seemed to be an indecisive battle that went on for over three hours, de Créquy, whose first mount that day had been killed beneath him by a round-shot, had no choice but to withdraw in haste and confusion, leaving behind on the battlefield over 2,000 prisoners, eleven guns and his entire supply train. The pursuit by the Imperial cavalry was so hard and fast that the marshal was lucky to reach Trier at all without further loss, although he had to desperately break through the newly-dug siege lines surrounding the place to be able enter the city with what was left of his command.

Less than a month later, on 9 September, and despite a gallant but doomed defence, with clearly no hope of relief and his hungry troops unpaid and near to mutiny, de Créquy had to submit and ask for a capitulation on terms. This was promptly granted by Duke Charles, although the marshal and his senior officers were briefly held in comfortable quarters as prisoners. The garrison were permitted to march out but, of course, had to leave their guns for the victors. Even after his defeat in open battle by the duke, that de Créquy had done his best in daunting circumstances, even to the extent of holding out in the church in Trier with a few of his loyal officers and men until their powder was exhausted, was to his credit and did a great deal to salvage his reputation subsequently. All the same, Louis XIV was dismayed at the reverse, and furious at the misconduct of many of the French troops involved. Those regiments who had actively mutinied in Trier were not allowed to go scot-free, and one officer, deemed not to have done nearly enough to maintain order, was executed by the public headsman, while one in every twenty of the errant rank and file were also to die, each soldier to suffer punishment being chosen by lot. The men were formed up on parade in their groups of twenty, while the lots were drawn, and the unlucky individuals were then marched forward to be promptly hanged from a cart in front of the assembled troops, as a stark lesson to all regarding their future conduct.

The dismal end to this campaign had, of course, been particularly mortifying for de Créquy, as he had been clearly outfought, although in fairness lacking numbers and with an army that was both poorly provisioned and in an exposed position. That he had pushed too far forward, and without adequate supports, was an inescapable conclusion. Louis XIV, although dismayed at the reverse that had been suffered, remarked that the marshal was known to be a brave man, who had met unusual misfortune. Nonetheless, there was something of a cloud over de Créquy for the time being, but, with Turenne soon to be killed in battle, and the Prince of Condé having had to retire due to poor health (he was gouty and unable now to ride a horse and had latterly to use a light carriage to get around a battlefield), the king was short of good commanders, so that de Créquy was before long summoned to go out on campaign again. He was then at the successful siege of the fortress of Condé in late April 1676, and subsequently at Bouchain of the river Escaut, where the king's brother, known to all as 'Monsieur', was in nominal command, while Sebastien le Prestre de Vauban conducted the siege operations themselves. As the Marquis de Louvois commented, 'The Marshal de Créquy had the honour of commanding under the orders of his majesty'.[5] The king had come to join the campaign and having taken up a position at the head of the covering army, situated between Valenciennes and St Amand, would have tried to force battle on William of Orange who was nearby, looking for a way to somehow lift the siege. Louvois wrote that,

> The king immediately mounted his horse and set out for Heurtebise, which was only a cannon shot from Valenciennes, followed by only eight squadrons of the guards, four of his gendarmes, and his light horse. His Majesty, on seeing thirteen squadrons in battle formation under the counter-escarpment of Valenciennes, thought at first that it was the garrison cavalry. He saw a moment later that the foe formed an extended cavalry wing . . . The king proposed to charge them. Monsieur arrived a little later with the Duc de Créquy and followed by twenty [more] squadrons.[6]

At a hastily-convened council of war, all the French generals were against making an attack, except for the typically aggressive Marshal de Lorges that is, as being both too risky and a needless distraction from the efforts to secure Bouchain. Louvois stepped in and agreed, urging that the main purpose of the army at this point was to see that the fortress fell without undue delay, and so Louis XIV reluctantly concurred with the advice, 'As you have more experience than me,' he said 'I concede [accede], but with regret'.[7] As it was, the decision not to undertake a battle there and then rankled with the king, and he never ceased to regret it.[8] However, the Bouchain garrison submitted the following day, and so the principal aim for the French was accomplished. The Prince of Orange turned instead to strengthen the garrison in Cambrai, while simultaneously raiding the French lines of communication across the river Somme with his cavalry, in an attempt to try to distract the attention of the king and his commanders.

In early 1677 de Créquy was sent to muster his army at Nancy and moved on to challenge Duke Charles when he marched into Alsace in mid-April; the marshal manoeuvred adroitly to prevent any combination of Allied forces with those of William of Orange who was at that time engaged in a siege at Charleroi. The attempt against that fortress failed, in part at least because of lack of numbers available to be employed, and so de Créquy's capable efforts to hold the duke off had paid a handsome dividend. 'By adroit moves, Créquy kept [Duke] Charles from joining William at Charleroi, thus helping to guarantee the failure of that siege.'[9] Baffled, Charles withdrew towards Trier, and the marshal took the initiative to march and threaten both the key Imperial fortresses of Freiburg in the Briesgau, and Offenburg. On 21 September de Créquy soundly beat an Imperial army under the command of the Prince of Saxe-Eisenach, and on 7 October, having withdrawn again into Alsace, inflicted a highly damaging defeat on Duke Charles in a fiercely-fought cavalry action at Kockersberg, a small town lying between Strasbourg and Saverne. As the cold months came on, and the general expectation that warm winter quarters would soon be sought for the troops, de Créquy instead moved swiftly on 9 November to again invest Freiburg. Duke Charles was taken entirely by surprise, no attempt was made to impede the French advance, and the place duly capitulated a week later, after a feeble pretence of defence by the garrison commander, who really should have done more to save the place.

As the campaign for 1678 gathered pace, de Créquy was tasked to ensure the continued security of the now rather exposed French forward stance in the Breisgau, although he was strictly instructed by Louvois not to engage in an open battle, but just to, 'Keep things on the same footing as last year, that is to conserve the king's fortresses and troops . . . without exposing himself to the risk of a general action'.[10] Duke Charles had wintered his troops in Alsace, and now had command of an army reported to be well over 30,000 strong (this was, in fact, found to be an exaggeration). Acting with considerable energy and skill, de Créquy ignored the repeated instructions to avoid battle, and after receiving reinforcements, inflicted two smart defeats on the Imperial commanders, firstly on 6 July fighting against Field Marshal Guido von Starhemberg at Rheinfeld near the Swiss border, and then on Duke Charles at Ortenbach on 23 July. He even went on to capture Kehl by storm, with its strategically-important Rhine crossing leading towards the free Imperial city of Strasbourg, on the 28th of that month. The marshal then crossed on a pontoon bridge and moved on towards Strasbourg itself, and destroyed what was left of the existing bridge over the river. He then took up a firm blocking position on the river Lauter, and with an Imperial army fast disintegrating through repeated defeat and a growing and chronic lack of supplies, Duke Charles had little option but to withdraw into the Palatinate; in consequence de Créquy had secured Alsace from further occupation for the time being.

This energetic and very well-handled campaign, understandably, did much to restore de Créquy's reputation and standing with Louis XIV and his formidable minister for war. The marshal could not, however, get along with the army intendant accompanying his troops, and he resented what was seen as interference with the issuing of orders. He wrote, 'To tell the truth, I do not believe that with an army of twenty thousand men, I should be treated on the same basis as a governor of a province'.[11] However, putting a rein on the powers of the marshals when they were out in the field was exactly what was intended in Versailles, and in the wider scheme of things the activities of the army intendants more often than not proved their worth to the commanders they served.

De Créquy acted as proxy witness for the king at the wedding of the dauphin to the Bavarian Princess Marie-Anne in late January 1680. To further cement his fast-recovering reputation, on 30 September 1681 he undertook another of his notable rapid marches to seize Strasbourg once more. Furthermore, this was accomplished after only a very short siege, almost by *coup de main*, so that bemused population awoke to find their defences securely in the hands of the marshal's troops and themselves become *de facto* French citizens. A delighted Louis XIV entered the city in appropriate state soon afterwards and ordered that the cathedral be returned to Catholic worship immediately, so that he could hear a *Te Deum* sung in celebration of the city being, once more, secure in French hands.

An interesting exchange took place in 1683, as an Ottoman army under Grand Vizier Kara Mustapha seemed about to set off and advance from Belgrade towards Vienna, and by doing so throw the whole of central Europe into turmoil. Louis XIV wrote to de Créquy, to explain why he had decided not to push matters forward with any real vigour in the Low Countries for the time being:

> I do not wish that those who should oppose the Turkish invasion could reproach me that my actions in the Lowlands [Southern Netherlands] to obtain my just rights, had made it impossible for them to wage war successfully for the defence of Christianity. I have resolved to end at once the business of the Lowlands by putting it to the arbitration of the King of England [Charles II].[12]

In fact, Louis XIV was just cynically trying to avoid being blamed if a catastrophe for Christianity should occur in the east, as it had been French policy for some time to actively encourage the Sublime Porte in Constantinople to engage Austria, and so distract the efforts and attention of Emperor Leopold from the Rhine frontier with France. Efforts were also made (with no success) by Versailles to persuade the Polish king, John Sobieski, to stay out of the conflict with the Ottomans, but it was also a simple fact that the king's dispute with Madrid was not proceeding all that well, and so, in reality a virtue was, perhaps, being made of necessity.

In April 1684 de Créquy had charge of the successful siege of the fortress of Luxembourg, although the great engineer Sebastien le Prestre de Vauban again actually supervised the work in the trenches. A preliminary bombardment of the fortress had failed to intimidate the Spanish garrison into giving up without making a fight of things, and the governor, the Prince de Chimay, put up a gallant defence with his 3,600-strong garrison, and a number of sorties were made to spoil the siege trenches. During one of the prince's counter-bombardments, de Créquy's unfortunate valet was decapitated at his side by a round-shot fired from the fortress; the marshal was splattered with his blood. Nonetheless, de Chimay had to submit on 3 June, and he was granted good terms, being permitted to march his men out with drums beating and colours flying. De Créquy had also been strictly warned by Louvois that the king's cherished engineer was not to be allowed to expose himself to danger during the digging of the approach trenches before Luxembourg:

> His Majesty recommends to the marshal to give Sr de Vauban all the time necessary to conduct the works required to reduce the place in such a fashion that it may be done with as few losses as possible. His Majesty also recommends to the Marshal to give such orders as needed to prevent Sr de Vauban exposing himself without great need.[13]

Almost inevitably, such orders were ignored by the gifted but strong-willed Vauban, whose renowned close attention to the entrenching work would not be lightly set aside in the name of ensuring his own personal safety. In any case, this was to be de Créquy's last campaign at age 65 as his health was now failing, and he retired from service in the field.

Remembered as one of the most dashing and brilliant of the young army commanders in the king's service at one time, cool under pressure and often daring in action, de Créquy could move fast and often showed that he could hit incredibly hard. Although the marshal never quite lived down the defeat at Konzer Bruck or having to briefly go into captivity with the fall of Trier, his numerous successes far outweighed his defeats, and although argumentative and occasionally over-confident, he could, much like Turenne, march more quickly than most of his contemporaries, and overall remained trusted and in royal favour to the end. De Créquy died in his house in the Rue de Nicaise in Paris on 3 February 1687, a few days before the death of his oldest brother, Charles. The marshal's widow, Catherine, lived on to a good old age, dying in 1713, and both were buried at the convent of Saint-Honore in Paris. Although the building was demolished in 1816, a fine memorial to the deceased soldier was largely saved and moved to the Church of Saint Roch where it still stands. The couple's surviving son, François-Joseph, was also a highly regarded commander in the service of Louis XIV, being made lieutenant-general in 1696, and director-general of infantry in 1702. He died in 1718 during the regency of the infant Louis XV.

Chapter 4

Marshal Luxembourg

François-Henri de Montmorency-Bouteville, who would become Duc de Luxembourg in time, was born on 8 January 1628, in Paris. The family setting was a troubled one, as his father, François de Montmorency-Bouteville, had been executed six months previously for having taken part in an illegal duel, an affair of honour pursued to an absurd length, with the Marquis de Beuvron. His mother, Elizabeth-Angelique de Vienne, was accordingly left in difficult circumstances (although she gamely lived on as a widow until her eventual demise in 1696). Accordingly, the young man was brought up in the household of Charlotte-Margurite de Montmorency, the Princess de Condé, who had him educated alongside her own son, the Duc d'Enghien, who would in time display his own brilliant talents as a commander and prove long to be a thorn in the side of the crown. Having taken an active part with d'Enghien (the Prince of Condé) in the Fronde civil wars, Bouteville, as he was generally known at the time, found it prudent to go and live in the Netherlands, until he was amongst those granted a pardon by Louis XIV in 1659. With the helpful influence of Condé, two years later he married Madeleine-Charlotte de Claremont-Tonnerre, Princess of Thingry, the wealthy heiress to the dukedom of Luxembourg. In consequence, François-Henri was created a peer of France with the title Duc de Luxembourg.

Although initially lacking an active command, Luxembourg eventually took part in Louis XIV's aggressive War of Devolution against Spain in 1667 and served alongside Condé in the occupation of the Franche-Comte region, holding the rank of lieutenant-general in the king's service. Having gained the favour of the minister for war, Louvois, in 1672 he was given a senior appointment in fighting the Dutch during Louis XIV's attempt to subjugate the doughty republic to French will and influence. Despite having to send a substantial number of his own troops to assist Marshal Turenne, Luxembourg remained active and alert, and a determined thrust by the Dutch forces under the robust command of John Maurice, Prince William of Orange's brother, towards the major manufacturing town of Naarden was smartly forced back. The Prince of Orange wrote to Maurice expressing his clear frustration, on 10 October:

> I am much grieved that M. de Luxembourg has prevented you from attacking Naarden and that he is worrying [harassing] you, which however I think he will soon have to give up doing, since I have resolved to march this evening to Woerden and attack it by force, and so doubtless he will return to Utrecht . . . I think it would be a very good thing if you would get some boats sent to the Zuiderzee and make some sort of cannonade against Naarden.[1]

However, Williams's subsequent attempt against Woerden on the road leading to French-held Utrecht failed when Luxembourg launched a night attack (a quite unusual event at the time), which resulted in five hours of heavy fighting in which the Dutch troops, although they stood their ground well for a while, were eventually driven off. A French attempt to pursue was thwarted by a stout rearguard action, maintained by their weary Dutch opponents who had recovered themselves sufficiently to be able to present a bold front.

The dramatic Dutch move in that year to breach their sea-dikes and open the sluices regulating water levels, had already made subsequent moves very difficult for the French army commanders. Louis XIV went back to Versailles at the end of July, and Luxembourg was left in charge of the troops facing the Dutch along what was known as the 'Water Line'. The minister for war wrote that, 'The king having realized that all the approaches to Holland are at present inundated, and that until the frost sets in it is not possible to penetrate them, had ordered the advanced guards to be withdrawn'.[2] Savage fighting in increasingly bitter cold weather went on winter approached, with little quarter shown by either side. Late in December, Luxembourg was responsible for the brutal sack of the small Dutch towns of Bodegraven and Zwammerdam, between Utrecht and Leiden, a place considered to be of high importance to the Dutch defensive effort, the loss of which would allow the French to move through the flooded stretches of land to reach drier country with the chances of access not only to Leiden, but also Gouda, Haarlem and even prizes such as Amsterdam and The Hague. Accordingly, orders had been given that Bodegraven should be stoutly defended and only abandoned in case of the 'utmost necessity'. The Dutch garrison commander, beset with contradictory advice and instructions, outnumbered and with his badly provisioned and raw troops having to man inadequate defences, plainly considered the case to be hopeless. On hearing that the French were on the march he withdrew his garrison rather than be cut off. Luxembourg approached, his troops moving on 28 December across the frozen polders in the moonlight, to reach sleeping Bodegraven. An unfrozen canal was encountered, which slowed progress, but this obstacle was soon bridged, and Luxembourg pressed on with a strong advanced detachment of 3,000 men. Finding Bodegraven and nearby Zwammerdam open and undefended, his French troops promptly burned both places and killed those citizens who had not been able to flee. On withdrawing towards Utrecht, Dutch troops did move to try and cut the French off, but proved unable to do so.

This quite unnecessary act of barbarity committed at the two small towns found little approval at court, even though French prisoners in Dutch hands at the time were often being treated with vengeful severity by their captors. Luxembourg merely shrugged off the critical comments; in the end, however, what had been achieved was a clear demonstration that the French could, if they put their minds to it, penetrate the waterlogged Dutch defences with little danger of meeting a concerted and effective resistance. Still, a risk had been run and a French officer wrote to a friend that, 'I cannot refrain from telling you that this action of forcing the enemy in their own positions is most fortunate, if it had failed there would have been no safety in retreat . . . for the waters are so high that there is no more road'.[3]

In a wider sense, faced with the widespread inundations limiting tactical movement, and moreover with the Dutch absolutely unwilling to consider negotiations while French troops remained in their land, Louis XIV began to look to give up the whole campaign. Louvois would write, rather unreasonably and seemingly without irony, that, 'If the Dutch were men, they would have made peace long ago'.[4] Well, the king and his field commanders had evidently failed in their efforts to subdue their opponents, and that was a simple if uncomfortable fact. During the early summer of 1673 Luxembourg was joined by the Prince of Condé, elderly and unwell, but who outranked him of course, a situation that suited neither man very well, particularly as the opportunities for achieving success in the ailing campaign were slimmer than ever. In an unexpected aside, however, the king's treasury saw benefits in the exorbitant taxation being imposed on the Dutch towns under occupation. 'The total has exceeded my hopes', Louvois wrote gleefully.[5]

In July the Dutch re-affirmed that all French troops must be withdrawn if discussions for a cessation of the war were to take place. Peace was plainly desirable at what had become, overall, an arid distraction on both sides of the conflict, while Condé wrote, almost despairingly, at the futile efforts being made to put some fresh life into the campaign. 'I have done nothing else but try and find a route for attack. M. de Luxembourg also employs all his astuteness without being able to find one, the waters being everywhere prodigiously high . . . All the dykes are covered by water at the shallowest up to the knee.'[6]

Spain formally entered the war in August 1673, although their troops had in fact been active in the campaign for some time. Condé was soon posted to Flanders on orders from Louvois, and on 13 September, Luxembourg now with much reduced strength, proved unable to save Naarden from being re-taken by Dutch and Spanish troops – the French garrison had prudently surrendered rather than face a storm and were permitted to march out unmolested, without their guns of course, and go to Utrecht to join the main body of the army still there. This marked a key moment in the war: the French were overstretched, and any slip would be bound to be severely punished. Luxembourg had written in forthright and blunt protest to the minister for war, at what had been a clear dividing of scarce resources in the face of a re-invigorated Dutch effort, bolstered now with the active assistance of their allies:

> I wish that you had not had good reasons for removing M. le Prince de Condé from Brabant; he obliged the Prince of Orange to keep troops there and do nothing as a result. Did you not know the strength of the Dutch, and did it not occur to you that they would undertake something? They would not have dared to think of it if M. le Prince had not left his position.[7]

In fact, Condé had needed to be sent with his troops to Flanders to confront the increasingly aggressive Spanish forces there, but the clear element of overstretch was evident, and with Turenne still dealing with the Elector of Brandenburg and the Imperial commander Raimondo Montecuccoli on the Rhine, Louis XIV's commanders were now strong nowhere and comparatively weak everywhere.

In November, Luxembourg skilfully conducted a withdrawal of his depleted army from Utrecht to Maastricht, which strong fortress had recently been taken by the French. He then moved on into France, eluding the efforts of William of Orange to intercept his march towards Charleroi. The losses amongst his troops had been significant, with Luxembourg being left with a bayonet strength of only some 20,000, but he deftly kept his army together in what had become disheartening circumstances, and extricated them from an increasingly exposed position. The movement, although the consequence of a clear French strategic reverse, was widely acknowledged as a very creditable operation, and earned him an appointment by the king as a captain in the prestigious Gardes de Corps in 1674, before being made a Marshal of France the following year. By then, and after so much effort, expense and bloodshed, all Louis XIV had to show for his war with the Dutch were the, not insignificant, fortresses of Maastricht and Graves on the river Meuse. All the same, Marshal Bellefonds loudly criticised the French withdrawal from Holland, claiming that it was premature and showed nothing but timidity, so that he fell from royal favour for a while, and was replaced by Marshal de Lorge, who was expected to be less outspoken.

In 1676, Condé gave up the command of the Army of the Rhine due to his increasing ill-health, and with Turenne recently killed in action, Luxembourg was appointed in his stead, moving to relieve the French garrison in Philippsburg, which had been invested early in May by Imperial troops led by the very able Duke Charles of Lorraine. Failing to either entice his opponent into open battle, or to move through the defences at Weissenberg, Luxembourg had to watch in frustration when Philippsburg fell on 17 September; 'This fortification had been the anchor of both the line of the Rhine, and the line that stretched to the Meuse, and so its loss was quite a blow to French power and prestige'.[8] Seeking a way to gain something from the year's campaign, the marshal crossed the Rhine and with little interference from his opponents embarked on a very successful grand raid, levying contributions, before wintering his army in Alsace and Lorraine. With the arrival of the warm weather of early spring, the following March he captured Valenciennes, where the impetuous attack of his infantry overwhelmed the plainly rather ill-prepared Spanish garrison; Louis XIV was present and highly pleased, being able to take the submission of the place in person. The city magistrates appealed to the king to be spared a sack, even though the French success had been forced 'sword in hand', and this request was graciously granted, although the magistrates were scolded for having resisted in the first place. Luxembourg went on to beat William of Orange at Cassel on 10 May 1677, operating with the king's younger brother, Philippe (known to all as 'Monsieur'), at his side and naturally enough holding the nominal command of the army; all the same, it took Luxembourg's robust repulse of the very capable attack the Dutch made to try and crush the French left to emphatically win the day.

The king and his entourage went back to St Germain, and the following year Luxembourg was left in command in the Low Countries, having strict orders to stand on the defensive. It could now be seen that Louis XIV felt the need to limit the escalating costs of the war, not just in money terms, and he wrote to caution the marshal, 'Make use of my cavalry rather than engaging yourself in an infantry battle, which causes the loss of a lot of men but which never decides anything'.[9] In truth, French finances were now in a wretched state after the formidable strains of the conflict, and Louis XIV managed to secure peace with the conclusion of the 1st Treaty of Nijmegen. Ironically, and despite the king's words of caution, Luxembourg and William of Orange clashed expensively on 14 August 1678, at St Denis to the west of Mons, neither commander yet being aware of the formal ending of hostilities. The news reached the respective camps that very same evening, too late to save the 8,000 or so casualties suffered across the two armies in battle that day.

Spain could not hope to carry on the conflict without Dutch involvement, and so Louis XIV had, in a limited sense, again made more secure his borders in the north and north-east, occupying the Duchy of Lorraine, and with such fortresses as Freiburg east of the Rhine now secure in French hands. 'I was resolved to make peace,' he wrote, 'but I wished to conclude it gloriously for myself, and advantageously for my kingdom . . . I wished to re-imburse myself by right of conquest, and to console myself thus.'[10] In fact, his war aims had not been achieved, other than in a highly limited sense, but French armies had, by and large, held off a powerful coalition that the king had not at the outset imagined could be formed against him. The subsequent 2nd Treaty of Nijmegen eventually ended the conflict between France and Spain.

In January 1680, Luxembourg was amongst several prominent notables detained in the Bastille prison in Paris, in connection with the notorious and scandalous 'Affair of the Poisons'. The highly spurious allegations against him seemed to refer to the rumoured telling of fortunes in an attempt to ensure yet greater victories in the field, rather than in the somewhat more dangerous art of conducting black masses, or trying to poison one's husband, wife, lover or rival. This all had much to do with a wearying ongoing quarrel the marshal was having with Louvois, previously a supporter, who was now anxious to keep a tighter rein on the highly ambitious soldier whenever he appeared to be shown too much favour. Before long, and perhaps rather predictably, nothing of real substance was found against the marshal so that he was eventually released. The Duc de St Simon recalled that, 'He was accused . . . not of poisoning, but of using spells to give him victories in the field. He was not a clever witness, and talked too much, but was finally exonerated on all counts. When he came back to the court, the king never mentioned the trial, but gave him great commands.'[11] Nonetheless, the moment had been one of real peril, as during the poison panic that gripped Paris at the time, a number of those suspected (mostly individuals of less elevated rank it is true), were executed while others were banished for life, or left to languish in miserable provincial gaols and, in effect, forgotten about by those in authority. For Luxembourg the dangerous moment passed, and he quickly resumed his duties as captain of the Gardes du Corps at court.

At the outbreak of the War of the Grand Alliance (Nine Years War) in 1688, Luxembourg superseded Marshal Louis de Crevant, the Duc d'Humières, and appointed to command the army in Flanders. He was able to call on the support of Marshal Boufflers, who was operating in the Moselle valley. Luxembourg moved quickly to cross the river Sambre at Froidmont and achieved a very neat and clear victory at Fleurus on 1 July 1690, where he boldly divided his army and enveloped both the flanks of the Dutch field commander, the Prince of Waldeck. The Allied horse broke as their outposts were driven in, and only the sturdiness of the Dutch infantry prevented a complete rout from taking place. Waldeck lost 17,000 killed, wounded or taken captive, almost half his strength, while the French loss was more modest, but not insignificant, at about 6,000, The marshal wrote of his beaten opponent that 'The Prince of Waldeck has good reason to resent his cavalry forever'.[12] Luxembourg had not had any significant advantage in numbers, if at all, so the daring he had shown, and the risk run, were quite clear, and Louis XIV was so delighted with the victory, that he sent word of it to the sultan in Constantinople as an example of what his commanders could achieve.

The Prince of Waldeck withdrew to Brussels, where he received reinforcements drawn from fortress garrisons, and also from Liège and Brandenburg, that more than make up his recent losses. Rather oddly, Luxembourg did not see the need to pursue the prince with much vigour after his recent victory, and instead levied 'contributions' on the surrounding countryside to re-provision his army. He was also obliged, with considerable reluctance, by instructions to send a substantial detachment of troops to support the army commanded by the king's son (known to all as the 'Grand Dauphin'), serving with Marshal Guy de Lorge against the Imperial-held fortress of Philippsburg on the Rhine. 'His Majesty knows,' Louvois wrote to the marshal, 'that this order will mortify you, but he expects you not to murmur since he thinks it to be for the good of his service.'[13] The dauphin was facing growing numbers of Imperial troops, so the move was certainly prudent, as the king would have been dismayed if his son had faced any hint of failure. De Lorge, as *de facto* army commander, was a safe enough pair of hands, but the concern for his son and his reputation haunted the king all the same.

During the French siege of Mons in late March 1691, Luxembourg had command of the 45,000-strong covering force, while Louis XIV supervised the actual operations against the fortress in person, accompanied as usual by his chief engineer, Vauban. On 8 April the garrison commander submitted after some heavy fighting, rather than face a storm and sack of the place; the decision to yield may well have been encouraged by the threat made that the citizenry of the town would be fined 100,000 crowns for each additional day that the garrison held out. The following month Luxembourg gathered his army between Menin and Courtrai, and seized Halle, after which he moved towards Brussels, but was confronted by Dutch and allied forces at Anderlecht, emplaced in so strong a position that he decided not to attack. Luxembourg went into camp at Soignies, where he received reinforcements that had been sent by Marshal Boufflers. After neatly blocking an attempt by William III to threaten Dinant on the Meuse, on 19 September he caught and almost overwhelmed Waldeck's ill-prepared rearguard yet again in an action at Leuze on the La Catoir stream. The engagement was marked by the rapid French marching pace over the 15 miles to get into action, and the sheer dash of their own horsemen who carried the day in fine style. The affair was, however, not entirely easy, and Luxembourg was himself involved in parrying a sword stroke from an enterprising English trooper who had valiantly broken through the French ranks to reach him. The marshal coolly deflected the blow with the cane which he habitually carried, before the gallant trooper was hauled off his horse and made prisoner.

French losses that day, at nearly 700, were more than outmatched by Waldeck's tally of 1,900 including some hundreds of prisoners, standards and kettledrums, but the onset of cold weather sent the opposing armies off to their winter quarters soon afterwards. The king was so pleased at reports of the action that he ordered a special medal to be struck in commemoration of the day, together with a special standard for the troop of Horse Grenadiers of the Maison de Roi, who had particularly distinguished themselves.[14] He was, however, less impressed that Luxembourg had omitted to report that his cavalry lad also lost several standards in the *melee.* The Marquis de Louvois died soon afterwards, and he was undeniably a hard man to replace (certainly not by the subsequent appointment in his place of his lacklustre son, the Marquis de Barbezieux), and Louis XIV in consequence came to rely on Luxembourg to a greater extent than before.

Taking the field once more in May 1692, Luxembourg with 60,000 men covered the French siege of Namur, conducted again by the king. He was incongruously once more accompanied by the a huge entourage including the principal ladies of the court, dressed appropriately enough as Amazons, and no doubt providing onlookers with quite a spectacle, although not increasing the bayonet strength of the army one bit. King William III (previously the Prince of Orange) came forward and attempted to confront the covering army, and so to open the road to relieve the Namur garrison who were commanded by the Duke of Barbançon, assisted by the efforts of the noted Dutch engineer Meinheer van Coehorn. However, the swollen spring waters of the Mehaigne stream prevented him doing so, and the garrison, who had withdrawn into the Namur citadel after bitter and costly fighting, submitted on terms on 30 June. The French success was only had at a high price, with some 7,000 killed and wounded, while the garrison suffered a loss of 4,000, including van Coehorn who was wounded by an exploding shell.

The weather had turned foul, and the royal party accompanying the army were in some distress, so that Louis XIV left along with his elegant entourage, and Luxembourg, now fully in command once he had gone, put his army into camp near to the villages of Steinkirk and Herne. The ageing king had for the last time gone on campaign, and he now at last fully entrusted matters to the capable hands of his marshals. He left instructions that the Luxembourg should move to shield Namur from any impending Dutch attack, but he was cautious, feeling that he had insufficient strength to do so with much prospect of success. Louis XIV was not too pleased at this inactivity, and he wrote urging him on. 'My intention is that you should march with speed, . . . fight him [William III] before he can establish his trenches. . . . I will not prescribe the route; you know better than anyone the best way to fall on him.'[15]

Luxembourg was in no hurry to move, and was still in camp at Steinkirk when, on 3 August 1692 William III surprised the French with a well-handled and wholly unexpected attack made over broken and wooded ground. Only after heavy and costly fighting did the marshal manage to hold his position, retake several batteries that had been overrun, and drive his opponents off. Both sides claimed a victory, as might be expected, although Luxembourg probably came away with most credit, having lost about 7,000 killed and wounded against the 10,000 casualties their opponents could count, but the withdrawal of the Dutch and their allies, although they had been repulsed, had been made in good order. Luxembourg sent his son to describe the battle in detail to the king, who was intrigued by accounts of the greater usefulness of flintlock weapons. Louis XIV was concerned to learn that his soldiers had been seen to discard their own matchlocks that day, eager instead to take up the fallen flintlock muskets of their opponents. He wrote to Luxembourg, instructing him to make enquiries.

> Look into it to see if you believe that it would be more useful to the good of my service either to have the infantry entirely armed with fusils or to leave the situation as it is. Talk to the old officers and tell me what they think. If you believe that it would be good to army my infantry with them, tell me, and I will order that they be distributed in the quantity that you desire.[16]

The days of the slow-firing matchlock, and the pike, were clearly passing, and the more efficient, but rather more expensive, flintlock together with socket bayonet would be widely accepted into French service before long. Louvois, conservative and cautious, was no longer on hand to offer strident but often ill-thought-out advice on such detailed military natters, and Louis XIV acted accordingly.

At the king's insistence, Boufflers was sent to bombard Charleroi, and then directed the Duc de Villeroi to seize the fortress of Huy on the Meuse, which was accomplished with only slight loss. Luxembourg then fought and achieved perhaps his greatest victory on 29 July 1693, when he soundly defeated the Allied army led by William III at Landen (Neerwinden), not far from what would be the 1705 battlefield of Elixheim. The reinforced army the marshal commanded that day was almost the largest that Louis XIV ever put in the field, some 99 battalions of infantry and 201 cavalry squadrons, and 71 guns (a force over 80,000 strong in total). William III had only about 50,000 troops on the field and while the contest that day at Landen was particularly severe, with heavy casualties on both sides (8,000–10,000 French and 12,000–14,000 Dutch and allies), the French at the close of the action were the clear victors. The contest for the village of Landen was particularly fierce and the place changed hands several times as the day wore on. 'We attacked at dawn, and after twelve hours of hard fighting, under a blazing sun, entirely routed [them].'[17] William III had to withdraw with his battered army to Louvain, and left most of his guns on the field, but his brave conduct that day attracted wide admiration. 'He retired with the Elector of Hanover only when he saw there was no longer any hope the victory was complete.'[18]

So many infantry colours and cavalry standards of the Dutch and their allies were taken and sent in triumph to Paris to be displayed, that Luxembourg was thereafter known by the witty nickname of 'the paper hanger of Notre Dame'.[19] The king was understandably warm in his praise. 'It is a pleasure to give orders to one who obeys them as you did.'[20] All the same, the scale of losses was a shock, and one keen observer at the court wrote that 'M. de Luxembourg had the victory, but it cost him dear, which occasioned the dauphin to comment that one or two more such victories would be enough to ruin the army'.[21]

The marshal then moved against Charleroi, albeit after expressing some reluctance, in the main pleading a lack of forage, but the king nonetheless insisted that he proceed forthwith. With the assistance of Marshal Villeroi, a formal siege was begun on 12 September[22] but an attempt to storm the place three days later, was smartly beaten off. All the same, the garrison submitted on 11 October, once French engineers under the charge of Vauban had laid mines under the main defensive works. So severe had the fighting been that of the 4,000 defenders at the commencement of the siege, only some 1,200 remained fit enough to march out, granted the honours of war by Luxembourg but as usual obliged to leave behind all their artillery. The king found it difficult to hide his satisfaction that he had been right all along, in urging that Charleroi be attacked, writing of William III, that 'He is accustomed to this sort of disagreeable surprise'.[23]

Luxembourg stood at that moment as arguably Louis XIV's greatest living field commander, but the two men were never close, as the king could not forget, and probably never quite forgive even after so many years, his early Frondist activities. All the same, the king did increasingly rely on him and his advice. Buoyed up by repeated success, Luxembourg was also getting a little above himself, claiming precedence over other nobles and citing as reason family descent, dated from 1571, traced as it had been through the female line (the male heir at one time having been declared mentally incompetent). Despite the discontent this clumsy presumption caused amongst the nobility, given his successes on campaign the marshal had supporters in this self-seeking endeavour, having, it was recalled, 'captivated the troops and the general officers'.[24] In the end, the discontent was rather overshadowed when it was announced in Versailles that the king's illegitimate sons were to be elevated in rank to just below that of the legitimate princes of the blood, and accordingly would stand above all other nobles no matter how ancient or august their lineage might be claimed to be.

Delays brought about by bad harvests and the growth of widespread famine in France made fresh campaigning again in Flanders in 1694 a hesitant business, conducted without particularly decisive results, while Luxembourg had to share the command of the army with the dauphin. The opposing army commanders all seemed reluctant to close and come to grips, while Luxembourg was anxious to prevent any move against Courtrai and Ypres, although as autumn came on Huy on the Meuse, and Dixmuide were recaptured by the Allies, which constituted almost the only result of a rather lacklustre campaign on all sides. Luxembourg returned to Paris as winter set in, where after a short illness he died on 5 January 1695, attended at the last by the renowned Jesuit priest Bourdaloe; command of the army in Flanders passed to Marshal Boufflers as a result.

Marshal Luxembourg and his wife, Madeleine (née de Clermont-Tonnere), had four sons, and one daughter, and the youngest boy, Christian-Louis de Montmorency-Luxembourg (born 1675), pursued in vain his father's claim to be ranked above other nobles. Despite this almost frivolous distraction he was, like his late father, a good soldier, particularly effective under Villars at the Battle of Denain in 1712, and was made Marshal of France in 1734 by Louis XV, while the eldest grandson, Charles Frederick de Montgomery-Luxembourg (born 1702), continued what clearly ranked as a family tradition and in 1757 in turn also became a marshal. Luxembourg's wife, Madeleine, died in 1701, just as the war for the throne of Spain was gathering pace.

The Duc de St Simon, in his witty and often barbed memoirs of life at court described Luxembourg in what, for him and given his dislike for the old marshal (and a feeling that somehow, he was not quite the thing), were rather glowing terms:

> Nothing could be surer than the grasp of M. de Luxembourg; no one could be more brilliant, more sagacious, more penetrating than he before the enemy or in battle, and this too, with an audacity, an ease, and at the same time a coolness which allowed him to see all and foresee all under the hottest fire, and in the most imminent danger. It was there that he was great. As for the rest, he was laziness personified. He never took exercise unless he was obliged to; his time was spent in play [cards] and in conversation with his intimate friends. Every evening there was supper with a few guests, almost always the same; and if there was a town anywhere nearby, care was taken that agreeable women were present.[25]

It should be mentioned that that Louis XIV was noticeably more inclined to take risks when issuing his orders to Luxembourg, than with other of his commanders, plainly having implicit faith in his abilities in the field. 'The letters between Louis XIV and Luxembourg, are most interesting evidence of Louis' willingness to accept a battle when he trusted his general.'[26] However, the darker side of this extraordinary soldier's life, as evidenced by the atrocities he allowed to take place in

Holland, is reflected when St Simon added the grim comment that he died, 'Much regretted by many people, but personally esteemed by none, and loved by very few'.[27] Nonetheless, he could justly claim to be one of that rare breed, a commander who had seen much action, yet had never lost a battle.

Chapter 5

Marshal Catinat

Born in the Rue de Sorbonne in Paris on 1 September 1637, to a family of respectable, but only modestly middle-class and relatively humble, origins, the eleventh of sixteen children, Nicolas Catinat de la Fauconnerie began his professional life studying to be a lawyer. He was remembered as 'A plain, modest man, and most remarkable for his humility'.[1] His father, Pierre de Catinat, was a magistrate for the Paris Parlement[2] and lived until 1679, but his mother, Catherine-Françoise (née Poisie), died when Nicolas was only 12 years old, in all probability due to the rigours of such frequent childbirth. Able to deploy only a little 'interest' from the nobility or influential friends, in 1665 Catinat, apparently having tired of the legal profession, managed to obtain a commission as a subaltern in the Regiment de Bignon, transferring five years later to the Chevaux-Léger cavalry,[3] where he served in the company commanded by the Marquis Henri de Fourille. He distinguished himself particularly at the siege and capture of the city of Lille in 1667, widely regarded as the most notable of Louis XIV's early military achievements (or, perhaps, the achievements of his generals while the king happily oversaw things). It was recalled on this occasion that 'Catinat charged in the attack on the counterscarp [defensive work] with a valour and signal intrepidity. This was noticed by Louis XIV, who asked his name.'[4] Such attention was most useful for a young man, with little influence, and with a way to make in a highly competitive world.

In recognition of his valour on this occasion, where coincidentally, an older brother was mortally wounded, Catinat was appointed by the king as lieutenant in the prestigious Gardes Françaises, a much sought-after rank, that he would almost certainly not have otherwise been able to afford to purchase. His younger brother was also elevated in rank, and that their deceased sibling had been serving in the Gardes at the time of his death before the defences of Lille indicated, or so it seems, that this promotion was a form of compensation for their loss. Continuing to build nicely, and rapidly, on a reputation as being both brave and a safe pair of hands, Nicolas Catinat was amongst the first to get across the Rhine at Tollhuis during Louis XIV's advance against Holland in 1672 and suffered a wound during an attack on a hornwork[5] at the siege of Maastricht the following year. At the grim Battle of Seneffe in 1674, he was severely wounded again, and commended by Condé for his valour, while after the capture of Besançon it was noted that he was still 'gaining a reputation as an officer of great promise'.[6] In 1675 he was promoted to be captain in the Gardes Françaises, a notable achievement for someone of modest bourgeois background and with hardly more than 15 years' service to count towards his credit. Perhaps predictably, his rise was not that popular in some quarters, and particularly François de Aubusson, who became Marshal de la Feuillade that same year, was opposed, seeming to regard Catinat as an encroaching parvenue. All the same, campaigning in Flanders under Marshal Luxembourg in 1677, Catinat was at the siege of St Ghislain, and instrumental in repulsing a potentially very damaging sortie by the garrison; when the place submitted shortly afterwards, he was appointed to be the governor. For reasons that are not clear, Catinat was then sent to Italy, on a confidential mission to do with the negotiations with the dissolute Duke of Mantua for Louis XIV to purchase the fortress of Casale on the river Po just to the east of Turin. On his return he was appointed to be governor of Longwy, and in 1680 made brigadier, and Marechal de Camp three years later, with the prestigious appointment as governor of the major fortress of Tournai, although his tenure there proved to be of only short duration.

Negotiations to acquire Casale having been concluded that summer, Catinat took possession of the citadel at the head of 8,000 French troops early in October 1681.[7] The Duc de Boufflers, who had command of a covering force during the occupation, then withdrew with his troops into the Dauphine, and Catinat was appointed governor of the fortress, which now formed a potentially rather exposed French outpost in northern Italy. In April 1685, with ten infantry regiments and ten squadrons of cavalry, he was sent to support Duke Victor-Amadeus of Savoy, and the following February, took part in the punitive campaign against the insurgent Protestant Vaudois rebels (also known as Barbets). The Vaudois had been harbouring Huguenot refugees from France, and Louis XIV was determined that an example be made of them, and much pressure was, as a result, put on the duke, when otherwise he might have left them well alone. The campaign against the rebels was brutal and grim, as so often when religion was involved, and despite his evidently humane instincts, Catinat was not slow to use repressive measures, reporting that 'The country is completely desolated; there are no longer any people or livestock at all. The Duke of Savoy has about 8,000 held prisoner. I hope that we will not leave this country, and that the race of Barbets will be entirely eliminated.'[8] By June the fighting was moving towards a tired end, and Catinat could return to his duties in Casale.

Becoming lieutenant-general in 1688, at the onset of the Nine Years War Catinat took an active part in the siege of Philippsburg, with the dauphin once again having overall command of the operations, albeit with the able assistance of Vauban. Catinat threw back a spirited sortie by the garrison, when fighting at the head of the Régiment d'Auvergne, and received a musket ball strike to the forehead. It was a near thing, and it was recalled that:

> He charged the enemy with all vigour and forced them to retire into the place. During this effective French charge, Catinat

> received a ball against his head, which pierced his hat, but did not inflict a serious wound, the great wig he always wore, as in his portraits and like his contemporaries, averted a mortal blow.[9]

Once again, his conduct was noted with approval, and an already good reputation appropriately burnished. 'The conduct of Catinat at the siege of Philippsburg, under the eye of the dauphin, and at the side of Vauban, shone a light on his brilliance as a commander.'[10] Sent south once more, later the following year, he had command of 4,000 French troops in besieging the returned and unreconciled Vaudois rebels in Basiglia near to the town of Ferrero, a lengthy operation that was only concluded the following May, when the rebels escaped, but not before brutally massacring over 300 of their own unfortunate French and Savoyard prisoners.[11]

In June 1690, Duke Victor-Amadeus adopted the apparently risky course of choosing to take the side of the Grand Alliance, and in the process turn against his erstwhile ally, the King of France. Things began badly for the duke on 18 August, at the Battle of Staffarda, near to Saluzzo on the river Po. Catinat, who now had the command of the French troops in the Dauphine and recently been busy levying 'contributions' in Piedmont, very capably inflicted on Victor-Amadeus a severe defeat. The French attack was constrained by the marshy water meadows of the river Po on their right flank, but the duke misread Catinat's determination and energy and pulled troops away from his left to reinforce his own right flank. In the event, the French infantry simply waded through the marshy water to overwhelm the newly-raised, and therefore relatively inexperienced, Italian-recruited Mondovi Regiment, and so neatly turn the left flank of the Savoyard position. In the process Catinat inflicted a loss of some 4,000 (including many prisoners) and eleven guns, at the expense to his own army of little more than 1,000 killed and wounded. A complete rout of the duke's army was only averted by the skilful handling of the subsequent rearguard action by the young Imperial commander, Prince Eugene, even though he had very few of his own Austrian troops on the field. The French had, however, problems with adequately supplying their troops, and after quickly taking the town of Susa in the second week of November, Catinat withdrew from Piedmont westwards into Savoy and the Dauphine once more, to find winter quarters in which to rest and replenish his small army.

Catinat advanced again in March 1691, when he neatly took Villefranche in the third week of that month, and then in early April he seized the town and port of Nice, an inexpensive victory, taking only three days to accomplish, and at the cost of the lives of only some 100 French soldiers. In consequence, the approaches to south-eastern France were made more secure, and only Montmélian, just to the west of the Alpes Maritime, remained in Savoyard hands, and even this place would fall to the French in time. However, 'It appeared to all the world,' an army intendant wrote in one of his reports to the ailing minister for war, Louvois, 'that Monsieur Catinat exposed himself very much [and] yesterday was wounded twice by musket balls'.[12] The loss of so enterprising a soldier would be much regretted, and the king, at that time in camp before Mons, wrote on 9 April to Catinat, 'You continue your good service to me . . . I understand the importance of the capture of Nice and, in consequence, the magnitude of the service you have given me'.[13] Meanwhile, the Marquis de Feuquières had advanced from Pinerolo, and combined forces with Catinat who had just taken possession of Avigliana, before laying siege to Cuneo on the river Stura. The operation went on frustratingly slowly, and when Prince Eugene and the Spanish commander in northern Italy, the Marques des Legânez, approached with a relief force of Austrian and Spanish/Italian troops, the French commanders found it prudent to withdrew in some haste, although not before seeing that the still isolated French garrison in Casale was reinforced and re-supplied. Concern for Catinat's own safety continued, and Louvois wrote to him in May, shortly before his own death, chiding the soldier with a mild but pointed rebuke, 'His Majesty is informed that you exposed yourself greatly in the attack on the Chateau [castle] of Veillane, and that you have done the same on numerous similar occasions'.[14]

Catinat seized Carmagnola in early June, but the place had to be given up again in October, once Victor-Amadeus and Prince Eugene had received fresh reinforcements from Vienna. For the time being the prince had to serve under the stern command of Count Antonio Caraffa, a veteran of many campaigns in the east against the Ottomans and the almost equally dangerous Hungarian rebels. Despite this, at the close of the year, Catinat had kept a firm hold on much of the Duchy of Savoy and Piedmont, together with the Dauphine region and the County of Nice, even though Carmagnola had of necessity been given up. Exposed Casale was held still, although Louis XIV's earnest attempts to bring Duke Victor-Amadeus back into alliance with France, on the general basis of letting bygones be bygones, were for the time being rebuffed.[15]

In 1692 Catinat had to campaign once more with wholly inadequate numbers and resources, as the king's main strategic effort was once more concentrated on confronting William III in Flanders, so that the 15,000 French troops he had under him were met by well over double that number led by Victor-Amadeus, together with the Austrian forces under Count Caraffa and Prince Eugene. An officer wrote that, 'Catinat remained strictly on the defensive in 1692, shielding several important places, which we occupied'.[16] In this way, he successfully managed to hold secure both Susa and Pinerolo, but an Allied incursion, led by Victor-Amadeus, into the Dauphiné region in southern France could not be prevented, and amongst other things, the town of Gap to the south-west of Briançon, was burned on 20 August although Grenoble was preserved. 'All the efforts of France were directed towards Flanders, where the king was in person . . . Catinat could not prevent the Duke of Savoy from taking the citadel of Embrun and making an incursion into the Dauphine.'[17] The Allied operation came to a halt when the duke became dangerously ill, it is thought with smallpox, and had to return to Turin, with not a great deal having been achieved; certainly Louis XIV was not immediately inclined to divert troops away from the campaign in the Low Countries.

Still, this Allied raid did prompt the king, on the face of things quite unmoved by what had been attempted, to at last change tack and order reinforcements for Catinat, drawing troops from the French forces operating against the Spanish in Roussillion. Their opponents had, in any case, already largely withdrawn from French territory, not having achieved a great deal, although an entry-port in the valley of the Barcelonette was retained for future use when the occasion should arise. Catinat was at Pinerolo by now, and on 26 September wrote that, 'I have arrived here at the residence of our friend [the Marquis de] d'Herbeville . . . The enemy troops have all returned to Piedmont.'[18] He noticed, however, that Johan Palffy, a highly regarded Imperial commander and another veteran of the wars in Hungary, was moving uncomfortably close to apparently threaten Pinerolo, but in the event he did not try to do so with any great effort and the danger subsided.

On 10 December 1692, after visiting Versailles to discuss the campaign with both the king and the newly appointed minister for war, the Marquis de Barbezieux (Louvois' son), Catinat left to resume campaigning in northern Italy. 'He was with the king in the morning, and in the evening; he set out immediately for Pinerolo . . . the opening of the campaign proved, in effect, very difficult.'[19] On 27 March 1693 momentous news was received that Louis XIV had made Catinat a Marshal of France, citing in particular, 'The services you have given me, so useful and agreeable. You have offered the qualities, and [now] reap the reward.'[20] The award of the marshal's baton was undoubtedly well merited, and a signal indication of the high regard in which he was currently held. However, when in the field, all too familiar difficulties of supply and adequate reinforcements persisted, so that, while still not expecting great things from the coming campaign in Italy, Catinat assembled his numerically inferior army to try and shield both Pinerolo and Susa, while simultaneously moving to clear the Barcelonette valley of troublesome Savoyard troops.

Duke Victor-Amadeus had moved against French-held Casale and constructed two new strongpoints after storming a defensive work at St George early in July. This enabled him to mount a very effective blockade of the garrison, but at the same time he hoped to maintain his hold on the Barcelonette and accordingly advanced on Susa, a move that Catinat had insufficient strength to challenge openly, at least until much-needed reinforcements arrived from the Rhine and Spain. When at last in place, these troops would bring his field strength to some 40,000 men, no more numerous, if at all, than those that were deployed by the duke and his Imperial allies, but at least allowing him to strengthen the garrisons in Briançon before advancing to Fenestrelle to the south of Susa. Victor-Amadeus had as anticipated begun a siege of the Comte de Tessé in Pinerolo, and on 14 August after seizing an outer work at St Brette on high ground close to the fortress, he moved against the main defences with a sharp bombardment beginning a week later. The instructions Catinat had meanwhile received from the king in Versailles were to the point, 'You cannot do anything more agreeable to me, in addition to the deliverance of Pinerolo, than to carry [achieve] considerable advantage over the enemy, which will convince the Duke of Savoy of the necessity of accommodating himself to me'.[21]

The Allied siege operations against Pinerolo proceeded slowly, and on 27 September Victor-Amadeus found that Catinat, newly strengthened in numbers now, was fast approaching, with every intention to raise the siege. The duke fell back towards Turin but was intercepted on the road and brought to battle on 4 October at Marsaglia, where both the opposing commanders employed the same tactic of attempting to envelope the other. The Savoyard troops and their allies were on the point of overwhelming the French left flank when a well-timed charge by Catinat's heavy cavalry, the elite Gendarmerie, who had only recently joined his army, firmly broke up the attempt. This effectively decided the outcome, and after over four hours of hard fighting, in which the French infantry's vigour was notable, Victor-Amadeus progressively lost control of the battle. His troops were forced off the field in confusion and breaking, fled towards Turin, with the significant loss of some 10,000, including a large number of prisoners scooped up in the rout, in addition to abandoned colours and standards and thirty guns, in all amounting probably over a third of the duke's bayonet strength. French casualties, at just over 2,000, were not slight, but clearly comparatively much less severe than that of their opponents who had been smartly out-fought that day (amongst the French wounded was the Duc de Vendôme's younger brother, Philippe, known to all as the Grand Prior). Seven days' later Louis XIV wrote with warm words of appreciation at the outcome, 'The perfect victory which you have reported over my enemies surpasses my hopes, augmenting the esteem that I have for you'.[22] Catinat replied courteously in equally warm terms, 'Sire, I am overwhelmed by the honour you do me, by the letter Your Majesty has written in your own hand'.[23]

As a direct result of this notable success, the pressure was eased on French operations, and the fortress of Casale was as a result safe for the time being, for the Savoyard blockade had inevitably been lifted two days after the battle at Marsaglia. The king hoped that Catinat could then march on Cuneo, but the marshal was resolute that he had insufficient strength to do so, and so the notion was, reluctantly and only after searching enquiries had been made, allowed to pass by. After re-supplying the garrisons there and in both Fort St George and Susa, Catinat withdrew his troops into the Dauphine to find winter quarters, although he took the opportunity to pillage as much of the

Piedmontese countryside as he could manage in the limited time left for campaigning that year.

With French attention, in the south at any rate, increasingly focussed on operations in Catalonia, 1694 passed relatively quietly for Catinat, whose army now had shrunk to only about 24,000 strong, as resources and men were diverted to more pressing theatres of war, and he was obliged to let much of his fine and experienced cavalry go to campaign elsewhere. Duke Victor-Amadeus was, however, newly and understandably cautious after the defeat at Staffarda and the more recent debacle at Marsaglia, although he did seize the French-held Fort St George late in August. Despite this seeming indecisive inactivity on the part of his opponents, Catinat could justly claim credit for having subsisted his army on the duke's territory in Piedmont throughout most of the year, while maintaining a firm hold on Savoy to the west of the Alpes Maritime, and in the circumstances, this was enough for the time being.

Amongst the many constraints that Catinat had to contend with, the most severe was the almost constant starving of his army of men, materiel and money with which to push has campaign in Italy forward. He was of course not the only French commander to suffer in this way, for the king's treasury was almost exhausted, and most attention was still largely centred on Flanders where Marshal Boufflers had replaced the recently deceased Luxembourg in command. The world had changed, and Louis XIV wrote to Catinat early in 1695 that, 'The only difficulty that presents itself for pursuing offensive war is the considerable sum of money that it requires . . . After having examined the state of my finances I have, despite myself, been obliged to resolve to pursue only defensive war during the coming year.'[24]

Confidential discussions between envoys from Versailles (including, amongst others, Renée de Froulay, Comte de Tessé) with Victor-Amadeus in Turin had been underway for some time, as Louis XIV tried to tempt the duke away from his alliance with England,

Holland and Austria. As a part of the preliminaries to such an arranged understanding, Casale was given up by Catinat in July, after a mock pretence of defence by the French garrison, but on condition that the fortifications should immediately be slighted and the place handed back to its previous owner, the Duke of Mantua. The French troops left Casale after their work of demolition had been completed, while Catinat maintained his hold on Savoy and the western parts of Piedmont. All the same, the conflict in northern Italy had run its course for the time being, and in July and August 1696 Duke Victor-Amadeus formally reached an understanding with France, at the conclusion of the Treaty of Turin, something that his erstwhile allies, Prince Eugene in particular, had long suspected was about to happen. Pinerolo was also to be given up to the duke by Catinat, and French and Savoyard troops, now nominally under his command, promptly moved against the Milanese. On 18 September the fortress of Valenza was invested, but before much else of note could happen the hostilities, in Italy at least, came to a formal end on 7 October with the Convention of Vigevano, 'which declared the neutrality of Italy'.[25]

His work in Italy done, for the time being at least, Catinat was summoned in 1697 north to join Marshals Villeroi and Boufflers in Flanders, where in mid-May he found that the siege of heavily-fortified Ath was to be the main focus of activity. The newly-arrived Catinat conducted the siege operations themselves with an army just over 40,000 strong, having once more the able assistance of the great military engineer Vauban, who had the distinct advantage of having designed the very same defences when they were still in French hands, and had quietly ignored instructions to level and spoil them when they left. Although William III approached at the head of a strong force to try and lift the siege, the operations proceeded with great rapidity, Vauban's precise knowledge of the layout of the defensive works proving particularly valuable. The lines of circumvallation were completed on 22 May, and two weeks later the governor, the Comte de Roeux and the garrison commander, the Prince of Anhalt, rather meekly capitulated rather than face a storm, and the garrison were permitted to march out with the honours of war, which not everyone thought to be that well deserved given their rather brief defence of the place. Still, the French bombardment, directed by Vauban (who was wounded in the cheek by a musket ball), had been particularly well directed and effective. Thirty-two artillery pieces had to be left behind by Anhalt under the terms of the capitulation, and Vauban wrote with some justifiable pride that, the siege had been conducted, 'With so much art and method, that it cost the king no more than one hundred men'.[26] William III, who belatedly had attempted to save the fortress, withdrew towards Brussels to avoid being cut off by the French under Villeroi and Boufflers. Hostilities ambled on to a weary end, with Catinat having his troops encamped around Courtrai, pending the welcome conclusion of the Nine Years War with the signing of the Treaty of Ryswick. Much was yet unresolved with many weighty matters remaining in contention, of course, not least the looming problem of who would occupy the soon to be vacant throne in Madrid, and few at the time can have been unaware of this.

Three years later, as the war for the throne of Spain approached, in May 1701 Catinat was sent back to Italy with instructions to secure Mantua and the middle reaches of the river Po valley for the French claimant in the dispute, the king's grandson, the Duc d'Anjou. 'I have sent Marshal Catinat to command my troops,' the King wrote, 'a man of such sagacity, experience and merit.'[27] Preparations for the coming campaign were complicated by the open animosity towards Catinat of the elderly Prince de Vaudemont, at that time the Spanish-appointed Governor-General of the Milanese. The Duc de St Simon remembered that:

> Vaudemont at once began to plot to overthrow Catinat, in conjunction with [Comte de] Tessé, who had expected the

> command and who was irritated because it had not been given to him. They were in communication with Michel de Chamilart, the Minister for War, who aided them, as did other friends at court . . . It was all the more easy because they had to do with a man who depended for support solely on his own talent, and whose virtue and simplicity raised him above all intrigue and scheming.[28]

That Vaudemont's very capable young son was a general officer in the Imperial service, and campaigning alongside Vienna's army commander in Italy, Prince Eugene, undoubtedly complicated matters. There was at least a whiff of suspicion that careless indiscretion, loose talk if not actual treachery, was in the air. All in all, not a very auspicious start to a new campaign on which such hopes were reposed. 'Catinat often complained of this; he sent word to the Court, [but] Prince Vaudemont had everyone in his favour.'[29] The marshal's probity and honesty were widely recognized, but being so straightforward in temperament he was perhaps not best suited to the counter devious and self-seeking in-fighting that could at times take place in an army headquarters.

As hostilities got underway, Catinat took up a defensive position with his left flank secured on Lake Garda. 'On 16 April . . . he established his camp at Castiglioni, and awaited the arrival of France's ally' (Duke Victor-Amadeus, who still tarried in Turin and appeared to be in no hurry to join the campaign).[30] Catinat was actually too confident in the strength of the position he had taken up, and Eugene wrong-footed him and neatly turned the clearly exposed French right flank by a daring march across inhospitable mountainous country. The French troops had to fall back from Castiglioni and Peschiera towards the river Mincio and beyond. Eugene wrote that, 'Catinat did not dare to give me battle . . . [he] retired upon Chiesa, and I became master of all the country between the Adige and the Adda, except

Mantua'.[31] Catinat had undoubtedly been constrained by instructions from Versailles that the neutrality of Venice be strictly respected, while on the other hand Eugene blithely ignored it, despite loud Venetian protests at his activities.

Louis XIV was understandably concerned at this early turn of events, writing rather peevishly to Catinat that he 'Trusted that my soldiers had done their duty'.[32] Early in July, having manoeuvred the marshal out of the way, Eugene struck at the detachment commanded by General St Fremont at Carpi, 'Surprised a party of French troops, and inflicted a severe defeat there, and the line of the river Adige was lost'.[33] Although the Comte de Tessé arrived with reinforcements in time to prevent a complete rout, the Duc de St Simon recalled that 'Our loss was very great'.[34] The king again wrote to Catinat, in terms of dismay, on hearing the news of further misfortune. 'My cousin, I have received with sadness the letter that you have written to me on the 1st of this month [August], that you have lost the battle.'[35] Catinat had not, of course been present on the day, but as the army commander the blame inevitably, if rather unfairly, attached itself to him all the same.

The simple fact was that Catinat, and his equally able subordinate Tessé, were having difficulty holding Eugene in check, whether in manoeuvre or on the field of battle. An added complication was that the commander of the Spanish/Italian forces in the region, the Prince de Vaudemont, was still hardly on speaking terms with Catinat, which was far from helpful, while Tessé who had hoped for the command of the army in the first place, had never quite got over his disappointment, and was not showing to be at his best. St Simon wrote that, 'Such was our first exploit in Italy; all the fault of which was attributed to Catinat. Tessé and Vaudemont did everything in their power to secure his disgrace [and] the king determined to take from him the command'.[36] Nonetheless, for all his undeniable talent, and the services he would yet render to the crown, the hopes of Tessé to succeed Marshal Catinat in command in northern Italy were to be dashed and fell away altogether.

Having lost the confidence of those in Versailles, who from a safe distance thought they knew better how to do these things, and hampered with contradictory instructions and advice but far fewer resources, on 21 August Catinat, having fallen back to a fresh position on the river Oglio, was replaced in command by Marshal Villeroi. 'This was a hard blow to Catinat . . . but he lost none of his *sang-froide* or his perfect self-possession.'[37] He loyally remained with the army headquarters, offering quiet support and advice, which predictably was largely ignored by an over-confident Villeroi, who was at the time riding what would prove to be an illusory crest of a wave. To many observers, this change of commanders in mid-campaign was felt to be a mistake:

> The surprise of everyone at this was very great, for no-one expected that the Marechal de Villeroi would repair the fault[s] of Catinat. When the command was taken out of his hands by the Marechal de Villeroi, he made himself admired on every side by the moderation and tranquillity with which he conducted himself. If Vaudemont was satisfied with the success of his schemes, it was far otherwise with Tessé, who had merely intrigued against Catinat for the purpose of obtaining the command of the army . . . Villeroi would have nothing to do with him, and his conduct was contrasted with that of Catinat, who, free after his fall to retire from the army, continued to remain there with rare modesty, interfering in nothing.[38]

When Eugene's position at Chiari on the Oglio was attacked on 1 September, an action in which the troops now actively commanded by Villeroi fought valiantly but suffered a severe reverse, Catinat was twice wounded by almost spent musket balls, while attempting to rally the shaken soldiers. 'The 7st September we learned of the troublesome battle at Chiari, where the Marshal de Villeroi acted against the advice of Marshal Catinat.'[39] Eugene recalled that:

> My post at Chiari, notwithstanding its excellence, was nearly forced by the unparalleled impetuosity of the French, the houses, walls and all were already carried . . . Never did I witness such valour . . . The worthy, the admirable Catinat rallied the troops, led them back to the attack and received severe contusions to the breast, and a shot in the hand.[40]

These wounds at least afforded him the opportunity to leave Italy and return to Versailles, with his dignity intact. Once there, a deeply depressed Catinat was kindly received by Louis XIV on 11 March 1702, who discussed with him at length the lack of progress of the campaign in Italy, and the reasons why this was so. 'The king, after his levée, invited Marshal Catinat into his cabinet [private chambers] . . . he said, "Explain to me with an open heart all that has taken place in Italy during the last campaign".'[41] The relevance of the interview was evident, and the king's solicitous interest was patently genuine, as the highly observant Duc de St Simon recalled:

> The king called Catinat into his cabinet. The conversation was amiable on the part of the king and respectful on the part of Catinat. The king . . . pressed him to explain what had really passed there [in Italy]. Catinat excused himself, saying that everything belonged to the past, and that is was useless now to rake up matters which would give him a bad opinion of the people who served him.[42]

Louis XIV was astute enough to read between the lines, as it were, and see that the in-fighting at army headquarters in Italy had hobbled much of what Catinat had tried to achieve, and that he had done his best in difficult circumstances. Nonetheless, the whiff of failure unavoidably hung around him for some time, and lowered the veteran marshal's spirits for the future.

Appointed to command the army on the Rhine, a rather reluctant and disillusioned Catinat left to take up the post early in April 1702. The strategic goal was to support Max-Emmanuel Wittelsbach, the Elector of Bavaria, who had just declared for the French claimant in the conflict. No longer the dashing commander of Staffarda and Marsaglia days, Catinat suffered once more from a lack of troops, having just some 20,000 foot and horse when facing the highly capable Louis-Guillaume, Margrave of Baden, who was reportedly able to deploy almost twice that number. Both Hagenau and Weissembourg were lost to Imperial forces, and the key French-held fortress of Landau laid under siege; that place submitted on 9 September after a resolute defence. Despite differences in their temperaments, Catinat later that month moved smartly to send Claude-Louis-Hector, Duc de Villars, enough reinforcements to be able achieve a notable success in battle at Friedlingen on 14 October, for which the younger man rightly got most of the credit and was soon made a marshal. This in effect opened the way for direct support to be sent from the French on the Rhine to the Elector of Bavaria, and incidentally, at one remove, would lead to the dramatic events of the field of Blenheim in the high summer of 1704.

In the meantime, the 71-year-old Catinat was increasingly unwell, and he was permitted to give up his command at the close of the year and return to Paris. Tired and lacking further offers of employment or real influence at court, he went into modest retirement at the Chateau of Saint Gratien. He lived with one of his brothers and a sister, and enthusiastically devoted his attention to tending his garden, 'which he scarcely ever left and where he only ever saw a few private friends'.[43] In 1705, when Louis XIV awarded the prestigious Order of the Holy

Spirit to all his marshals then living, a world-weary and apparently deeply disillusioned Catinat politely but firmly declined the honour.[44] Two years later, with his experience of campaigning in the Dauphine and Savoy-Piedmont, Catinat offered well-considered advice to Tessé (by now made a marshal) on how the defence of Toulon should be conducted while under attack that summer by Prince Eugene and Duke Victor-Amadeus. Active employment still eluded him, but he seemed now not to regret very much at all that his campaigning days were truly at an end.

Catinat never married, and left no descendants, but he remained fond of his large family of siblings, nieces and nephews, and often corresponded with this brother; three of his sisters entered convents. He remained well regarded and highly respected, and it was remembered that he 'was not the typical soldier of this period . . . with no advantage of birth and [had] made his way by sheer merit. He was a careful general, thorough and sparing of the lives of his men.'[45] St Simon numbered Catinat amongst those few men he openly admired, and wrote of his death at St Gratien on 12 February 1712:

> I have so often spoken of Marshal Catinat, of his virtues, wisdom, modesty and disinterestedness; of the rare superiority of his sentiments, and of his great qualities as a captain, that nothing remains for me to say except that he died at this time very advanced in years at his little house at Saint Gratien . . . where he had retired and which he seldom quitted although receiving there but few friends. By his simplicity and frugality, his contempt for worldly distinction, and his uniformity of conduct, he recalled the memory of those great men who after the best-merited triumphs, peacefully returned to their plough, still loving their country . . . He had intelligence, good sense, ripe reflection; and he never forgot his origin; his dress, his equipages, his furniture, all were of the greatest simplicity.[46]

An added compliment may perhaps be slipped in, for the Imperial commander in the east, Prince Eugene of Savoy, when reflecting on his great victory over the Ottoman sultan at Zenta on the river Thiese in Hungary in 1697, commented wryly that he could not have hoped for such a complete success had he been facing his wily old adversary, Marshal Catinat, that day.[47]

Above left: Louis XIV, the Sun King.

Above right: Marshal de Fabert.

Below: Marshal Turenne.

Above left: Marshal de Créquy.

Above right: Marshal Boufflers.

Left: Marshal Luxembourg.

Above left: Marshal Villeroi.

Above right: Marshal Catinat.

Right: Marshal Vendôme.

Above left: Marshal Vauban.

Above right: Marshal Tallard.

Left: Marshal Villars.

Above left: Marshal Berwick.

Above right: Cardinal Mazarin.

Right: Duke Victor-Amadeus II of Savoy.

Above left: Prince Eugene of Savoy.

Above right: John Churchill, 1st Duke of Marlborough.

Left: William III.

Above left: The Duc de Bourgogne.

Above right: Louvois.

Right: Max-Emmanuel, Elector of Bavaria.

Above: The Margrave of Baden.

Below left: Emperor Leopold I of Austria.

Below right: James Stuart, the 'Old Pretender'.

Chapter 6

Marshal Boufflers

Born in Crillon en Oise in Picardy on 10 January 1644, Louis-François de Boufflers, who in time would become Duc de Boufflers, was the second and youngest son of François II, Comte de Boufflers, and his wife Louise, née de Vergeur. Entering the army at the age of 19, as a cadet (aspirant officer) in the Gardes Françaises, Louis-François first saw action when taking part in a punitive expedition against the Berbers at Gigeri in North Africa. He then served at the hard-fought siege of the Imperial-held fortress of Marsal in the Moselle valley, where he attracted favourable notice for his calm manner and cheerful indifference to enemy fire. Advancing in rank to lieutenant in February 1666, he was present the following year at the triumphant campaign during the war with Spain which saw Louis XIV gain Douai, Tournai and most notably the city and fortress of Lille. Made Major in the Gardes Françaises in 1668, the following year Boufflers was then appointed Maitre de Camp with command of the highly regarded Colonel-General Regiment of Dragoons. He served under the command of Marshal de Créquy in 1670 during the nimbly conducted occupation of the Duchy of Lorraine, and he continued to demonstrate considerable skill in handling his troops to avoid heavy losses, together with notable personal bravery. Both his parents had died by 1668, as did his older brother in February 1672, but the title Comte de Boufflers passed to an infant nephew, and so Louis-François was permitted to style himself Marquis de Boufflers for the time being. He had three sisters, but other than that they all in time entered a convent, there is little known of them.

In April 1672, at the commencement of the war with the Dutch, Boufflers took part in the rapid advance of Louis XIV's armies into southern Holland, and was present at the seizure of Burick, Rees and, most importantly, Arnhem in June that year. Less happily, he was with Marshal Luxembourg at the controversial sack and pillage of the villages of Bodegraven and nearby Zwammerdam in the closing weeks of the year, and was entrusted with the command of the hard-pressed rearguard as the French troops withdrew across the flooded and rapidly freezing countryside in the face of a sturdy Dutch counter-move. On 4 October 1674 Boufflers was present with his dragoons and a strong body of musketeers, fighting under the command of Marshal Turenne at the Battle of Ensheim. He went forward with his reinforced ad-hoc brigade to scout the Imperial dispositions and when coming under heavy and unexpected fire soon got embroiled in an unplanned and fierce skirmish in wooded country, an affair that quickly brought on a general action, during which he was wounded by a musket ball. Although tactically the battle was a drawn affair, with the French too exhausted at the end of the day to follow up their opponents' withdrawal, once again the valour and dash displayed by Boufflers had been noted, and on the recommendation of Turenne he was appointed on 12 March 1675 to the command of a brigade of cavalry. When the marshal-general was mortally wounded at Salzbach that July, Boufflers had command of the army's rearguard in the subsequent withdrawal while under severe pressure. Had the difficult operation not gone as well as it did, then the movement might well have been turned into a rout, and Boufflers' calm handling of the situation attracted much praise, although his own brigade had suffered severely in the action and was at one point almost overwhelmed before managing to extricate itself. Continuing to campaign in Germany, in 1677 Boufflers was made marechal de camp, and was actively involved with de Créquy in the brief and successful siege of Freiburg that November, and in the following summer was at the battles of Rheinfelden (a town now in Switzerland) and Seckingen. In August 1678, he was appointed Colonel-General of Dragoons, a prestigious move as the dragoons were proving to be increasingly effective, and had become highly regarded, in both their mounted and dismounted roles.

With the onset of the campaign of the Reunions, Louis XIV had simultaneous ambitions to build on the French strategic posture in northern Italy. Prolonged, but eventually successful, negotiations were undertaken to acquire the fortress of Casale from the all-but-bankrupt Duke of Mantua. Boufflers had been appointed lieutenant-general in 1681, and late that September he was entrusted with command of the troops that took possession of the Casale citadel. This was his first independent command, albeit with the able support of Nicholas Catinat, who was left in possession of the place when Boufflers, his task accomplished, withdrew to Pignerol. Two years later, campaigning against the Spanish once more, he was at the successful siege of Courtrai in November, while serving under the overall command of Marshal Louis de Crevant, Duc d'Humières. In May 1684 he was posted with his cavalry brigade, substantially reinforced and now some 5,000 strong, between the Sambre and Meuse rivers, to provide cover for the flank of the main French army operating under de Créquy against the fortress of Luxembourg.

Although active hostilities had technically come to an end in August 1684, with the 'Truce' of Ratisbon, Boufflers was sent to command troops in Bayonne and Béarn at a time of continuing tension with Madrid. However, with the revocation of the Edict of Nantes and the resultant increase in persecution of the French Huguenots, he was tasked with their suppression in Bearn, which he did with both considerable dexterity and occasional severity, and continued to do so in the regions around Bordeaux, Montauban and Saintonge. Such a ruthless campaign, for which Boufflers was commended by the king, added to the general flight into exile of those Protestants who could not bring themselves to convert.

On 4 August 1686 Boufflers was made governor of Luxembourg and appointed to the prestigious Order of St Esprit two years' later. With the commencement of the Nine Years War in 1688 he had the command of the army in the Moselle, and scored a notable success on 15 October that year with the capture of Mainz, a fortress strongly held by an Imperial garrison. The city of Coblenz, which under the orders of the Elector of Trier had refused to admit French troops, was also bombarded by Boufflers, and considerable damage done. In 1689 he took the small, fortified town of Cochem on the Moselle, after a stout and courageous defence, with heavy fighting in the breaches in the defensive works that had been made by the French guns. He was then ordered to the river Sambre, marching to combine forces with Marshal Luxembourg in time to participate in the very successful Battle of Fleurus on 1 July 1690, where the Dutch commander, the Prince of Waldeck, was severely defeated. The following year Boufflers campaigned under the personal supervision of Louis XIV, although he held the actual field command at the hard-fought siege of Mons that March, being once again wounded during an attack on the defences. He was clearly very much in royal favour. 'I praise above all your wisdom [and] take great pleasure,' the king wrote to him, 'in giving command of my armies to men enough in control of themselves to prefer the good of the state to my advantage . . . I am well satisfied with you.'[1]

Sufficiently recovered from his wound to take up campaigning again, Boufflers was present at the siege of Liège in 1691, where once again a heavy bombardment was undertaken, and at Namur in May and June 1692. The king, rather inevitably, was present with a large and distinguished retinue, very interested in all that was going on and generally getting in the way, but the siege went ahead at a good pace all the same. The overstretched garrison at first did not put up much of a fight, and it was remembered that:

> The Prince of Condé, Marechal d'Humières, and the Marquis de Boufflers each led an attack. There was nothing worthy of note during the ten days the siege lasted. On the eleventh day, after the trenches had been opened, a parley was beaten and a capitulation made almost as soon as the besieged desired it. They withdrew to the castle [citadel] . . . the rains sadly interfered with the siege; the trenches were full of mud and water, and it took often three days to move cannon from one battery to another.[2]

Nonetheless, the operation ground remorselessly on, and the governor of the fortress, the Prince de Brabançon, offered to submit on 1 July. 'A fortunate circumstance for the besiegers, who were worn out with fatigue . . . It is certain that without the presence of the king, the siege might never have been successful.'[3] Once the fortress was secure, Boufflers was sent to threaten Charleroi, but after feinting towards Huy and drawing his opponents' attention away, he turned aside in a sudden move against Furnes were the garrison capitulated on 6 January 1692, and this success enabled the French to move on and take Dixmuide without much difficulty.

Boufflers fought alongside Luxembourg at the desperate Battle of Steinkirk on 3 August, when William III and his Dutch and allied troops surprised the French army in camp and all but carried the day before being driven off with heavy losses. The next year he was rewarded with his appointment as a Marshal of France, and before long created Duc de Boufflers. He also found time in a what was evidently a busy round of military affairs to marry Catherine-Charlotte de Grammont, daughter of the duke of that name. Appointed to the command of an army on the river Meuse, he operated with some 35,000 troops in support of Luxembourg's efforts in Flanders, where Louis XIV, increasingly suffering from gout and as it proved, having taken part in his last active campaign, left early to return to Versailles. Later in the same year, Boufflers moved with reinforcements to the Rhine to combine forces with Marshal de Lorge in besieging Heidelberg, where they were joined by the king's son, the rather ineffectual Grand Dauphin, who naturally assumed overall command by virtue of his royal status. Bad weather hampered the operations, which achieved little of real worth, and at the end of August Boufflers took his troops back north. He had however, been appointed as colonel of the Gardes Françaises, a highly coveted post which he was subsequently permitted by the king to sell to the Comte de la Guyiche for 500,000 francs.[4]

In 1694, although the French negligently lost the fortresses of Dixmuide, Deynse and Huy to William III's troops, the year saw relatively few decisive military enterprises, Boufflers was appointed to be the governor of French Flanders, a region much expanded during the recent campaigns of course, and of the key fortress of Lille. His close acquaintanceship with the city would pay handsome dividends during the epic siege of the place which would begin fourteen years later. In April the following year, the marshal was given the task to oversee the construction of elaborate lines of defence between the rivers Lys and the Scheldt. So well organized was the work, carried out by 20,000 labourers covered by a similar number of troops, that only seven days were required to accomplish the task. He then went to take command of the garrison in Namur, which he had been substantially reinforced, and which by early July 1695 was put under a close siege by William III. Boufflers managed to enter the fortress just before the Dutch investment was complete, and he maintained an admirably dogged and aggressive defence against the Allied siege operations which were supervised by the noted engineer Meinheer van Coehorn. The formidable outer works known as 'Terra Nova' and the as yet incomplete 'Fort William' proved hard nuts to crack, with days of particularly hard fighting before they at last fell, and which saw remarkable displays of courage by the soldiers on both sides. Only on 4 August 1695 did the marshal give up the town, withdrawing with his troops across the river Sambre to hold out in the massive citadel. All the bridges over the river were blown or broken down behind the withdrawing soldiers, only 8,000 of whom remained on their feet and in a condition to fight on. So robust was the morale of the garrison, that when Boufflers offered to release any man from service who did not wish to fight on, not one stepped forward to take up the offer. While it may be suspected that no individual relished the prospect of attracting the derision of his comrades, this staunchness and loyalty was, nonetheless, quite remarkable given the severity of the fighting so far.

William III at this point was employing some 80,000 troops in the Namur siege and the necessary covering force, and so Boufflers, by his admirable defence of the place, was very effectively hamstringing the Allied operations for the whole summer and autumn. An astutely conducted defence is no passive thing, and not for the last time, a well-motivated garrison under his command would dictate the pace and direction of an entire campaign, wasting away the good-weather months when greater and more promising projects might otherwise have been attempted. Boufflers put in a damaging sortie on the Allied siege lines on 18 August, but after heavy fighting this was beaten back by troops led by General John Cutts (the 'Salamander')[5] and the Comte de Rivera, the Elector of Bavaria's master of horse. On 1 September when the increasingly heavy toll of casualties made the hold on the citadel no longer tenable, and with Marshal Villeroi showing little intent to intervene, so that no relief effort was in prospect, Boufflers offered to submit. Good terms were agreed the following day, and the citadel was given up on 5 September 1695. Perhaps understandably, the casualties in this gruelling operation suffered by William and his allies had been severe.[6] All the same, it was noted that, 'It was something new in the history of the age for a Marshal of France to hoist the white flag on one of the greatest fortresses in Europe'.[7] This is, of course to overlook both the prolonged and admirable defence put up by Boufflers and his gallant troops, together with the failure of Villeroi, albeit still lacking firm direction from on high, to intervene decisively to relieve the place.

To widespread surprise, Boufflers was then held as an honourable captive by the Dutch, despite the explicit terms of the capitulation, on the rather specious grounds that the French were refusing to honour an agreement to exchange the 7,000-strong garrisons recently taken prisoner at Dixmuide and Deynse. As a part of the dispute, the French had asserted that an agreed ransom had not been paid by the Dutch, but this was disputed, while an Allied officer wrote of Boufflers' fury at being accosted in this way. Detained while on the road leading out of Namur:

> He demanded with heat to know if it was thus that we treated a man of his rank, one of the first men in all of France . . . he claimed that all Europe would cry out against the affront now being made to him, and that the Allies would be able to boast with cause that it was the first advantage they had ever gained over him . . . he was by this time verily spitting fire and brimstone . . . He is still here in Namur without guards, the town being his prison.[8]

The marshal was eventually taken to Huy, but the Dutch and English prisoners concerned having been belatedly released, he was soon set at liberty, going with his servants and personal baggage to Dinant. Still bristling with indignation, he returned to Versailles where he met general and warm applause for his valiant conduct at Namur, and sympathy for being held, albeit briefly, by the Dutch. Perhaps understandably there was certainly a good deal of bad feeling over the whole affair, including how the Allied prisoners in the dispute had been treated while in French hands. A Dutch officer who was amongst those captive at the time, wrote that, 'I cannot sufficiently express the ill-usage we received from the French . . . they took away our swords and led us with guards as if we were criminals. We are in a place where they put their galley slaves, yet this does not trouble us so much as the concern [felt] for the poor soldiers.'[9]

Boufflers had all the same gained a good deal of credit for his handling of the defence of Namur, and Louis XIV wrote to him on his release, in solicitous terms. 'If you wish to command an army, you may do so, but after the fatigues that you have suffered, if you think that you need a rest, I will permit you to come to me to tell me about the siege.'[10] Amongst the rewards that came to the marshal from a grateful king was the dukedom he had looked forward to for some time, although this caused some surprise and comment, as he had in the end had to yield Namur, and in effect suffered a significant defeat, honourable without doubt, but a defeat nonetheless. On the other side of the hill, the unfortunate Allied garrison commander in Deynse, Major-General Ekenberger, a Danish officer of previously good reputation and who had risen through the ranks on his own merits, was much less fortunate. He was executed in Ghent for negligence and dereliction of duty, apparently being picked out as a convenient scapegoat by William III for what, the capture of Namur aside, had been a generally lacklustre Allied campaign that year.

In 1697 Boufflers had command of the covering army for the very successful and notably short siege of Ath, conducted by Catinat along with Vauban's invaluable assistance. He was also soon able to demonstrate that his skills as a soldier were matched by his agility in the conference room, playing a notable role in the negotiations in that same year that led to peace with the Treaty of Ryswick, bringing as it did a tired end to the war. Much of the details of that treaty were apparently agreed by Boufflers and Hans William Bentinck, Earl of Portland and William III's confidante and close adviser, while walking and talking in easy conversation in an orchard without the help of other eager and overly busy parties.[11] The Marquis de Langallerie, in his highly entertaining memoirs, wrote that, 'Marshal Boufflers (who passed at court as a man of no great genius in making treaties, but more properly to appear at the head of an army) at last agreed the affair with the Count [*sic*] of Portland [and] it was agreed between them that the king of France should for the future acknowledge the Prince of Orange for king of England'.[12]

Not that the onset of what would prove to be but a temporary peace afforded Boufflers the chance of much leisure. In 1698 he was entrusted by Louis XIV with the organization of a grand military spectacle, remembered as being the 'Manoeuvres at Compiègne', attended by the royal family, principal minsters, and almost the whole glittering French court. This affair was intended to demonstrate French military prowess, and advance the knowledge of the Duc de Bourgogne, the king's eldest grandson. Sixty thousand troops were involved in parades, marches, reviews and drills, together with a mock battle and siege, in which over 80,000lbs of gunpowder were expended. 'The king wished to show the court all the manoeuvres of war; the siege of Compiègne was therefore undertaken, according to true form, with lines, trenches, batteries, mines etc. On 13 September, the assault took place.'[13]

The after-action entertainments were equally lavish on a grand and spectacular scale and inevitably costing a great deal of money, with Boufflers reported as having to deploy:

> More than seventy-two cooks and at least 340 servants, of whom 120 wore livery. There were 400 dozen napkins, 80 dozen plates of silver, and six dozen of enamel besides plates and silver bowls for fruit, and everything else in proportion. On an ordinary day they consumed fifty dozen bottles of wine and when the king and princes came to eat, eighty [dozen] bottles. In one day, 2,000 pounds of coffee were consumed, and 268 litres of liqueurs.[14]

Given Louis XIV's dislike of excessive drinking and his own preference for watered wine, these figures are remarkable, and indicate that a convivial time was clearly had by all, so that what lessons were learned from the military spectacle may have been rather slender or partially remembered. Inevitably Boufflers' own pocket took a hammering from the affair, so that the king was obliged to help defray part of the expense. The Duc de St Simon recalled that, 'To Marechal de Boufflers [the king] provided 100,000 Francs . . . I leave it to be imagined what 100,000 Francs were to him whose magnificence astonished all Europe, who day after day could hardly believe their eyes.'[15]

Boufflers had command, together with the governor-general of the Spanish Netherlands, Max-Emmanuel Wittelsbach, of the troops sent by the king to take possession in February 1701 of the Dutch-held 'Barrier Towns' (Luxembourg, Namur, Mons, Oudenarde, Ath and Nieuport), ostensibly in the name of his grandson, Philippe (soon to be Philip V of Spain). These were seen as vital to the defence of Holand against any fresh French attack, and so this rash move caused great offence in both The Hague and London and did much to ensure that open war would result. With the active onset of the war for the throne of Spain, Boufflers was then appointed to command the 62,000-strong army in north-eastern France with the principal task being to drive the Dutch out of the fray before the troops in the pay of Queen Anne, commanded by the then Earl of Marlborough, could take the field in significant numbers. Although the nominal command of the French army lay with the young Duc de Bourgogne, eventually to be heir to the French throne (had measles not carried him off first), regarded as 'a talented young man who tried hard . . . the king's soldiers tried to teach him to command the army',[16] his practical inexperience was a handicap with which Boufflers had to contend, and he would prove to not be the last army commander to have to do so.

Once hostilities commenced in earnest, the marshal's efforts were initially very successful, and the Dutch commander, Godert Rede van

Ginkel, Earl of Athlone, was robustly forced back towards Nijmegen on the lower Rhine and looked likely to face certain defeat. However, Boufflers had outrun his supplies, and an unforeseen Dutch raid under van Coehorn into western Flanders to 'levy contributions' proved a worrying distraction, so that when Marlborough arrived in June 1702 to take over the command of the rapidly strengthening Allied army, the French had little option but to fall back. This move exposed cities such as Liège, Bonn and Cologne, and wide areas of Guelderland, to the Allies' ready attentions. In the process of withdrawing the French army had to cross the Heaths of Peer, with their flank glaringly exposed to an attack by Marlborough, and a clear defeat beckoned if only the Dutch had been less reluctant to risk a general action at that point.

Boufflers was plainly at something of a loss to how to deal with the confident and rapid movements conducted by Marlborough (who was soon to be made a duke for his efforts) and his close colleague, the Dutch Veldt-Marshal Henry of Nassau, Count Overkirk. The marshal had extensive lines of defence rebuilt and improved, within which he could manoeuvre to foil his opponent, but the Walloon nobleman the Comte de Merode-Westerloo was sceptical of the real worth of these works, on which so much labour was expended, writing that they were 'More profitable to the purses of the engineers who built them than for the country they were supposed to protect'.[17] In fact, much of the defensive works were laid across the comte's own estates, and he deeply resented the fact, and the inevitable damage done to his crops.

With the further loss of the fortresses of Venlo, Ruremond and Liège, the campaign in 1703 saw yet further successes for the Allies in the north, who also captured Bonn and Huy, although Boufflers adroitly surprised and routed an Allied detachment at Tongres. Soon afterwards, a spirited attempt by Marlborough to take Antwerp miscarried badly when his Dutch allies ventured too far and too fast and were surprised and severely mauled on 30 June in an action at Eckeren. Dutch general Opdham got lost, and only the stout rearguard action led by the usually obstructive and argumentative Baron van Slangenberg saved the hurried withdrawal from turning into a complete debacle. Boufflers had hurried his troops, covering 30 miles in a single day, to the scene of the action to snatch a welcome success, at a cost to the Dutch of a quarter of their troops on the field. He was able to write to his king, in some justifiable pride, that, 'Yesterday, Sire, a very rough and dogged combat took place between the army of your Majesty in Brabant and that of the enemy commanded by [General] Opdham, in which your majesty's army carried off all the advantage and all the marks of victory'.[18] Not everyone was that convinced as to what had been achieved at a strategic level, and Merode-Westerloo, who had command of an infantry brigade in the action, remembered that, 'Following this combat we did nothing for the rest of the campaign except march and counter-march'.[19] All the same, Boufflers had the command in the north at a rather arid period, when many of the cherished conquests achieved by Louis XIV as a young man had been lost or put at risk, and all without fighting a major battle (the hard-fought action at Eckeren excepted) being attempted. To no great surprise, the marshal was replaced in command in Flanders and lacked active employment for some time, although his replacement, the Duc de Villeroi, hardly did any better.

In July 1708, with the stinging defeat suffered by the army commanded by Marshal Vendôme and the Duc de Bourgogne at Oudenarde, the way lay open for Marlborough and Prince Eugene to pierce the borders of northern France, and after some debate on the best way forward their chosen target was the massive and important city and fortress of Lille. 'Some anxiety was felt for Lille, which it was feared the enemy would lay siege to. Boufflers went to command there, at his own request, and found the place very ill-garrisoned with raw troops.'[20] The veteran marshal, who had the valuable assistance of De Puy Vauban, the recently deceased great engineer's nephew, rallied the city militia, levelled suburbs that had been permitted to crowd the formidable defensive works, and sent away as many of the citizenry as possible to avoid having to provide for and feed them; he displayed considerable ability and energy, and the siege soon proved to be a prolonged and bitterly-fought affair, with the French garrison once more putting up an admirable defence, so that St Simon remembered:

> The besieged under the guidance of Marechal de Boufflers, who watched over all, and attended to all, in a manner that gained him all hearts, made a gallant and determined resistance . . . Our troops disputed the ground inch by inch, but eventually [Boufflers] retired into the citadel after two months of resistance [26 October]. He offered the discharge to all the soldiers who did not to wish to enter the citadel, but [as at Namur 13 years earlier] not one of the 6,000 he had left to him accepted.[21]

Eugene, who had command of the siege operations themselves, signed the articles for the capitulation of the city (but not yet the citadel) without reading the proffered document, declaring that there was nothing that so valiant a soldier as Boufflers could ask that he would ever refuse. The marshal's success in holding on to Lille for so long was a significant tactical achievement, dragging to a halt the hitherto (after a hesitant start) successful Allied summer campaign, and this was widely acknowledged both in Versailles and in the Allied camp. The classic role of the fortress, to hamper the operations of an opponent, was seldom seen to better effect.

Early in December, when Boufflers at last gave up possession of the citadel, Louis XIV, having given permission for the submission, wrote to the old marshal who had done so well, commending him in warm terms on his achievement in the campaign:

> I cannot sufficiently praise your vigour, and the pertinacity of the troops under your command. To the very end they have

backed up your courage and zeal. I have given the senior officers special proof of my satisfaction with the manner in which they have defended the town. You are to assure them, and the whole of the garrison, that I have every reason to be satisfied with them . . . I shall have the satisfaction of telling you myself that the latest proof you have given of your devotion to my service strengthens the sentiments of respect and friendship which I have for you.[22]

St Simon added that, 'The Marechal de Boufflers returned to court from his firm but unsuccessful defence of Lille, and was received in a triumphant manner, and overwhelmed with honours and rewards'.[23]

Falling ill in the spring of 1709, Boufflers was not offered the command in Flanders, Marshal Villars receiving the appointment instead, but once recovered in the autumn, he joined the army on campaign as a volunteer. 'Boufflers, loaded with honours and glory, might well have hoped to pass the rest of his life in repose. It was hardly possible, do what he might, that he could add to his reputation . . . He thought only of the welfare of the state.'[24] He declined the courteous offer made by the younger man to assume the leadership role himself, but on 11 September 1709, during the bitter fighting in and around the woods at Malplaquet, Boufflers hurried to take up the command when Villars was gravely wounded by a musket ball. He very capably managed the difficult withdrawal from contact of the battered French army later that day. In less assured hands, such a taxing operation under extreme pressure might well have spun out of control and into disaster. Still, the exhaustion of the troops led by Eugene and Marlborough that day made any close pursuit unlikely, and his own report to Versailles of the battle attracted a degree of ridicule for claiming that he could assure the king that misfortune had never before 'been attended by such glory'.[25]

As it stood, the battle at Malplaquet had been a defeat for France, albeit after heavy losses had been inflicted on their opponents who could only claim a highly qualified success. Madame de Maintenon, the king's morganatic wife, wrote rather dismissively that, 'The Marechal de Boufflers has described the battle as glorious and unlucky, for we have lost despite the courage of our soldiers, not one of whom deserted during the action or the retreat. God's will is clearly apparent.'[26] The lady had perhaps not heard, or did not want to hear, that the much-vaunted Gardes Françaises had abruptly taken themselves out of the line rather than stand the ferocious Allied preliminary bombardment, denuding the centre of the French position of much of its bayonet strength, and that it was just here Marlborough eventually broke through, almost splitting the French in two.

With an army much reduced in numbers and capability after that day, with 'the men were without bread and without pay'[27] and despite the active assistance of the very able Marshal Berwick, Boufflers was unable to prevent the fall of Mons some six weeks later. The Allied casualties could be replaced, whereas the loss to France of that fortress, for the security of which the battle had been fought in the first place, was difficult to rectify, and it would remain in Allied hands until the end of the war. The measure of the lack of French success in this campaign, then, was that the awfully expensive battle at Malplaquet, on both sides, had only been fought to ensure the security of Mons, and in that endeavour the French commanders had failed, no matter what cost in casualties they had inflicted on their opponents. Boufflers now stepped down, and newly-created Marshal Pierre d'Montesquieu temporarily took up the command of the army, until Villars had recovered sufficiently to resume campaigning in 1710.

Tragedy struck Boufflers in his declining years, in the most severe form, when his eldest son died shortly after having been savagely whipped by Jesuit teachers while at school, as punishment for what was apparently a minor offence, almost a boyish prank. The lad was not, in a real sense, beaten to death, but the punishment was so severe (probably more so given the stature of his father and family connections, so that no suspicion of undue favour or leniency should arise) that the reaction in his young body soon took him remorselessly off. 'He was carried to the marshal's house, but it was impossible to save him; in four days it was all over . . . The king, who was much touched by it, sent one of his gentlemen to testify to them [Boufflers and his wife] the share he had in their loss.'[28] Bowed by understandable grief, and in increasing ill-health and frailty, the old marshal died at Fontainebleau on 22 August 1711.

Perhaps not always remembered as an outstanding field commander, but as evidenced by his epic defence of Namur in 1695, and Lille in 1708, Boufflers undoubtedly had proven himself to be a loyal servant and a safe pair of hands, who on many a good day would more than repay the trust put in him, and friendship shown to him, by his king.

Chapter 7

Marshal Villeroi

Born on 7 April 1644, the second son of Nicholas de Neufville, and with a fairly humble family background (his grandfather reputedly having been a fishmonger at one time), François de Neufville, who would become in time Duc de Villeroi and a Marshal of France, nonetheless benefited from the simple fact that his own father, Nicolas, was gifted enough, and prospered sufficiently, to become the Secretary of State under King Louis XIII.[1] Nicholas de Neufville was also the governor of the infant Louis XIV, and therefore his son immediately gained an entrêe into the innermost circles of the French court. His mother, Madeleine née de Créquy, was of noble stock, which undoubtedly helped things along, but their first-born son had died when only 12 months old. The young king and François became firm friends, despite the six-year gap in their ages, a relationship which, however tested in the heat of active campaigning and repeated misfortune, would firmly endure to the end of the reign. In the meantime, the two boys were much indulged and allowed to lay mock siege to toy castles, even being permitted to use blank cartridges in a miniature cannon. One day one of these cartridges accidentally ignited and exploded, causing much noise and smoke but luckily no injuries. Anne, the queen regent, was horrified at what had occurred, and as a result it was clearly necessary to put a stop to such exciting childhood escapades, the pleasing memory of which, no doubt, endured.

Villeroi's active military career began in Hungary, at the age of 19, when on campaign with other French volunteers alongside Austrian

Imperial forces fighting against the Ottomans. He fought under the command of Raimondo Montecuccoli, at the notable success in battle at St Gotthard in 1664, where the youthful volunteer sustained a flesh wound to the arm. He was in all likelihood one of those dashing long-haired French cavaliers who were mistaken by the astonished Ottoman commander that day to be 'young girls' seen riding into battle. Two years' later Villeroi was sent to Venice as French ambassador, where his easy charm and courtly good manners did him much favour. Appointed to the command of the Lyonnais Régiment in 1667, Villeroi accompanied the king to the sieges of Douai, Tournai and most significantly that of Lille. While campaigning under Turenne, he was marechal de camp during the occupation of the Franche-Comte in 1674, but his progress was steady rather than spectacular, and only in 1677 was he made lieutenant-general in recognition of distinguished service at the sieges of Condé and Bouchain, and he received at the same time appointment to the prestigious Order of St Esprit. In 1682 Villeroi married Margueritte-Marie de Cossé, and the union was apparently happy and particularly fruitful, as the couple had seven children, three boys and four girls, all of whom happily survived to adulthood, rather against the general trend at the time.

After an appointment as governor of the Lyonnais region, and serving on campaign under Marshal Luxembourg, Villeroi attracted favourable notice for his efforts when under heavy musketry at the close-fought Battle of Steinkirk in 1692, and the following year was made Marshal of France. He soon afterwards neatly captured both Huy and Charleroi, and on the death of Luxembourg in 1695, was appointed to the command of the army in Flanders, together with being granted the vacant captaincy of the prestigious Gardes de Corps. Constrained by contradictory orders from Versailles and urged not to run risks. 'You must apply yourself to be sure that they [the Allies] do not penetrate my lands . . . I am convinced of the opinion that it is important to think of defending my country, and conserving my troops the best way possible.'[2] The campaign that summer hinged largely on Bouffler's well-handled defence of Namur, but Villeroi's indecision in not trying to and actively lift the siege was not much to his credit, although the varying instructions coming from the court were far from helpful. The marshal was at that point relatively unhindered and free to manoeuvre to threaten Louvain, Maastricht or Liège, but lacking firm instructions from the king, he decided not to directly intervene – a forthright course that a Turenne or a Luxembourg would almost certainly have taken, whether holding instructions from Versailles or not. However, on 13 July he did attempt to catch and overwhelm an Allied detachment under the command of the Prince de Vaudemont, but the slowness of the king's illegitimate son, the lame Duc de Maine, in the end prevented the closing of the net and he managed to escape.

> Maine wished in the first instance to reconnoitre, then to confess himself [take Confession] in effect so long that M. de Vaudemont was able to commence his retreat. The general officers cried out at this, but to no avail . . . Maine could not be prevailed upon to charge, and so allowed M. de Vaudemont's army to escape.[3]

Villeroi refused to blame Maine publicly, but when Louis XIV learned what had happened, and the missed chance for a victory, owing to his son's inaction he very uncharacteristically lost his temper and broke his cane over the back of a servant who had offended him by pilfering a biscuit from the royal table. Despite all this, Villeroi did eventually go on to attempt to draw off the attention of William III in mid-August by mounting a heavy three-day bombardment of Brusssels, more than 3,000 mortar bombs, and 1,200 heated round-shot being fired, but this was ineffective in its aim, although obviously doing considerable damage, and attracted some sharp criticism for its patent and needless brutality. Villeroi than advanced to threaten William III's dispositions, but hampered as he was by the persistent slowness of the Duc de Maine, in the end decided against making an attack. This sealed the fate of Namur, so that Boufflers submitted in early September, and gave up the fortress, but the campaign for that year soon afterwards came to an end. Despite a general lack of success in the field that year, St Simon was able to note rather acidly that, 'As for the Maréchal de Villeroi, he grew more and more in favour with the king'.[4]

Louis XIV now actively looked for an advantageous peace, France was gripped by poor harvests, taxation was burdensome but still the king had an all but empty treasury. The year 1696 in Flanders saw Villeroi manoeuvring in conjunction with Boufflers, facing William III and his astute ally the Elector of Bavaria, but not taking part in any major action, Villeroi was then engaged in covering the short and very well-handled siege of Ath conducted by Catinat and Vauban in May and June 1697, before active hostilities came to an end with the conclusion of the Treaty of Ryswick.

On the commencement of the War of the Spanish Succession in 1701, Villeroi had command of the French forces on the upper Rhine, but after Marshal Catinat's relative lack of success in northern Italy, particularly at his being outmanoeuvred by Prince Eugene prior to the defeat at Carpi, he was sent to take of over the command of the French, Spanish and Savoyard forces in the Po valley. The king wrote to him on 4 August:

> I cannot accommodate myself to Marshal Catinat's slowness, if he had chosen his tactics well, the war would not be in the middle of Italy . . . I believe that it is to the good of my service to send you to command my troops. You know how important it is for the beginning of a campaign to be fortunate . . . I will leave Marshal Catinat with you. I am convinced that with a body of

> troops so superior as the ones that I have in that land, you will not miss an occasion to act.[5]

Louis XIV added thoughtfully, 'Take care of yourself, you know how important you are to me'.[6] This fresh appointment was, arguably, a mistake, as Catinat might have cautious, but he did not lack skill and energy. In addition, Villeroi's rather high-handed manner went down badly with Duke Victor-Amadeus, France's ally in Turin. There was also the possibility of the perils of an overly divided command, with Catinat still at army headquarters and the Comte de Tessé truculent and resentful at being passed over for the command. Still, the marshal's good manners and common sense avoided any notable friction. Matters got off to a poor start, all the same, on 1 September 1701 with Villeroi making a rash and poorly prepared frontal assault on Prince Eugene's entrenched troops outside the walled town of Chiari on the river Oglio. This resulted in heavy losses, almost 3,000 killed or wounded (including 291 officers), although the French soldiers had certainly fought with considerable valour.[7] Catinat had warned Villeroi that the position taken up by the prince was too strong to be assaulted in such a clumsy way, but the new army commander would not listen, saying rather blithely that, 'The king has not sent so many brave men just to look at the enemy through their spyglasses'.[8] The French attack was pressed far too long, when it was plain that success was not to be had, and Catinat was amongst those wounded.

When news of this dismal affair at Chiari reached Versailles, Louis XIV was understandably dismayed at the expensive reverse suffered, writing to Villeroi in tones rather more sharp than usual when addressing his old friend:

> I see by your letter that you attacked the enemy trenches with twenty battalions . . . on the assurance that the enemy had retreated leaving only a detachment of infantry. That this

attack was made on the advice of the Duke of Savoy and the unanimous agreement of the generals. It would be desirable that you had better advice. . . . I understand that Marshal Catinat was in great danger. I ordered you to seek out the enemy, to keep as near to them as possible, but that ought to have been carried out with prudence.[9]

Villeroi's own account of the day rather lamely went that, 'If the enemy had not been entrenched and reinforced by walls, the affair would not have lasted very long, we hope to find more favourable occasions later'.[10]

Relations between Villeroi and Duke Victor-Amadeus were increasingly strained, both men being too proud to deal easily or effectively with the other, while the marshal's airs and graces did him few favours. On one infamous social occasion, the duke insulted his French ally openly and rather pointlessly, in front of the assembled senior officers of the army, as the Duc de St Simon recalled with scarcely concealed relish:

The Duc de Savoy being in the midst of all the generals and of the flower of the army, opened, while talking, his snuffbox, and was about to take a pinch of snuff, when M. De Villeroi who was standing near, stretched out his hand and put it into the box without saying a word. M. de Savoy flushed up, and instantly threw all the snuff on the ground, gave the box to one of his attendants, and told him to fill it again. M. de Savoy continued the conversation that he had not interrupted, except to ask for fresh snuff.[11]

Considerably more mortifying for the marshal than this ill-mannered snub was that in early February 1702 he was captured in his headquarters in Cremona, during a daring night-time surprise attack by Eugene. Some scurrilous reports had it that Villeroi had been taken prisoner while still in bed, but this was not so, for 'The Marechal de Villeroi, already up and dressed [and], was writing in his chamber'.[12] Hurriedly throwing on his coat and rushing into the street, he was gallantly attempting to rally his troops in the Grande Place, when he was rushed and hauled off his horse. 'At the turning of one of the streets he fell into the midst of an Imperialist *corps de garde*, who surrounded him.'[13] Despite offering a handsomely-filled purse to his captors in order to be released, the marshal was instead taken away. 'Marechal de Villeroi whispered his name to the officer and promised him ten thousand pistoles . . . to be allowed to escape.'[14] Instead, he 'passed the day, guarded, in the coach of Prince Eugene'.

St Simon wrote that 'The news of this, the most surprising event that has been heard of in recent ages, was brought to the king in Marly on 9th of February 1702 . . . It was no fault of the marshal who had [only] arrived at Cremona the day before the surprise.'[15] The night-time attack on Cremona proved to be an expensive failure overall for Eugene, but the capture of a Marshal of France was widely reported and caused considerable surprise. 'Marshal de Villeroi was treated as those who excite envy and then become unfortunate are always treated. The king, however, took his part [and]M. de Vendôme was appointed successor in command of the army in Italy.'[16] Eventually Villeroi was sent into comfortable confinement in Graz, as an honoured guest and captive, and was only released by exchange some nine months later.[17] He would attempt, without success, to scrupulously pay Eugene for the expense of his upkeep during this time, but the chit authorizing such payment remained uncashed.[18]

In a curious way, the detention of Villeroi proved to be a boon for French interests in Italy, as with the Duc de Vendôme being sent as his replacement, Eugene found him far harder to handle. Villeroi's plight as a prisoner was generally regretted at court as he was much liked, and Louis XIV wrote to him, while in captivity, in kindly terms:

> My cousin, I would desire nothing more for the glory of my troops and my own satisfaction than to have you share the honour that they have earned by the defence of Cremona. I am touched by your fate. You know for a long time the friendship which I have had for you; it will not diminish by your absence, and I will never forget that which you have a right to expect of a good master.[19]

Duly released, and welcomed back at Versailles, Villeroi was appointed to command the French army in Flanders in 1703, as Boufflers had been asked to step aside, He found no ready opportunity to achieve success against the Duke of Marlborough, who took possession of both Huy and Limburg without much interference. The marshal did, however, seize Tongres on 9 May, taking one Dutch and one Scottish battalion (a unit in Dutch pay) prisoner in the process. By then refusing to offer them good terms, despite their stout defence, he attracted some criticism from his opponents for such seeming ungenerous conduct. 'This handful of allied troops [had] resisted for twenty-four hours.'[20] The soldiers were, however, not ill-treated, and were eventually exchanged. Then, in a move to prise Veldt-Marshal Overkirk away from Maastricht, Captain Robert Parker wrote that, 'Villeroi advanced to attack us, and began to cannonade us with great fury [but] upon hearing of the approach of the duke [Marlborough] he made what haste he could to get within his lines'.[21] The duke continued to be frustrated by the cautious but perfectly astute defensive tactics employed by his French opponent, who had the already formidable lines of obstacles and extended and improved (the Lines of Brabant) behind which he could manoeuvre and shelter, thereby avoiding risky clashes in the open.

When Marlborough marched south in May 1704 to eventually join Prince Eugene and the Margrave of Baden on campaign in Bavaria, Villeroi soon understood the necessity to shadow the march. He had obtained the express consent to do so from Versailles, otherwise the whole French strategic disposition along the Rhine might well be outflanked. Still, the choice was at first not that that clear, so that he was temporarily in something of a dilemma as to what to do for the best, and had appealed to the king for instructions, to be promptly told to march south too, and combine forces with Marshal Tallard in Alsace. Accordingly, there was no viable alternative option open to advance and attack the remaining rather slender Dutch forces under the command of Veldt-Marshal Overkirk, whose reduced numbers remained to guard the borders of Holland. Whether Villeroi would have taken the initiative and move forward to do so, and how he would have fared against the very able veldt-marshal, we can never know.

Tasked to hold the line of the Rhine secure while the campaign in Bavaria went forward, Villeroi came across that river to Villingen, after Tallard had been so comprehensively defeated at Blenheim in August. He met and shepherded to relative safety the remnants of the battered Franco-Bavarian army under the Elector of Bavaria and Marshal Ferdinand Marsin. This was done by Villeroi without authority from Versailles, a potentially risky course of action, but clearly the correct one and very much to his credit. Once again, he had to adopt a strictly defensive posture in the face of a confident Allied advance across the Rhine. Although in falling back Villeroi necessarily exposed the fortress of Landau to attack, he operated in the certain knowledge that to risk another defeat in open battle, so soon after Blenheim, would have had the most serious consequences for France. Louis XIV certainly approved of his caution at this time of peril, although Landau eventually fell, after a valiant defence undertaken by the blinded Marquis de Laubanie, with Marlborough concurrently clearing out French garrisons out of the Moselle valley. All the same, the autumn campaign was less successful for the tired Allies than might have been expected after the recent dramatic French reverses, and Villeroi's cautious strategy at the time was arguably the correct one

After such devastating events as those in the high summer of 1704, France had to stand on the defensive in 1705, and once more commanding the army in Flanders Villeroi was closely instructed to take no risks, with the king writing, 'The situation requires great precautions on your part to avoid having a combat forced upon you. You understand the smallness of the advantages if you should win, and the terrible results of losing.'[22] Marlborough meanwhile had devised a plan to advance in the Moselle valley, where Marshal Villars was in command, but on learning of his absence from Flanders, Villeroi moved out and struck at the Allied-held fortress of Huy, seizing it on 10 June in a very neat little operation. Veldt-Marshal Overkirk was in a state of some alarm and summoned Marlborough to return from the Moselle, where his campaign was, in any case, not going at all well. On the duke's approach, Villeroi fell back from threatening Liège towards Tongres, where he once more had the protection of his prepared defences behind which to stand.

However, on 17 July Marlborough decoyed the marshal's attention away to the south, sending Overkirk and his Dutch troops that way, but then moving swiftly northwards to breach the almost denuded French lines near to the village of Elixheim. He went on to maul and drive off a force of Bavarian and French troops under the command of the highly capable Comte d'Arco who had hurried to the spot. Max-Emmanuel, the Elector of Bavaria, recalled that:

> The enemy surprised the barrier between Wanghen and Espen, and at four o'clock in the morning broke through. It was not discovered until five o'clock. When I was alerted, I went with the Marshal de Villeroi with all diligence, but too late to remedy the situation for we found a great number of the enemy army had passed through in spite of the charges that were made without success because the enemy forces were superior [in number] to those that we could oppose against them. The army was too spread out to attempt a general engagement.[23]

The simple fact was that Villeroi had been completely deceived by Marlborough's astute moves and had taken himself off in pursuit of Overkirk's distracting march southwards, while the duke nimbly thrust through the now exposed defences at Elixheim.

Marlborough then attempted to turn Villeroi's exposed right flank and moved up to confront a temporarily isolated French detachment under the Marquis de Grimaldi, found at pretty well what 110 years later would become the field of Waterloo. The Dutch, concerned at the likelihood of heavy losses, were reluctant to go forward, even the normally reliable Overkirk being apprehensive, and so nothing came of the promising notion, nor did a subsequent attempt to surprise the French in position along the Yssche stream.

The unfortunate associated side effect of all these missed opportunities was that the relative lack of success for the Allies in Flanders that year apparently gave Villeroi as well as those eager to offer advice in Versailles a false sense of security, with the comfortingly happy thought that Marlborough had, in reality, simply enjoyed good luck and little more in 1704. In an interesting but rather mistaken comment given the sharp reverse suffered at Elixheim, the Duc de St Simon, secure in the rigid comfort of the court, remembered that, 'Nothing of importance occurred during the campaign, and the two armies went into winter quarters at the end of October'.[24]

With his treasury once more in a sorry state, and a growing desire to achieve a good, negotiated peace, always allowing, of course, that his grandson should remain on the throne in Madrid, Louis XIV was concerned in 1706 to demonstrate to all concerned the continued vitality of the French war effort. His opponents were to be browbeaten to the conference table; accordingly he instructed his principal field commanders to attack on all fronts. Villeroi had these instructions: 'The king had more than once pressed him to engage the enemy.'[25] He hesitated, waiting for reinforcements to join him from the Moselle valley, but was prompted by Versailles to get on with things and not delay. St Simon went on: 'The marshal was irritated by these reiterated orders, which he considered as reflections upon his courage [and he] determined to risk anything in to order to satisfy the desire of the king.' Villeroi considered that Marlborough would probably move first against the French-held fortress of Namur on the river Sambre, and without waiting for the arrival of all the promised reinforcements being sent by Marsin from the Moselle valley, on 19 May 1706 he moved out of camp with his 60,000-strong army, newly strengthened and equipped as it was, to take up a position on the Ramilles-Offuz ridge-line between the headwaters of the Mehaigne and Gheete streams. This feature was a watershed, almost the only dry passage giving easy access from east to west in the central part of the Spanish Netherlands. From there, he could threaten the exposed flank of Marlborough's army should it move southwards against Namur, and in the meantime the French and Bavarian army could settle into a firm defensive position with flanks that could not easily be turned, and wait to see what transpired as events unfolded.

On Whit Sunday 23 May, Marlborough moved to confront Villeroi's army in position around Ramillies. The duke was familiar with the ground, having scouted the area carefully the previous year when his troops levelled the defensive lines there. In a fine display of tactical skill, he both turned the French right flank at the hamlet of Taviers in the south, and then mislead the overly confident marshal as to the true nature of his intentions, obliging him to undertake a wasteful and unnecessary reinforcement of the French left to the north on the plateau of Mont St André. Too late, Villeroi realized the trap into which he and the Elector of Bavaria had fallen, but there was no time to put matters right, and that early evening a slashing Dutch and Danish cavalry charge overwhelmed the right of the French army, sweeping it entirely off the field in utter rout, along with their Bavarian and Walloon allies, with the loss of thousands of prisoners and all guns and baggage. He recalled that as the catastrophe unfolded that afternoon, with his attention almost entirely on his left flank:

> One came to tell me that our right wing had been absolutely defeated. I went there and saw a disorder even greater than had been indicated . . . Now I saw the enemy squadrons established on the terrain that had been occupied by our right wing. There was no other possible action than seeking a way of retreat.[26]

Villeroi was almost captured in the scramble to get off the field, as Major-General Cornelius Wood saw him nearby, not far from the small village of Offuz but did not recognize the marshal as being an officer of such high rank. Had Wood not turned aside in search of more promising prey, Villeroi might well have had the unhappy distinction of having been made a prisoner twice within four years.

The French governor of nearby Namur did show enough enterprise to sally out and recover some of the guns abandoned and strewn about on the field, as the victorious Allied army pursued their broken and fleeing opponents towards Louvain, Brussels and beyond. With almost no effort, other than brief siege operations against such places as Ostend, Dendermonde and Ypres, almost the whole of the Spanish Netherlands were in Allied hands within a few weeks, as the French were too broken, physically and morally, to put up much resistance to Marlborough's surging and confident advance. The Marquis de Tarazena, the Spanish governor of the great port and fortress of Antwerp, in one example, prudently changed sides and declared for Archduke Charles with remarkable speed.

News of the disaster made its way only slowly to Versailles, and 'Days seemed like years in the ignorance of everybody as to details . . . the king was forced to ask one and another for news'.[27] Villeroi, despite the scale of the awful defeat his army had suffered, had to be kept in post until his replacement could arrive from Italy, and on

10 June, the king wrote 'Your presence is necessary in Flanders until the arrival of the Duc de Vendôme. Until that I recommend that you pay attention to everything and give the orders you believe necessary for the good of my service.'[28] In time, Villeroi proved reluctant to give up the command and return to Versailles, so that in the end, as the scale of the disaster became more clear, Louis XIV had to give out that his old friend had actually resigned after all, and recalled him. 'He was informed in language which admitted of no misapprehension that he must return . . . M. de Vendôme had orders to leave Italy and succeed to the command in Flanders.'[29] The defeated marshal was treated kindly on his return, the king's affectionate memories of their boyhood spent together being quite clear, but understandably perhaps Villeroi was never offered another field command.

Despite his manifest shortcomings as an army commander, Villeroi remained favoured at court, and nine years' later, as Louis XIV lay dying, he presided at the final council meeting held at the king's bedside. He could not conceal his horror when the surgeon changed the bandages on Louis XIV's gangrenous leg and could see that the entire limb had turned black with mortification, so that, hoping to hide his feelings as best he could, he hurried to his own apartment in tears. Appointed under the terms of Louis XIV's will to be governor and mentor to the infant Louis XV, Villeroi was also directed to take command of the household troops and to take them with the young boy to Vincennes, a place thought to be easily defensible in case of need. The implication was clear, that Louis XIV feared a *coup d'etat* taking place at his death, with his heir an infant still falling prey to the ambitions of others. The King's nephew, Philippe, Duc d'Orleans, and the legitimatized Duc de Maine and the Comte de Toulouse all had their adherents, and even Philip V (the Duc d'Anjou) in Madrid, might move to try and secure the throne; accordingly, his great grandson was thought to be better protected at highly defensible Vincennes than anywhere else. When it came to it, Villeroi was instrumental in ensuring that the bastard sons of the late king remained firmly excluded from the succession, while no opportunistic moves were made by Philip V, however impractical they might have been, given the dictates of time and space.

Villeroi was the head of the council of finance under the regency which was in place during the minority of young Louis XV, although this was a largely symbolic appointment. He was often at odds with the Duc d'Orleans, in place as the Regent of France. He also showed an unfortunate tendency to be overbearing with the infant king, occasionally frightening the boy with largely fanciful tales that his life was at stake unless he, Villeroi, took the closest care of him. This undoubtedly stemmed from a genuine concern for young Louis' well-being but was also intended to cement Villeroi's position as a force at court, and as a key member of the regency council. At last, his antipathy towards the regent and his immediate circle was too much, and in August 1722, he rashly picked an argument with Cardinal Dubois and publicly lost his temper. '"You are all powerful', declared [Villeroi], "everybody bends before you; nobody resists you . . . employ all your power, put yourself at ease, and arrest me if you dare".'[30] Dubois and the regent were close, and rather predictably a week or so later the marshal was indeed arrested and bundled away from Versailles in a sedan chair, escorted by a body of Grey Musketeers under the command of a Captain d'Artagnan. Loudly protesting at this treatment, but powerless, he was conducted to his coach. 'The marshal had not ceased to cry out against the outrage committed upon his person, the audacity of the regent, the insolence of Dubois, or to hector d'Artagnan all the way for having lent himself to such criminal violence.'[31] Villeroi eventually calmed down, and found it prudent to behave with rather more dignity in accepting what had taken place, so that after a short interval being kept under watch at his home, he was sent to be governor of Lyons, almost a post of internal exile for such an exalted personality at court. Tempers calmed on both sides, and the marshal was certainly not forgotten, so that when Louis XV attained his majority, he remembered his old governor with genuine affection, and permitted Villeroi to return to Versailles, to take up once more his agreeable life as courtier. Now something of an elderly roué, and almost a curiosity from a bygone age, predictably ill-health increasingly dogged him and he died in Paris on 18 July 1730. His wife had died some years previously, quite soon after the debacle at Ramillies.

With the valuable, but seductively dangerous, benefit of hindsight, it is easy to view Villeroi as something of a dilettante lightweight, overly indulged by his boyhood friend, the Sun King, out of his depth and in time responsible for one of the most crushing defeats that the armies of the French ever had to endure over the course of the eighteenth century. However, Villeroi undoubtedly had many good qualities, quite apart from his skill as an accomplished courtier at Versailles and Fontainebleau, and he had his successes, such as the cautious but strategically valuable autumn campaign on the Rhine after the Blenheim defeat. His bravery and honesty, and his loyalty to the crown, were never in doubt.

Chapter 8

Marshal Vendôme

Louis-Joseph de Bourbon was born in Paris on 1 July 1654, a Prince of the Blood, if only on the wrong side of the blanket, by virtue of his grandparents being King Henry IV of France and his mistress Gabrielle d'Estrees. He was also the first cousin of Prince Eugene of Savoy, as his own Italian-born mother, Laura Mancini, was the sister of the notorious court gossip Olympia, the prince's rather wayward parent. Louis-Joseph's father, Louis, Duc de Vendôme, died in 1669 and in consequence the future marshal inherited a substantial fortune to be enjoyed on his maturity. The money derived from a legacy from his great-grandmother, the Duchesse de Mercoeur et Penthièvre, and the young man had been known, up to the time of his father's death, as the Duc de Penthièvre. Louis-Joseph was raised in the meantime in the home of his vivacious and promiscuous aunt, another of the remarkable Mancini girls, Marie-Anne, who had also married well and become the Duchesse de Bouillon, of whom it was remembered, that she was 'An intellectual, she had a salon'.[1] The inevitable and intimate connection with the rather raffish Mancini clan would prove to be a highly intriguing one, as time would tell.

Vendôme entered the service of Louis XIV at the age of 18, as a junior officer in the Gardes Française, and was soon displaying both remarkable courage and commendable enterprise in the Dutch War, serving under both Turenne and Condé. He campaigned vigorously in the conflict as it escalated with the growing involvement of Brandenburg and Spain, and attracted favourable attention for his energy and tactical skill, so that by 1688 he had risen to the rank of lieutenant-general. With the onset of the Nine Years War, he was active with both Marshal Luxembourg at the Battle of Steinkirk in the Low Countries in 1692, and with Nicolas de Catinat at the Marsaglia victory in northern Italy. Vendôme was noted at the time to be something of a brawler, and while securing a firm reputation as a bruising fighter of great energy, also rather given to bouts of indolence and self-centred boredom. Admired by his soldiers for his hard-fighting qualities, when the mood took him, there was a scurrilous doggerel rhyme on their ruffianly commander that ran through the ranks: 'Our big, fat blondy, Courageous and poxy, with his bold marauders, goes his own way, and don't wait long for orders.'[2]

He was also remembered by the wittily observant Duc de St Simon (who was highly disapproving of his uncouth manners) as being of:

> Ordinary height, rather stout, but strong, hearty, and active. He appeared handsome and well-bred, had the grand manner and was naturally graceful in speech and bearing. . . . He was a most polished courtier and managed to escape the consequences of his worst excesses [because] of the king's respect for his noble birth. He had a vast knowledge of the world, the court and its various personalities, and beneath an air of carelessness, hid a very keen eye to his own popularity with the common people, he affected a hearty familiarity.[3]

Vendôme was involved at one remove in the dangerous scandal known as the 'Affair of the Poisons' as his aunt, the Duchesse de Bouillon, was summoned for questioning over her alleged involvement in the highly febrile matter. On 29 January 1680, she arrived before the special tribunal looking into the affair. 'Lovely, rosy, smiling and surrounded by her adoring relatives', she was hand in hand both with her indulgent husband (who it was suggested she had tried to poison), and with Vendôme, who spoke ardently in her support; it was widely thought that the duchesse favoured her nephew as a potential lover. The Duc de Bouillon was a man plainly deeply in love with his rather wayward wife and declared that he did not at all mind her love affairs, so long as he still got his fair share of the lady's attentions.[4] Rather predictably, she was acquitted of any wrongdoing, but her already rather shady reputation had taken something of a battering. She was inclined to gossip about the affair, which annoyed the king, so that she found it convenient, as from time to time the other Mancini girls had also found it prudent to do, to live in quite retirement away from the court for a while until the dust settled.

Vendôme married late in life, and his personal behaviour in the meantime was reportedly rather dissolute, of that there seems to be little doubt, although he was perhaps not quite the gross debauchee that some observers maintained (the much-biased comments of St Simon have to be treated with more than a little caution). Vendôme did however, have to undergo the Grand Cure (involving the administering of copious amounts of mercury) for the treatment of syphilis, on at least one occasion:

> Vendôme began at last to think about his health, which his many excesses had thrown into a very bad state. He took public leave of the King and of all the Court before going away, to put himself in the hands of the doctors . . . His going in triumph, where another would have gone in shame and secrecy, was startling.[5]

He was often hot tempered, given to boorishness, and disinclined to listen to the advice of others, but despite this he was acknowledged as an undoubtedly tough fighter and gifted commander. In 1695 he was made Marshal of France by Louis XIV, and soon afterwards appointed to the command of French forces operating in Catalonia, in place of Marshal Noailles who had fallen ill and had left the field. There on campaign Vendôme distinguished himself particularly by his skilful conduct at the head of some 20,000 troops. After initially falling back to Gerona, he attacked his Spanish opponents at Ostalric in 1696 and then in the following year, with a substantially reinforced army, and in what was widely regarded as resembling a triumph, he besieged for two months and eventually took the key city of Barcelona. '[The city] made a better defence which gave time for the viceroy of Catalonia to march with a Spanish army to its assistance, but M. de Vendôme left his siege works and defeated him. The town, then, seeing relief impossible, capitulated.'[6] The garrison under the able command of the Prince of Hesse-Darmstadt had fought very well, and casualties were heavy on both sides, with a French naval bombardment and the planting of French mines under the defence being required to gain the submission of Hesse-Darmstadt. The garrison had suffered severely but were granted good terms by Vendôme at the capitulation on 10 August 1697, although as was the custom they had to leave their guns behind when they quitted the city.

With the onset of the War of the Spanish Succession, Vendôme was sent to command the army in northern Italy, where first Catinat and then Villeroi had struggled to hold Prince Eugene in check, at the head of an Austrian army and their allies. On 26 July 1702 he mauled a detachment of Eugene's troops at a bitterly-fought action at Santa Vittoria, although the French casualty toll that day was significantly greater than that of their opponents. The following month the two armies clashed at Luzzara beside the river Po, in what was effectively a drawn battle, as neither commander made much effort to find an exposed flank to their opponent's dispositions. Although Vendôme typically claimed it as a resounding victory as he held the ground at the close of the day, such rather specious claims were becoming the norm for a man who showed himself to be naturally boastful. St Simon was amongst those not overly impressed by what had been achieved. 'In Italy our armies were not more successful than elsewhere. From time to time, M. de Vendôme attacked some unimportant post and having carried it, despatched couriers to the king, magnifying the importance of the exploit. . . . All these successes led to nothing.'[7] It was true, however, that the marshal's astute moves had pushed the highly capable Eugene back from many of his hard-won successes of the previous year and obliged him to retire a fair way towards the shelter of the Trentino region. France's strategic hold on the Po valley, and consequent ability to exert pressure on Duke Victor-Amadeus of Savoy, was still very much in place.

The following year, as the campaign waged by Marshal Villars and the Elector of Bavaria to drive Austria out of the war gained pace, Louis XIV instructed Vendôme to march north, through the passes of the Tyrol, to join forces with them to force the issue on the upper reaches of the Danube. He took no action in response to what was demanded, concerned in the main that Victor-Amadeus might be about to desert his alliance with France, and that accordingly, it would be rash to leave the Po valley. Vendôme did move towards the town of Trent and bombarded the place in early September for no particular gain, but then withdrew southwards, as his concerns for the security of the rear areas of his army, and the overly extended lines of communication and supply, remained lively. These concerns would, before long, prove perceptive, for Victor-Amadeus was indeed on the point of changing sides, but Louis XIV was far from amused at this seeming lack of action, and he wrote quite tartly to Vendôme that:

> One could not be more surprised than I to see that you have taken upon yourself to defer the execution of an order which would have been of such great importance . . . Do you think that when I give you an order as precise as the one you received, that I do not have reasons stronger than yours for sending it? You allow yourself to be engaged by what is before you, and I see things that are in the distance which can have effects,

> and which cause me to make resolutions suitable to one who is charged with the weight of government. I ran [run] the risk of losing my army [that of Villars in facing the superior numbers enjoyed by the Margrave of Baden] and that of an ally who can alone contribute to the maintenance of an honourable war and open to one the route to a peace. The conquest of the Tyrol would have been easy.[8]

This last rather blithe sentiment may be held to be in some doubt, as Max-Emmanuel's Bavarian troops had turned aside from pressing the Austrian forces covering the approaches to Vienna, and instead advanced into the Tyrol and got as far as Innsbruck before receiving a severe mauling from local peasant militias and forced to withdraw in some disorder. Concurrently, matters moved fast in northern Italy, where Vendôme, in receipt of confidential information that the duke really was about to defect, disarmed much of the Savoyard army at the end of September, just in time it might be thought, as the duke duly declared his new allegiance to the Grand Alliance on 8 November. The French king wrote sharply to Victor-Amadeus, rebuking him for abandoning his alliance with France, 'Since religion, honour, interest, this alliance, and your signature mean nothing to you, I am sending the Duc de Vendôme, at the head of my armies, to explain to you my intentions'.[9] Although he soon had the able assistance of the Imperial Field Marshal Guido von Starhemberg, Victor-Amadeus was before long confined, more or less, to the fortified city of Turin and its immediate environs.

Pushing forward his campaign in 1704, Vendôme was unable to entice Victor-Amadeus out from the security of the walls of the city, for the duke would almost certainly have been overwhelmed by the considerably more powerful French forces in the region. The marshal did manage to take Vercelli in July, and invested Verrua on the Po in mid-October, although the place would be stoutly defended and hold out for a very creditable six months. Still, in time Victor-Amadeus must face ruin, or having to humbly seek to make amends for his behaviour with the king in Versailles, as the French net tightened around him in Turin. In the meantime, after considerable marching and countermarching, and a good deal of frustration felt by the commanders on both sides, who each complained to their respective masters at a lack of resources, Vendôme took Mirandolo in early May 1705, and soon after both Nice and Villefranche fell into French hands. (The Savoyard garrison in the citadel of Nice, however, stoutly held out for another six months.)

On 16 August 1705, Prince Eugene almost overwhelmed an exposed French detachment led by Vendôme's negligent younger brother, Grand Prior Philippe de Bourbon, at Cassano on the River Adda. The marshal arrived in time to push reinforcements into the escalating fight, and the hotly-pressed Austrian attack across the key feature of the Ritorta stream was repulsed with great loss, after an afternoon and evening of hard fighting. 'He was on foot,' an officer wrote of Vendôme's conduct in the battle, 'sword in hand, his horse having been killed. His coat and waistcoat were unbuttoned, his face all in a sweat, his shirt full of tobacco and dust, he looked like Mars, the God of War.'[10] That a serious reverse for the French and their allies had been narrowly avoided was much to his credit, and clearly demonstrated the energy that Vendôme was able to deploy, at a most difficult moment. 'He did not fail,' St Simon spitefully recalled, 'to claim all the honours of this victory, which in reality was a barren one, and sent word of his triumph to the king . . . In the end the Grand Prior was obliged to give up his command.'[11] This was to no one's great surprise, as he had demonstrated quite breathtaking incompetence in allowing Eugene to close up to his encampment and yet take almost no measures, at first, to meet the threat in the preliminary phase of the action that day at Cassano.

Returning to Versailles in February 1706, Vendôme met general applause for what he had achieved so far, at least how he related the facts at any rate, and where 'It was evident that everyone had resolved to raise Vendôme to the rank of a hero'.[12] Well, heroes were in woefully short supply in France at the time, and the marshal's achievements in Italy, while inconclusive and perhaps amplified in the telling, had nonetheless caused considerable difficulties for Vienna and the newly enthroned Austrian Emperor Joseph's new ally, Duke Victor-Amadeus. Such blind adulation from those at court was of course dangerous, and Vendôme clumsily mishandled things, undoubtedly getting above himself.

> He claimed to be appointed commander of the Marshals of France [in effect to be made Marshal-General], and although the king refused him this favour, he accorded him one which was but the stepping-stone to it. Vendôme went away towards the middle of March, to again command the army in Italy, with a letter signed by the king himself, promising him that if a Marshal of France were sent to Italy, that person was to take commands from him, and with that, M. de Vendôme was content.[13]

With the onset of the 1706 campaigning season in April Vendôme smartly defeated the Austrians and their allies at Calcinato, at the time under the command of Graf von Reventlau (Eugene had not yet arrived to actively take up the command) and inflicting over 3,000 casualties and as many again taken as prisoners, together with twenty standards and ten guns. The king wrote in warm appreciation, to Cardinal de Noailles, on receiving the news:

> I could not hope for a more happy and glorious advantage at the beginning of this campaign, than that which my cousin, the Duc de Vendôme has signally obtained in Italy . . . the experience of the Duc de Vendôme, the courage of my soldiers,

> and the just confidence that they have in him, have surmounted all obstacles. A victory so complete is the more welcome, and the more advantageous by thee enemy abandoning the posts that they were emplaced on the [river] Adige where they had entered five years since.[14]

The marshal then arranged his army to counter any moves by Eugene to relieve Turin, where Victor-Amadeus was besieged by a French army under General de la Feuillade, joined latterly by the king's nephew, Philippe, Duc d'Orleans, and Marshal Ferdinand Marsin.[15] The city defences were very strong, having been designed by Vauban, and the siege itself was marked by lacklustre planning and preparation, and arguments amongst the senior French officers on how best to proceed; Victor-Amadeus had managed to leave the place with his cavalry, in order to harry the French operations. Helpful advice was sent by the elderly Vauban, the master of such kind of measured warfare, but this was largely ignored. The engineer was so scathing of the way in which the operations limped almost aimlessly on that the Minister for War, Michel de Chamillart, wryly wrote to de la Feuillade that, 'Vauban announces to his friends and the world at large that he is willing to have his throat cut if you ever succeed in taking Turin'.[16] In any event, sceptical that Eugene would be able to move to the relief of his cousin so far or so fast in the face of superior French numbers, Vendôme was caught out and failed to intercept the prince's long march along the length of the Po valley to reach Turin. Fortunately for his reputation, he would not stay to see the sorry result of a campaign that he was in the process of bungling but was called to take over the command of the shattered French army in the Low Countries, following the heavy defeat inflicted in May 1706 on Villeroi by the Duke of Marlborough at Ramillies.

Hurrying north in response to the king's summons, Vendôme was once more rapturously received at Versailles, being regarded as the saviour so badly needed at this critical moment. Undoubtedly, his relentless energy when roused, and his undoubted popularity with the troops did a great deal to restore French fortunes after the calamity:

> The entire staff surrounded his coach [and] he had scarcely reached his room when a flood of visitors appeared. The Princes of the Blood, hitherto so jealous of the favour shown him in the service, were the first to pay their respects . . . He was almost born on the shoulders of the crowd to the salon [where] the King embraced him many times.[17]

Taking advantage of the moment, Vendôme again asked for the appointment as marshal-general, a post last held by Turenne, and which would give him authority over all the other marshals. Louis XIV agreed, but when the patent was issued, Vendóme curtly returned the document as it made no mention of any authority over the royal princes when on campaign. This was both absurd, as by virtue of their status no-one but the king could have authority over these younger men, but also rather clumsy and impertinent on the part of the marshal. The appointment never came into being, which was perhaps just as well as the other marshals would almost to a man have refused to accept his authority.[18] The possible exception was Marshal Matignon, who, it was widely thought, had only been appointed to the rank by the king simply because he would indeed accept Vendôme's orders.

As it was, Vendóme set off for Flanders on 1 August 1706, and his restless, fitful, energy did much to restore things and slow the remorseless advance of Marlborough's victorious army, stabilizing the otherwise perilous situation facing France in the north-east. He continued to ruffle feathers with his boastful demeanour, and the Duc de St Simon recalled that:

> As he rose in rank and favour, his arrogance and self-will rose in proportion, to a point where he became impervious to advice

> of any kind and refused to listen to any but a very small number of intimates . . . [he] gradually accustomed his junior officers to call him 'Monseigneur' and 'Votre Altesse'. As no one opposed him, this spread to lieutenant-generals and other distinguished persons, not one of them dared address him otherwise, so that after a time the improper title became a right.[19]

Monseigneur' 1707 Marlborough tried without much success to pin Vendôme down long enough to have to fight a major action in the open; but the marshal's adept and cautious manoeuvring foiled the Allied commander-in-chief on several occasions, although bad luck (and foul weather) also dogged Marlborough's efforts from time to time. Vendôme was in turn hampered by having troops drawn away from Flanders to bolster the French war effort in other theatres, particularly in southern France where the major French naval base at Toulon was under threat, while a proposal made that he should move to seize Huy was refused by the king. All the same, the course of the year was one of general disappointment for the Grand Alliance, with the cause of the French claimant to the throne in Madrid prospering with a ringing victory at Almanza, and the Allied attempt to seize Toulon failing amidst much acrimony over who was most at fault.

In 1708, however, and at his own request, the Duc de Bourgogne, the king's eldest grandson and eventual intended heir to the French throne, joined the army in Flanders. This was a move which Vendôme apparently approved of, initially at least, as it was likely that the young man would try to exercise less control over the commanding general than did the Elector of Bavaria, who had technically at least held the overall command appointment, as he still held the now rather redundant role as the governor-general of the Spanish Netherlands.

> In the spring of 1708, the Duc de Bourgogne besought his grandfather to employ him again. The king thought that he

> could not well refuse him, especially as the Duc de Vendôme, who had the command in in Flanders, seconded his wishes, expecting, no doubt, to be less liable to control under a young Prince, without experience, than under the Elector whose life had been dedicated to the service, and who, for four and twenty years had been used to command in chief.[20]

Elector Max-Emmanuel duly went off to campaign on the Rhine, hoping in the process to raise his homeland of Bavaria in his support (a hope which predictably remained unfulfilled), while in the north a promising start was made with a daring and sudden stroke which saw the recapture of the important cities of Ghent and Bruges, together with the French obtaining a grip on the important waterways of northern Flanders, without which Marlborough had acute difficulty in moving his army's supplies given the poor state of the roads of the time: This was to the undisguised delight of many of the local citizenry, who were tired of onerous Dutch and Austrian taxation.

> Early in July we took Ghent and Bruges by surprise, and the news was received with the most unbridled joy at Fontainebleau It appeared easy to profit by these two conquests, obtained without difficulty, by passing the Escaut [Scheldt], burning Oudenarde, closing the country to the enemies, and cutting them off from all supplies.[21]

The advantage gained was then squandered, because Vendôme could not agree with the Duc de Bourgogne as to the next best course of action. The two men had by now formed a hearty mutual dislike which was not at all helpful, as their respective staffs took their lead and tried to ignore each other as much as could be done. So, the question on the next steps had to be referred to Versailles for the king to give his ruling. With the French campaign hobbled in this way,

Marlborough, who had been joined by Eugene, recovered his tactical poise and moved to close with the French army on the river Dender. Caught out by the speed with speed with which the Allies moved, and unable to hold the line of that river, Vendôme and Bourgogne fell back to the Scheldt, from where they hoped to attack the Allied-held fortress of Oudenarde. On Wednesday 11 July the French found that Marlborough's army had force-marched from the Dender and was closing up to them as they made their almost leisurely way across the river at Gavre, just downstream from Oudenarde.

The fault-line in the French command and control arrangements that afternoon was stark, with Vendôme and Bourgogne ignoring each other still, while the marshal allowed himself to be drawn into a bitter infantry battle alongside the Scheldt. Bourgogne, meanwhile, was irresolute and uncertain to how to deploy the uncommitted wing of the army that was under his direct command, and while Vendôme looked for, and rightly expected, his support, in the end none was forthcoming. Although Marlborough was unable to deploy his full strength in time to destroy the French army in position, he inflicted a severe defeat on them whose losses were some 14,000 killed, wounded and as prisoners (Marlborough and Veldt-Marshal Overkirk's casualties were slightly over about 3,000 all told). The beaten French had to withdraw in complete confusion northwards, to find sanctuary behind the Ghent-Bruges canal. 'Vendôme set out without giving any orders or seeing to anything.'[22] The day at Oudenarde had from start to finish been woefully mishandled, and Vendôme was the *de facto* army commander whatever shortcomings the young Bourgogne may had exhibited, and the fault lay firmly at his door.

The intrinsic perils of divided command have, perhaps, rarely been better displayed. Vendôme was in command, and his orders were those to which attention should be paid, but the young royal prince, by virtue of his rank, attracted attention and deference from all around him, and yet he was a relatively inexperienced campaigner, with little liking or aptitude for the rigours and attendant horrors of warfare, for all that his grandfather pushed him forward to get to know, and get to be known by, his soldiers. The marshal, on the other hand, for all his faults, relished campaigning and was, on his day, a most formidable opponent, but this is not to disguise the calamity at Oudenarde, over which he presided:

> He embarked on the one thing that the king had always forbidden, an infantry battle in broken and enclosed country. He then indulged his love of hand-to-hand fighting, crashing about like an enraged animal instead of remaining at the post of command [and] after the *debacle*, he subsided into a sulky lethargy, and left Bourgogne in full control.[23]

Predictably, he wrote to the king in highly disparaging terms, regarding the lack of support he had received on the day of battle, 'The princes are a fearful burden on the army . . . It appears to me that the movements required during the remainder of the campaign do not in any way require their presence.'[24] Referring to the king's grandson in this way was risky, but Vendôme was often cuttingly outspoken, trading on his royal lineage and generally getting away with things that others would not. An observer commented that, 'Vendôme, after spending several days in sleeping off the effects of Oudenarde, had relapsed into a false sense of security, and persisted in believing that the enemy were planning nothing of importance [saying that]. It is simply a matter of standing firm.'[25]

Marlborough and Eugene having moved to threaten the city and fortress of Lille that August, Louis XIV wrote to Vendôme with an unmistakeable call to move forward and foil their operations. 'The train of [Allied] siege artillery which they have withdrawn from Maastricht, must by now be at Brussels. It would by highly advantageous to attack the escorting troops with a stronger force, and one could take no more serviceable [valuable] action.'[26] Despite this, almost no effort was made to impede the preparations for the siege, in a clear case of misjudgement and neglect by the senior French commanders at this time. The low state of morale in their troops after Oudenarde was also very evident. The bickering continued and the Duc de Bourgogne, who must carry his share of the blame for this sorry situation, wrote to Versailles that, 'The king is gravely mistaken in having so high an opinion of him [Vendôme]. I am not the only one to say this.'[27] The exasperation felt in Versailles that more was not being done to save the city, cherished prize of Louis XIV's early conquests, was plain:

> The king wrote to him to go with his army to the relief of Lille . . . losing his temper he despatched another courier, with orders to Monsieur de Bourgogne, to lead the army to Lille. At this Vendôme awoke from his lethargy, he set out for Lille, but took the longest road and dawdled as long as he could on the way . . . The king demanded news of the siege from his courtiers and could not understand why no couriers arrived. It was generally expected that some decisive battle had been fought. Each day increased the uneasiness.[28]

In fact, it was soon understood that with an army so disheartened after the calamitous failure at Oudenarde, any offensive moves to lift the Allied siege were most unlikely to succeed, and even the minister for war, Michel de Chamillart, when sent by Louis XIV in mid-September to see that the most active steps were taken, soon agreed that little could really be done. He did report, however, that Vendôme intended to move against the Allied lines of supply and communication that ran back to Brussels and Ostend. All the crossing places over the Scheldt were indeed seized in October, apart from Allied-held Oudenarde, but Marlborough was deftly able to re-open them with hardly a pause in the siege operations, and a simultaneous attempt by the Elector of Bavaria to take Brussels failed dismally. 'We gave our armies four months to raise the siege and during those four months we were able to succeed only in small enterprises.'[29]

With the subsequent fall of Lille in early December, despite the valiant defence conducted by Boufflers, Vendôme's attempts to blame others for what had been a lamentably poor campaign were too much. 'He had a short interview with the king, in which he made many bitter complaints.'[30] Louis XIV had already spoken to several of the senior officers involved in the campaign, notably the highly capable Jean de Chasteney, Marquis de Puyesgur, and was not deceived. He removed Vendôme from command, and temporarily ordered him into retirement. 'The end came swiftly, Vendôme, thrown out of service, sold his military equipment, dismissed his household, and retired.'[31]

However, the talents Marshal Vendôme clearly possessed, when the mood took him, could not be left idle at a time of great danger for France and the French claimant to the throne in Madrid, so that the following year, at the particular request of Philip V, he was sent to take command of the French and Spanish forces fighting the Austrians and their allies in the peninsula.

> The King of Spain was desperately in want of generals, and M. de Vendôme knowing this, and sick to death of banishment, had asked some little time before to be allowed to offer his services. At first, he was snubbed, but the King of Spain, who eagerly wished for M. de Vendôme, despatched a courier, begging the king to allow him to come and take command. The king held out no longer [and] the Duc de Vendôme had prepared everything in advance.[32]

Before that, and to general surprise given the widely held, and equally widely believed, rumours as to the precise details of his private life, on 21 May 1710, Vendôme took as his wife the homely

Marie-Anne de Bourbon, a granddaughter of the Great Condé. The wedding ceremony took place in the chapel at the Chateau de Sceaux.

Philip V's army had been badly beaten by Imperial Field Marshal Guido von Starhemberg at Saragossa on 20 August, and matters for the French claimant in the dispute were in some disarray. 'M. de Vendôme learned of this defeat while on his way to Spain.'[33] His arrival at Valladolid on 17 September 1710 was therefore timely, and he swiftly took matters in hand, moving to adroitly blunt a well-handled, but clearly under-resourced, offensive against Philip's forces, during which Madrid was briefly occupied by the Allied army. They could not hold the city, however, in part due to the hostility shown by the population, and withdrew towards Catalonia. After a stiff fight on 8 December 1710 Vendôme overwhelmed a small British force commanded by the Earl of Stanhope at Brihuega, going on to batter the main Imperial army under von Starhemberg the next day at Villa-Viciosa. 'The day was, in fact, won just as night came on . . . But Starhemberg, having all the night to himself, succeeded in retiring in good order.'[34] The marshal was, accordingly, unable to prevent his opponent from withdrawing pretty well intact, even though having to leave much of his spiked artillery and stores behind, with one rather specious report stating that, 'The debris of the enemy army retired in much haste'.[35] Rivalries amongst the commanders in the Allied camp had been unhelpful, but Vendôme had certainly conducted a very effective campaign with slender resources all the while under the watchful eye of Philip V and he richly deserved the credit gained. The Spanish and French success at Villa-Viciosa was undoubtedly important. 'Never had victory been more complete, and this day will change the face of affairs in Spain.'[36] The Allied campaign to secure the throne in Madrid for the Habsburg claimant, Archduke Charles, had fallen to pieces, and would soon prove to be beyond recovery, so that Vendôme's successes in this campaign can be seen as strategically highly significant. St Simon wrote perceptively, that,

'When we consider the extreme peril the Crown of Spain ran in these engagements, and that this time, if things had gone ill, there was no resource, we tremble still'.[37]

Vendôme was able to pursue von Starhemberg back into Catalonia, where before long Gerona fell, being occupied by French troops on 25 January 1711. As the year progressed only the Imperial hold on the environs of Barcelona remained of what had been the long and costly Allied effort to secure the Spanish throne. After taking some leave in France, Vendôme returned to Spain in January 1712, and joined his troops at Tortosa and Valencia, but once there he suffered what appeared to be a bout of food poisoning and died on 11 June at Vinaròs at the age of 58. His final few days were miserable, and as so often at the time when sudden illness occurred, dark deeds were suspected:

> He became unwell [and] his illness increased so rapidly, and in so strange a manner, after having for a long time seemed nothing that the few around him suspected poison and sent on all sides for assistance. But the malady would not wait; it augmented rapidly with strange symptoms. Vendôme could not sign a will that was presented to him; nor a letter to the King, in which he asked that his brother [the Grand Prior] might be permitted to return to Court . . . He remained in the hands of three or four of the meanest valets, while the rest robbed him of everything and decamped.[38]

Although in some ways a controversial figure, dissolute, brawling, idle and often behaving uncouthly (but much and most unfairly maligned by a waspish St Simon), Vendôme was much liked by his soldiers, and proved in on numerous occasions to be a very adept and effective campaigner, with the brilliant, albeit fitful, courage of the true soldier. This was acknowledged by Philip V, and he was buried with full honours in the Escorial Palace outside Madrid. 'This was the crowning glory of Marshal Vendôme; for no private persons are buried in the Escorial.'[39] He and his newlywed wife Marie-Anne had not had children, but on his death on campaign in Spain she inherited in her own right the Duchy of Étampes, and when she died in 1718, the estate went to her niece, the Princess de Conti. Vendôme's younger brother, Philippe, the Grand Prior succeeded to his titles, although that of the Duc de Penthièvre had been sold in 1696.

Chapter 9

Marshal Villars

Born in Moulins on 8 May 1653, Claude-Louis-Hector de Villars was from a family tainted by Frondist connections, although his grand-uncle was the renowned Marquis de Bellefonds (Marshal of France 1668). The year following the birth, his father, Pierre de Villars, entered the French foreign service and eventually became the ambassador to Copenhagen and then Madrid. Educated at the Oratorian College at Juilly, the young Claude early on sought a military career. His father's carefully constructed connections at court, despite the animosity shown by the Marquis de Louvois (who heartily disliked his grand-uncle Bellefonds), managed in 1670 to secure for him a commission as second lieutenant in the prestigious Chevaux-Léger cavalry. Although denied permission to accompany his grand-uncle as an aide-de-camp, Claude was noted for his bravery in action in 1672 at Zutphen, when fighting the Dutch, and then appointed as lieutenant in the Burgundy Régiment of Cavalry, on the death in action of his predecessor, the Marquis de la Rochefoucauld.

Villars' remarkably gallant conduct won him the notice and growing approval of Louis XIV, and after briefly serving on a diplomatic mission to Madrid, he again saw action in the war against the Dutch, at the siege of Maastricht in 1673. There, he earned for himself a smart reprimand for disobeying orders and rashly leading his cavalry in a headlong charge, as he was irked and frustrated at the slow pace of the French infantry's advance. Nonetheless, the intention had been good, and Turenne cited him for his bravery, and Louis XIV was persuaded to endorse the citation. The king was also apparently rather taken by Villars' free and easy manner and took no offence when the young man neglected to bow to him on one occasion. At the hard-fought battle at Seneffe on 11 August of the following year, when only the onset of darkness called a weary halt to the killing, Villars served under the Prince of Condé and was wounded three times, but staunchly refused to leave the field to be treated. In this way he gained for himself another commendation for bravery, and soon afterwards received the prestigious appointment as colonel of the Courcelles Régiment of Cavalry. However, he fell seriously ill with dysentery while recovering from wounds in hospital in Charleroi, and was lucky to recover his health at all.

Campaigning in Alsace in 1675 under Marshal de Créquy, Villars led the forward screen of cavalry in the approach to the Imperial-held fortress of Kehl on the right bank of the Rhine, where an expensive frontal assault had eventually to be undertaken to seize the place. At the head of his regiment in an action leading to the seizure of St Omer in 1677, he again disobeyed orders and charged and broke William of Orange's right flank; the smart reprimand he received on this occasion was tempered by the undoubted success of his unauthorized manoeuvre, which did much to secure the French success on the day. He particularly distinguished himself at the Kockersberg cavalry action in October that year but all the same, by 1679 and the peace that came with the Treaty of Nijmegen, Villars had not managed to secure any further promotion. Fresh opportunities for renown appeared, however, with the major Ottoman incursion into Hungary and Austria in the summer of 1683, when the city of Vienna was laid under siege by Grand Vizier Kara Mustapha and his reputedly huge army. Louis XIV somewhat reluctantly allowed numbers of French officers to go and fight in the East, and Villars was amongst their number. This reluctance on the king's part stemmed, no doubt, from the fact that he had actively encouraged Constantinople to make as much trouble for the Austrians as they could to divert Emperor Leopold's attention from French activities in the West.

In 1687 Villars served under the Imperial army commander, Charles IV, Duke of Lorraine and Bar, at the siege of Buda, and had command of the Bavarian cavalry in the decisive action at 2nd Mohacs (Berg Hazan) on 12 August. His gallantry was commented on by, amongst others, the young Prince Eugene of Savoy, with whom he formed a close friendship. When Elector Max-Emmanuel of Bavaria left Hungary, apparently affronted that his efforts were not better appreciated in Vienna, Villars accompanied him to Munich. However, the renewal of war in the West, once the Grand Alliance had been formed to challenge Louis XIV, promptly recalled him to the French service. In 1689 he fought at the Battle of Walcourt, where he brought his cavalry forward in timely fashion to support the French infantry who were being very roughly handled by their Dutch opponents. and was promoted to Brigadier-General of Cavalry on the earnest recommendation of Marshal d'Humieres. The recent death of the Marquis de Louvois helped matters, as he had long harboured a quite unreasonable dislike for Villars.

Appointed to the command of the cavalry campaigning in Flanders under Marshal Luxembourg, Villars shone at the Battle of Leuze in September 1691. He led the charge at the head of the squadrons from the du Maine, de Rohan and de Prâlin Régiments, during which he was set upon in the *melée* by several opponents, and only narrowly escaped with his life. 'The Marquis de Villars,' it was recalled, 'had no other armour than a double buff-coat, and a handkerchief under his hat, which saved his life, for his coat and his hat were pierced in seventeen places, yet his body was not touched.'[1] The Duc de Chartres, illegitimate son of the king who was present on the day, also wrote appreciatively that, 'It was his agility that stopped the enemy's rearguard, and he always led on the left Wing to the Charge with great advantage'.[2] As it was, the Dutch commander that day, the Prince of Waldeck, managed to extract his troops and retire more or less unhindered, although he undoubtedly had the worst of the scrambled affair.

Villars had now established a well-merited reputation for dash and enterprise, but he clearly knew when to apply caution, as on one occasion when a fellow officer, in command of a group of foragers, suggested impetuously charging a larger and threatening force of Imperial cavalry. 'Sir,' Villars chided him, with only mild sarcasm, 'when I am at a loss what to do in the morning, it is a pleasure to me to have twelve or fifteen grenadiers lose their lives', adding that he should 'learn how to fight'.[3] Instead, Villars had his dragoons move to a flank and open fire as a preliminary to making an attack, and confronted in this way, the opposing cavalry prudently withdrew. 'By this means he . . . saved the foragers and gave a lesson to the Horse with regard to the conduct necessary to be observed in the presence of enemies.'[4]

Two years after the affair at Leuze, Villars served under Marshal Boufflers at the siege of Furnes, where he had command of the covering force. In the bitterly cold weather of early January, he took post at Courtrai, between the rivers Scheldt and Lys, ready to intercept any Allied attempt to raise the siege, and when the Elector of Bavaria advanced towards Nieuport, he made a deft countermove towards Dunkirk to forestall him. This was successful, and the elector drew off, so that, despairing of relief, the garrison commander in Furnes submitted on 7 January 1693. '[It]was horrid weather, it was remembered, 'and the trenches full of water.'[5] Boufflers was summoned to return to Versailles, and Villars was left in command in Flanders, with the appointment both as Lieutenant-General and Inspector-General of the French armies, a post of considerable influence and importance. In mid-May, after a brief visit of his own to court, he was sent to command the cavalry on the Rhine under the overall command of Marshal de Lorge. There, he had to warn his officers, at the risk of his severe displeasure, not to allow their men to continue to wantonly plunder and burn, as the discipline of the French troops had temporarily broken down with the seizure of Heidelberg.

> The [Imperial] governor surrendered on the seventh day, and to punish him for his poor defence, he was tried in a court martial, and sentenced to be degraded of his arms, a kind of infamy more dreadful than death itself to a man of honour. Our troops plundered and burnt the city of Heidelberg, in spite of the endeavours by the officers to prevent this calamity; but it must be confessed, that the soldiers of the army were inexpressibly licentious. Marquis de Villars spoke to all the regiments of Horse, and declared, that if they did not behave more discreetly for the future, they should be punished with great severity.[6]

While Marshal Luxembourg was battering the army of William III at Landen, the French troops on the Rhine rather lost their way and sense of purpose and did not achieve a great deal other than looting and levying contributions. 'An army under the command of the Dauphin, and in the presence of three Marshal of France [d'Huxelles, de Lorge and Boufflers] was seen to behave in a most dissolute, abandoned manner . . . the soldiers were often punished, and sometimes twenty were hanged up in a day.'[7] At last reinforcements had to be sent south from the army to bolster the efforts of Catinat in northern Italy, and the remaining French troops took post at Breisach on the Rhine. Villars had in the meantime been sent to take up a command in Flanders, but was replaced by the Comte de Montrevel, and initially lacked employment that winter, a sidelining partly due to the dislike shown by the Marquis de Barbezieux (lacklustre son of the deceased Marquis de Louvois), the newly installed minister for war, had for him. The king, however, would not let his talents lie idle for long, and appointed Villars to be governor of both Breisach and Freiburg, rather to the discomfort of Barbezieux. Almost immediately, though, Louis XIV directed that Villars be sent to Italy where he served under Catinat for a brief while, earning more praise for his skill and dash in action. 'The King was pleased to give him testimonies of the satisfaction his services gave.'[8] Villars was then appointed to inspect the French cavalry in Savoy, Franche-Comte, Alsace and Lorraine, although the order to do so was inexplicably delayed, and had to be repeated before he took up the post.

Villars accompanied Marshal de Lorge in early 1694 when he advanced to again challenge Louis-Guillaume, Margrave of Baden, who had taken up a position with his Imperial troops on the upper Rhine. The French crossed the river at Philippsburg on 8 June, but the region was so devastated and stripped by armies in recent campaigns, that it was impossible to remain there for long. A sharp engagement took place on 25 June at Visloc, which saw Villars forcing the way across a boggy stream, 'The passage across the rivulet was found pretty difficult, and the enemy making a great fire . . . the dragoons of the army plunged into the rivulet, whose great depth and oozy bottom, was very incommodious to the soldiers.'[9] He was clearly eager to come to grips with his opponents, in what became a hectic and toughly contested action, during which the Imperial commander Count Claude Mercy fell under Villars' own horse and was trampled on. Eventually, after this modest success de Lorge retired to the left bank of the Rhine, to manoeuvre to thwart any further attempts by the margrave to attempt an incursion into Alsace. Lacking supplies and opportunities for forage, Baden had to fall back, and other than obliging him to do so, the campaign had really produced few results. Villars returned to Versailles for the winter, where he was gratified to be received in private audience by Louis XIV on two occasions.

Marshal de Lorge being unwell, his place at the head of the army on the Rhine in 1695 was taken by Marshal Jean-Armand de Joyeuse. Under his command Villars with a body of reinforcements was soon engaged in a sharp skirmish with Baden's advance guard. Superior numbers obliged him to fall back, which he did with only slight loss, and when the de Joyeuse came up in support, he was fulsome in his congratulations on a generally well-handled affair. Apart from some sparring and marching to and fro, there was little other of note in the campaign, although Villars was again engaged in a sharp cavalry action against Count Johan Palffy, who had been a close colleague of Prince Eugene when on campaign against the Ottomans in the East; the Imperial commander was wounded in this engagement.

Sent to once more support Catinat in northern Italy for the 1696 campaign, Villars was introduced to Duke Victor-Amadeus Savoy, who had renewed his alliance with France and in the process abandoned that with Vienna. Villars took a prominent part in the hard-fought siege of Valenza in September. 'It was natural that we must go and besiege Valenza, for the indispensable necessity we were under of making use of the [river] Po, to transport our stores. The river being very low at that season, the boats could go but half loaded . . . We invested Valenza on the 20th.'[10] Four days later the trenches were opened, and Villars was in command of the works when, on 30 September, the Imperial garrison made a sharp and very well-handled sortie to spoil the siege works. Villars was able to beat back the attempt, but only after suffering some serious losses before matters could be concluded:

> Villars commanded the trenches the 30th of September, when the enemy made a considerable sally. He marched against them with the Marquis de Chatelet, Colonel of Horse, heading his squadron, repulsed them to the covered way [but] his colonel was very dangerously wounded on this occasion.[11]

With the arranging soon afterwards of a 'convention' of neutrality in Italy (the Treaty of Vervagno), active operations came to an end, and the garrison in Valenza could be left in peace. Villars was almost immediately sent to join Marshal Claude de Choiseuil on the German frontier, but the Treaty of Ryswick brought the wider war to what would prove to be but a temporary pause in 1697. In that same year Villars' father died, so that he formally assumed the title of Marquis de Villars.

In 1698, Villars was appointed by Louis XIV to act as his diplomatic representative in Vienna, with the rather contrived title of Envoy Extraordinaire, explicitly not as ambassador, apparently in order to avoid offending the resident Spanish ambassador to the Imperial court. His equipage for the journey was remarkable, and was described as follows; 'Marquis de Villars sent from Paris three coaches with eight horses each, four wagons with the same number of horses, and five or six carts, to carry the furniture he designed to use in Vienna; six pages, four gentlemen [valets], and a great number of domestics'.[12] On arrival the warmth of his reception was rather mixed, with entrenched suspicion of Louis XIV and his often dangerous plans telling heavily against the French interest. Once in post Villars was able to observe and comment, not too kindly it would seem, on the character of Leopold's eldest son and heir, 'The King of the Romans [Archduke Joseph] was young and addicted to his pleasures. He was a prince of good sense, but his mind was still unsettled and might be brought to either good or evil.'[13] Joseph's younger brother, Archduke Charles was described as 'extremely mild [with] the gentleness and humanity of the House of Austria', although in time he proved in fact to be both obstinate and rather dull.

Villars' efforts at the court in Vienna were thorough and effective enough, in difficult circumstances, but the opening moves of what would be the war for the throne in Madrid inevitably meant that he would soon be *persona non grata* and have to return to France.

> On the 18th of November [1700], the Marquis de Villars received a letter from the king which informed him of the King of Spain's

> death . . . News was brought in that His Catholic Majesty [Carlos II] had made a will in favour of the Duc d'Anjou. Villars was informed at the same time that the king had acquainted Great Britain and the United Provinces [Holland] with his having accepted the donation; and was ordered to acquaint the court of Vienna that the Duc d'Anjou had already been treated as King of Spain, and in consequence thereof would set out on the 1st of December, to take possession of his kingdom.[14]

This news was, of course, highly unwelcome to Leopold and his ministers, as Archduke Charles also aspired to the Spanish throne. Villars was able to alert Louis XIV in March 1701 that the emperor was quietly moving troops into northern Italy but was ordered back to France on 18 July that year.

Appointed to be chief-of-staff to Catinat when taking the campaign trail once again in northern Italy, Villars was not at the expensive and ill-judged Battle of Chiari in September when the newly-appointed army commander, Marshal Villeroi, rashly attacked Eugene's army in a strong defensive position and got badly beaten for his trouble. Recalled to Versailles in November 1701, Villars was once more warmly greeted by the king, and informed that he was to command the French forces being sent to bolster the position of the Elector of Bavaria, who had now openly declared for the French claimant to the Spanish throne.

In the meantime, Villars married Angelique Roque de Varagneville, a young and wealthy ward of Louis XIV, and 30 years his junior standing then, as he did, at the good age of 50. In the meantime, he was sent back to serve under Catinat, now recovered from wounds suffered in Italy, and in place with the command on the Saar and upper Rhine. There the two men clashed over what appeared to Villars to be a needlessly hesitant campaign waged by Catinat, with the possibility that the key fortress of Landau would risk being lost to their opponents unless more active measures were taken to save the place. In early September, before this could happen, Villars received orders to assume an independent command and proceed to Munich with a force some 15,000 strong, to join the elector in facing the Imperial troops on the stretch of the upper Danube between Ulm, Donauwörth and Ingolstadt. Matters became considerably more complicated when, as predicted, Landau fell on 9 September, after a stout resistance of some 84 days. The Imperial commander, the Margrave of Baden, was now free to manoeuvre against Villars, and Elector Max-Emmanuel took alarm, and withdrew his troops, under the very able Count Jean d'Arco, who had been intended to assist Villars in his crossing of the Rhine and forthcoming march towards Bavaria.

Once reinforcements had been received which brought his numbers to some 17,000 troops and 30 guns, Villars set off at last, seemingly full of optimism and felt able to write to Michel de Chamillart on 23 September that, 'I wish to take the liberty to say that nothing is impossible for these men For such men, the priority is to meet the enemy on the field of battle'.[15] Five days later, riding ahead with a small party, he reached Hüningen on the Rhine, and found the Margrave of Baden with a 15,000-strong force in a position of defence nearby at Tuttlingen. Villars quickly drew up plans to confront the Imperial troops, decoying their attention away with work parties attempting, or so it was made to appear, to build a bridge of boats across the river. He then marched 21 miles up the course of the Rhine and neatly effected a crossing near to the fortified post of Nürnberg, and promptly swung back towards his opponent who was still motionless at Tuttlingen. On 14 October a sharp action was fought near to Fort Friedlingen in the Black Forest, with quite significant losses on both sides, and a fleeting degree of panic taking hold in the two armies, but Baden was at last forced to withdraw from the field, leaving behind twelve guns and thirty-three standards and colours. His losses stood at just over 4,000 killed, wounded and prisoners, while Villars reported to Versailles his own casualties as being 1,152 killed and 2,839 wounded, with just a few prisoners lost. The battle had been remarkable for the way the Imperial cavalry fled, paradoxically just as the French infantry did so, but the tactical advantage plainly lay with Villars at the end of the day.

Fort Friedlingen was stormed by French troops that same night, and the way was, in theory at least, now open for Villars to march with little hindrance to join the elector on the Danube. For this strategically significant success, allowing Louis XIV to establish direct contact now with Max-Emmanuel, the most significant of his key allies, Villars was at last awarded the marshal's baton by the king, and this was gazetted on 28 October 1702. That his rather misleading report on the degree of success gained in the battle at Freidlingen had stood him in good stead was, all the same, widely commented on.

Baden withdrew with his battered army to Freiburg, and Villars would have pursued him there, but the elector refused to move forward in support and called instead for at least 10,000 French troops to be sent to bolster his position in and around Munich. Villars had been instrumental in firmly binding the allegiance of Max-Emmanuel to the French cause in the war, but the brief friendship that had initially existed between the two strong-willed men would not last for very long. Villars protested to Versailles at the fresh change of plans and the apparent timidity now being shown by the elector, but the king reluctantly agreed that no further moves should be made as the cold weeks of winter set in. The newly-appointed marshal's troops went into quarters in Metz, and at the end of December he returned to Paris to see his new-born son for the first time. In the meantime, Max-Emmanuel came under renewed pressure from Vienna, although he did seize the fortress of Neuburg, and so on 12 February 1703, still in the depths of winter, Villars re-crossed the Rhine at Hüningen and a week later reached the Imperial-held fortress of Kehl, on the far bank just cross from Strasbourg. The place fell to French assault after a modest resistance of 22 days, and on 18 March Villars, having in this way secured an important bridgehead across the river, prudently retraced his steps to Strasbourg, to rest, refresh and re-equip his army after the arduous task of successfully conducting such an operation in bitterly cold weather. The elector in the meantime stirred himself to gain a small but important success over an Imperial detachment at Siegharding, so that the Duke of Marlborough, at the moment looking forward to a fresh campaign the Low Countries, was moved to write rather despondently to Antonius Hiensius, the Grand Pensionary of Holland, 'I wish we could hear any good news from the Upper Rhine'.[16]

Baden had occupied a strong defensive position known as the Lines of Stollhofen, to cover the crossings of the upper Rhine, and Villars, with support brought by the Duc de Tallard, probed the works, but could find no inviting weak spot to attack. Urged by Louis XIV to get on and effect a lasting junction with Max-Emmanuel without further delay, Villars left Tallard on the Rhine and evaded the Stollhofen position to begin his march through the passes of the Black Forest. The Imperial garrison in Villingen was screened on the way, and the junction of the French and Bavarian armies, a key strategic objective for Versailles, was at last achieved at Reutlingen on 9 May 1703. The two commanders, both veterans of the wars in Hungary against the Ottomans, greeted each other warmly enough, and Villars proposed an ambitious plan to force the Austrian emperor to seek peace. This entailed Max-Emmanuel, suitably reinforced now with French troops, to operate south of the Danube against Passau and Linz, while Villars with the bulk of his force, advanced to the north of the river.

The added advantage would be that French and Bavarian troops would be able to forage freely in enemy territory, and so relieve Louis XIV's treasury of much of the growing burden of the expenses of the war. All seemed very promising, particularly as renewed rebellion in Hungary against Vienna's overlordship and tax-gathering activities provided a heavy distraction for the hard-pressed emperor (the rebels were fortified by substantial cash subsidies from Versailles). However, on 27 May Villars learned to his chagrin that Louis XIV had agreed that he should consider himself to be under Max-Emmanuel's direct orders. Simultaneously, the unexpected but relatively unimportant defeat of a small Bavarian detachment at Amberg made the elector cautious once more, so that as a result Villars' promising plans to advance and threaten Vienna came to nothing.

There then followed a squabble over whether the marshal's young wife would be permitted to join him on campaign. Much mischief was made for Villars at Versailles where it was gossiped by the Duc de St Simon and others that the older man was losing interest in the campaign on the Danube, while longing for the more obvious comforts of marital bliss at home. Louis XIV was none too amused, but at last reluctantly gave his consent, although the inability to gain a pass of safe conduct for the lady from the Imperial general Count von Styrum brought the plan to nothing in the end. The episode had, however, done little to enhance the marshal's reputation which was now in distinct danger of flagging, with carping comments from many who had from the outset viewed his growing reputation with some scepticism.[17]

In mid-June, Villars had to watch, with scarcely concealed frustration, when Max-Emmanuel took his own troops southwards into the Tyrol, getting as far as Innsbruck before having to halt in the face of rapidly growing fierce local resistance. A plan for the French commander in Italy, the Duc de Vendôme, to advance northwards through the Brenner Pass into the Tyrol in support of the elector's excursion failed to materialize. The months of summer sped by with little being achieved, while the Margrave of Baden managed to get possession of the key Bavarian fortress of Augsburg. Once the elector had withdrawn his army from the unfortunate adventure into the Tyrol at the end of July, he and Villars could field some 23,000 troops and they managed to corner von Styrum, who had just 18,000 men, on the Plain of Höchstädt some few miles to the west of Donauwörth on the Danube – coincidentally virtually the same ground on which the Battle of Blenheim would be fought nearly a year later. On 20 September 1703, von Styrum was soundly beaten in a confused and hard-fought battle and forced to retire with the loss of 2,000 men killed and wounded, with almost 3,000 more left behind as prisoners along with thirty-two standards and colours, and thirty-three guns. The precise loss amongst the French and Bavarian armies is uncertain but cannot have been light given the ferocity of the fighting that day. Knowing the king's dislike for expensive pitched battles and lengthy casualty lists, Villars almost certainly played down the scale of his losses.

Despite this tactical success for the French and Bavarians, the Margrave of Baden had maintained his firm grip on Augsburg, and a sharp fresh disagreement arose between Villars and Max-Emmanuel as to the best next step. Louis XIV had already written to the marshal with a few, meant to be helpful, words of advice on how to deal with the elector. 'I cannot recommend strongly enough, not to be haughty with a man of his birth and rank. You should be firm in important things, but present them frankly and you will gain more influence over his conduct than you can by other means.'[18] It was no good; each man complained loudly to Versailles about the obstructive attitude of the other, so that the king, anxious, after the recent loss of his ally the Prince-Archbishop of Cologne, to maintain the link with Bavaria, decided that he had to replace Villars, who in the end had proved too strong-willed to co-operate fully with the equally highly opinionated and obstinate Max-Emmanuel. Newly-promoted Marshal Ferdinand Marsin, described as 'A man with fewer talents but a softer tongue'[19] and not yet fully tested perhaps, was sent to take his place. Villars duly returned to Versailles to find a rather cool reception and little employment immediately waiting for him. He soon learned to his chagrin that Marsin and Max-Emmanuel had managed to regain

Augsburg without too much difficulty with Baden obliged to withdraw. Currently not in the royal favour, without an active role, and with no taste for the life of just being one courtier amongst many, Villars retired to his estates in the Dauphine, where he could at least enjoy the company of his wife and young son. Never one to underestimate his own worth, he drily commented that, 'I do not know whether the king will leave me without a command. If that happens, I shall have enemies at court who will rejoice, But the enemies of the king will rejoice even more.'[19]

He was not to be left idle for long, and in the spring of 1704, Villars was instructed by Louis XIV to end the Camisard revolt in the Cevennes region, where the previous repressive efforts of Marshal Nicholas-August de Montrevel had so far borne little fruit, other than some limited tactical successes. Although rather sporadic in extent, the revolt was nonetheless a distracting running sore for the king, as its origins were in the suppression of the Protestant religion after the revocation of the Edict of Nantes in 1685. Arriving in Nimes on 21 April, Villars publicly announced the most severe measures against anyone who remained active in the rebellion, but at the same time offered a general amnesty to those who submitted and gave up their arms within eight days of the proclamation. 'I will endeavour to end the misfortunes by kindness,' he wrote, 'as severe measures appear to me not only useless, but totally contrary.'[20] In the first week of May he moved sharply against those rebels still active, and after some local successes renewed the offer of amnesty on 5 June. Villars' adept policy of 'carrot and stick', mixing aggressive pursuit with generous offers of clemency, worked well enough, and one of the leaders of the revolt, Jean Cavalier, duly submitted. However, a diehard group of recalcitrant rebels, apprehended on 14 August, were publicly broken on the wheel as a warning to others who still held out.

Gradually resistance trickled away, and on 1 October 1704, Villars was able to report to Versailles that the region had been pacified, with a measure of toleration having brought a beneficial effect in restoring order in the region. Amongst the terms agreed with Jean Cavalier, was this rather surprising and benevolent clause, which ran, in part:

> That all the Protestants of the Languedoc, without being obliged to go to Mass, shall be permitted to assemble together, without any reproach or molestation. They shall not be permitted to build a church but shall have the liberty to meet in the fields. The inhabitants, who have had their houses burned, shall pay no taxes for seven years.[21]

The king was both relieved at the news, coming as it did in the dismal aftermath of the French debacle at Blenheim, and warm in his appreciation of this outcome, so that before long the marshal was made Duc de Villars as a result.

On 3 February 1705, Villars was appointed to the command of the Army of the Rhine, and he took up a strong defensive posture at Sierck in the Moselle valley, shielding the approaches to Saarlouis and Thionville in the process. He was soon confronted by the Duke of Marlborough, who had not been able to make the most of his successful summer campaign in the face of a well-handled tactical withdrawal by Villeroi and the robust defence of the fortress of Landau later in that year. The duke's fresh plan was to drive into northern France by means of the route along the Moselle, but he found no easy way of manoeuvring the French out of position. In mid-June, Marlborough had to hurry back to the Low Countries, as the fortress of Huy had been lost to Villeroi, and the Dutch had taken alarm that Liège might also fall. 'Villars out-manoeuvred Marlborough in a manner that would have done credit to the greatest general. Marlborough, compelled to change the plan of campaign he had determined on, returned into Flanders.'[22] In actual fact, little of this Allied failure had to do with Villars, as the duke's supply arrangements in Coblenz had fallen apart through barefaced embezzlement by the senior commissary officer involved, while the Margrave of Baden was unwell and late in joining Marlborough, and when he did come brought with him fewer Imperial troops than expected. Whether Villars could have been forced out of his well set out defensive lines in the Moselle can never be known, although it could not have been a simple done thing to do, but nonetheless, Louis XIV congratulated the marshal for the successful holding of the line along the river.

Taking advantage of Marlborough's departure, although reduced in numbers by having to send reinforcements northwards to Villeroi, Villars moved robustly against Baden, seized Trier, and on 4 July in concert with Marshal Marsin, attacked and routed an advanced Imperial detachment at Wiessenbourg,[23] forcing the margrave back all the way back to the safety of the defensive Lines of Stolhoffen.[24] On 1 August Villars crossed the Rhine at Kehl and Gambsheim, looking once more to raise contributions in the vicinity, but on 1 September he withdrew on receiving instructions from Versailles not to venture too far forward while largely unsupported and potentially exposed. Furthermore, Baden had unexpectedly roused himself, and adroitly crossed the Rhine at Lauterbourg to lay siege to the French-held fortress of Hagenau. This place fell on 5 October, but not much more was attempted or achieved, so that after some ineffectual sparring and marching around each other, with no good opportunity being found to strike, the opposing armies went into winter quarters late in November.

Working still with Marsin, Villars opened his campaign in 1706 to push Baden away from Hagenau, and the place was duly taken on 12 May. He had, however, resisted a suggestion from Versailles that he might also attempt to recover Landau, feeling he did not have the required bayonet strength to do so. In any case, once the calamity of the terrible defeat at Ramillies only a week or so later was known, Villars had yet again to send substantial numbers of troops north to Flanders to help Vendôme re-establish the French position there. As a result, he was able to do little more on the Rhine but to observe his opponent, the increasingly frail Baden, levy contributions in the Palatinate, while taking the opportunity to seize a small island on the Rhine which would allow him to outflank the Lines of Stollhofen, when the right moment came.

Allied attention in 1707 largely concentrated on the lamentable campaign to capture the great port and naval base at Toulon, and simultaneously for Marlborough to try and bring Vendôme to decisive battle in the Low Countries. Both endeavours failed, and meanwhile Villars was sent with his cavalry on a raid into central Germany. This was intended to both sow alarm and to distract the notice of the princes and margraves of the Empire who provided such excellent troops for the cause of Archduke Charles in his struggle for the throne in Madrid. 'Finding himself feebly opposed by the Imperial [commanders] he penetrated deeply, after having made himself master of Heidelburg, Mannheim and all the Palatinate . . . He gathered immense sums – treasures beyond all hopes.'[25] Villars, like other marshals, had a reputation for plundering at times, but he again warned his senior officers against too unbridled a foraging campaign on this occasion, for to drive the civilian population into hiding would inevitably prevent his troopers from obtaining food and fodder, and he cautioned them, 'If you burn, if you make the people run away, you will die of hunger'.[26] All the same, the booty collected and sent back to France was considerable, and when those in Versailles, always envious of the lively marshal's success, called the attention of Louis XIV to his activities in enriching himself, the king simply said that he had benefited also, and therefore saw no reason to complain.

Villars was then appointed to command the French troops in the Dauphine region, facing Duke Victor-Amadeus of Savoy and the Imperial General Philip von Daun. Villars took up a position covering Montmêlian, and on 29 July his opponents moved to cut the road between Grenoble and Briançon. Villars remained alert, so that, thwarted in this endeavour, Victor-Amadeus had to fall back, and on the second week of August was soundly beaten in an action at Cestana. He was obliged to withdraw into Piedmont and make for the security of Turin, but not before taking the chance to occupy Fenestrelle on the way. That small success was all that the Allies could count in the region that year, and the ability of Villars to hold the ring secure in this way, with what were relatively modest resources, was counted as much to his credit.

In the awful aftermath of the French defeat at Oudenarde, and the loss of Lille in the late autumn of 1708, the king appointed Villars to take command of the battered army in Flanders, and to save what might be had, from what had every appearance of being a complete wreck. That winter was bitterly cold, and privation and near starvation was rife in some French towns, which in places saw bread riots. Louis XIV had written, almost despairingly, to the marshal, 'I put my faith in God, and in you'.[27] The troops that Villars was sent to command were ill-equipped, unpaid, hungry and downcast by recent defeat and command mismanagement, while the garrisons in such key places as St Omer, Arras, Mons, Valenciennes, Tournai and Le Quesnoy had been driven to the verge of mutiny. His boundless energy and enthusiasm revived their spirits to a surprising degree, while the king was bluntly confronted with the truth of the poor state of his army, and commissaries, sutlers and tradesmen were bullied into providing what was necessary. Foraging was expanded, and supplies commandeered without compunction, but there was, however, a limit to what could be achieved. One miller, when threatened with being hanged if he did not provide enough flour, simply shrugged and said that he might as well put the rope around his own neck on the spot, as what was demanded was simply not available. Villars had to write to the king in sombre mood: 'We can go some time without money, but without bread it is impossible.'[28] What actually happened to the sturdy, but unfortunate, miller is not known for sure. As it happened this remarkable turnaround in the French effort in the north, for all its limitations, was helped by the unwise arrogance shown by the Allies who assumed, wrongly, that peace was at hand on any terms they wished to dictate, and so Villars was allowed the necessary time to re-organize his army for the coming campaign in the summer of 1709. He was also able to assure Louis XIV, when presented by the overly-confident Allies with particularly harsh demands to obtain a negotiated peace, that he could now rely on the army no matter what.[29]

Concerned with the likelihood of a threat to Ypres in the summer of 1709, Villars concentrated his army to cover that fortress, even drawing troops out of the garrison in Tournai for the purpose. It soon proved that he had been mistaken, and that Tournai was the intended target for the opening attack by the Allies. Once underway, the siege proved to be a particularly gruelling one as the value of the Vauban-designed defences, and the fine performance of the French garrison under the Marquis de Surville-Hautfois (recently recovered from a wound received at the siege of Lille), were both remarkable. Despite this, Villars lacked the numbers to save Tournai from capture, after a long and hard-fought siege which came to an end in the first week of September.

The king feared that Mons would go the same way and instructed Villars to take active steps to save the place. 'Should Mons follow the fate of Tournai,' he wrote, 'our case is undone; you are by every means in your power to relieve the garrison; the cost is not to be considered.'[30] In effect, Louis XIV was giving an instruction to his army commander to go out and seek battle, if that was what it would take. Villars needed little urging and moving forward from his own lines of defence, took up a strong position in the Gap of Aulnois, close to the border between France and the Spanish Netherlands, threatening to disrupt any attempt by Marlborough and Eugene to proceed directly with an immediate attempt to seize Mons. Of course, the Allied commanders' strategy had all along been to try and lure the

French army into the open to face battle by threatening key fortresses, and so it seemed, on the face of things, that Louis XIV and Villars had neatly played into their hands. This was not so, for the marshal was a most astute operator and prudently stood his ground, having chosen a naturally strong defensive position, between two belts of dense woodland which should, he felt sure, protect his otherwise exposed flanks. On Wednesday 11 September 1709, a bitterly fought and terribly expensive battle took place close to the small village of Malplaquet, from which the action took its name, and although the French were obliged to quit the field at the end of the day, the cost to the Allied army was simply dreadful, with a casualty list far exceeding that suffered by Villars and his sturdy troops.[31] Marlborough acknowledged this in a letter sent to the Dutch Pensionary, Hiensius, that very evening, 'The French have defended themselves better in this action than in any battle I have seen'.[32]

Villars was gravely wounded in the battle, receiving a musket ball to the knee, and he had to be helped from the field, in agony and fast losing blood, so that Marshal Boufflers took over the command and got the battered French army away that afternoon in fairly good order. Louis XIV wrote shortly afterwards that 'I have lost some brave officers, and I am much disturbed by Marshal Villars' wound, which I fear might be dangerous'.[33] Although suffering badly from a fever in addition to his wounded leg, Villars wrote to the king that 'The [army] dispositions were so good, that I had reason to hope for success. The truth is that I hoped to be attacked.'[34] His surgeons proved unable to remove the ball, despite the most testing attempts, and although amputation of the limb was not found to be necessary, Villars from then on limped along with the mangled leg often held fast in an iron brace. His partial recovery and convalescence were hastened by Louis XIV who was anxious to have perhaps his best field commander back in action, and in May 1710 the marshal rejoined the army during the energetic but ultimately unsuccessful attempts to relieve the besieged fortress of Douai. Although armed with permission from the king to fight another general engagement if necessary to save the place, Villars, even with the able assistance of Marshal Berwick, was unable to manoeuvre his opponents into a position where such a prospect held much chance of success, and the greatly reduced Douai garrison submitted on good terms on 27 June.[35] The defence of the fortress, which had been very well handled, had cost the Allies 63 days, valuable time that they could ill afford. Although Villars now increasingly felt reluctant to openly challenge the Allied operations, his defensive strategy did work well, as his opponents were obliged to spend the remainder of the campaign season in reducing still more fortresses – Bethune, St Venant and Aire-sur-La Lys – at considerable cost in casualties and the sick languishing in field hospitals, for what were plainly rather limited strategic gains. Dismay was felt nonetheless at Versailles, and 'All fell into the hands of the enemy during this campaign,' the Duc de St Simon wrote ruefully, 'who thus gained upon us more and more while we did little or nothing'.[36] Villars was by now so unwell that he took leave, handing over the command to Marshal d'Harcourt, and went to take the waters at Bourbonne. In the meantime, the stout defensive system constructed under Vauban's supervision was able to take the weight of the heavy blows directed by Marlborough and Eugene, and France was effectively saved from a major and deep-penetrating invasion in the process.

The campaign in 1711 in many respects matched that of the previous year, with the Allies trying to find a way through the gradually thinning French fortress belt, only to be blocked by while Villars, once more in command, kept far enough out of reach to avoid being cornered and having to stand and fight again in the open. Eugene had been detained in Vienna by the unexpected death from smallpox of Emperor Joseph, and while his younger brother, Archduke Charles, secured his own election to the Imperial post, a process which was slow and overly formal. However, the strong defensive lines, constructed by the French, and known as Non Plus Ultra, in the event proved capable of being breached, when Marlborough decoyed Villars away towards Arras in the west, and then very adroitly swung to the east and force marched to get over the river obstacle at Arleux, without having to fight or lose a man to do so. The duke was as a result able to lay siege to the French fortress of Bouchain at the confluence of the Escaut and Sensée rivers. He did so with such skill that Villars, although in close proximity (and with Eugene still absent able to deploy superior numbers), was reluctant again to risk a major engagement in open field and could not prevent its capitulation on 12 September. This success, it was widely felt, would open the road leading to Paris, but this was not so, and Allied efforts were frustrated and ultimately proved unavailing.

Early in 1712, Marlborough was dismissed, and British troops were soon to be withdrawn from active campaigning, as Queen Anne's ministers in London had quietly reached an agreement with Louis XIV. All the same, Prince Eugene, now in command of the Dutch forces as well as his own much-reinforced Imperial troops, pressed on and took Le Quesnoy, and then began an attempt to besiege the larger fortress of Landrecies close to the southern edge of the Forest of Mormal. The confidence that the aged king had in his principal army commander may be seen in an account of his leaving Versailles on 16 April 1712 to begin the fresh campaign. Measles had just swept the court in deadly fashion, carrying off many of the young royal family, and the extent of this tragedy for Louis XIV can be seen expressed most starkly. 'On that day', Villars remembered:

> the self-control of the monarch yielded to the feelings of the man. The king shed tears and said to me in a voice that went to the heart 'You see in what state I am, Monsieur le Marechal. Few have known what it is to lose, as I have lost in the space of a few weeks, a grandson [the Duc de Bourgogne], a grand

> daughter-in-law [the Duchesse, eldest daughter of Duke Victor-Amadeus II of Savoy], and their son, all of great promise and tenderly cherished. God punishes me, and I have deserved it . . . But now let us leave sorrowing over my misfortunes and see what can be done to avert those of my kingdom. I have shown clearly what confidence I have in you, since I have entrusted you with the armed forces and the security of the state. I know your own zeal, and the worth of my soldiers.'[37]

Villars was aware that Eugene's lines of communication and supply had become over-stretched, reaching as they did back to a fortified camp at Denain on the river Escaut, and then on to a massive supply depot established at Marchiennes on the Scarpe. Subtly concealing his real intentions, on 19 July the marshal came out of his lines of defence and five days later surprised and overwhelmed the outnumbered Dutch and German garrison in Denain, commanded by Arnold Joost van Keppel, 1st Earl of Albemarle, inflicting in the process a heavy loss in casualties, prisoners and guns. 'There was an overflowing of joy at Fontainebleau,' St Simon wrote, 'about which the king was so flattered that he thanked his courtiers for the first time in his life.'[38] Worse was to happen for Eugene, as on 30 July the French captured and looted the supply depot at Marchiennes, with another great haul of prisoners, effectively ruining the Allied plans against Landrecies and obliging him to withdraw in some haste. This undeniable French triumph, achieved with no great superiority in numbers against so able an opponent, was greatly to Villars' credit, and widely acknowledged as such. So well had the initiative passed from the Allies that by the third week of October the marshal had recovered Le Quesnoy, Douai and even Bouchain, doing much to restore the integrity of the rather battered French fortress belt. Furthermore, the Dutch were downcast as this dramatic turn of events, and edged more quickly towards a negotiated peace.

Commanding the army on the Rhine in 1713, Villars reached Strasbourg in May, and advanced to besiege and capture the key fortress of Landau on 20 August, as Eugene had insufficient strength to actively challenge the operation. Although the Imperial garrison had put up a good defence Villars, in an untypically mean move, refused to grant good terms, and they were marched away as prisoners of war. The French then quickly moved against Freiburg, which was invested on 20 September and the trenches opened 10 days later. The garrison resisted stoutly and only after Villars had threatened to raze the town and turn out the citizenry into the bitter weather of approaching winter did the garrison commander, the Baron von d'Arsch, agree to give up the citadel, which he did on 16 November (having obtained permission from Vienna to do so). Within a fortnight, however, the war had run its course, and Villars was entrusted by Louis XIV in the complex and taut negotiations to formally achieve peace, talks that were held in conference with Prince Eugene at Rastadt, the home of the late Louis-Guillaume, 'Turken Louis', Margrave of Baden.

The two old adversaries had of course known each other in youth, when campaigning together against the Ottomans in the 1680s, and they had both stared across numerous fields of battle, both real and potential, in recent years, so that the mutual respect and rapport they felt greatly facilitated the progress of the discussions. Eugene remembered, however, that Villars proved to be hesitant and poorly prepared during the tangled negotiations and overly eager to reach an agreement for peace. It was generally understood, as a simple fact, that Louis XIV earnestly sought an end to the war, but the marshal's' attitude smacked of a weakness that was not really reflected in the hard-won successes had achieved in his recent campaigns. It was also understood that Vienna also needed peace, for the Imperial treasury was, as so often, empty, but agreement proved elusive, particularly over the requirement by the king that his ally, the Elector of Bavaria, should be reinstated and even compensated for his losses in the war. This was too much for Emperor Charles, who with some reason regarded Max-Emmanuel as little more than a turncoat, with ambitions to set himself up as emperor with French assistance. For weeks the talks proved incapable of settlement, and Villars had to ignore a ridiculous instruction from Versailles to prepare his, now totally unprepared, army for the renewal of active hostilities. A tentative solution appeared to have been reached at the end of December, but both Vienna and Versailles still had reservations on points of detail. Agreement was only reached on 7 February 1714, when Louis XIV in effect gave way on several points, doing so with the outward appearance of kingly good grace, and the treaties were formally signed a month later. As Villars was not too fluent in Latin, he insisted that the documents be made out in French, and Eugene accepted this, but stipulated that this must not set a precedent for the future.[39]

Whatever were the qualities of Villars as a soldier and army commander, and he demonstrably was gifted in those respects, it can be seen that the subtle skills and patience required for complex negotiations were really not his to deploy. He had been outmanoeuvred by Eugene at the conference table at Rastadt, and the terms of the agreed treaties were considerably more favourable to Vienna than many, including the emperor, had expected or dared to hope for.

The death of Louis XIV in 1715 saw the creation of a regency under Philippe, the Duc d'Orleans, during the infancy of the old king's great-grandson, Louis XV. Villars played an active part as a member of the regency council and was also appointed to head the war council. His opposition to the plans laid by another prominent council member, the highly capable Cardinal Guillaume Dubois, was noticeable, although the cardinal's influence was key in helping to maintain peace, of a fragile kind, in western Europe, in particular when Philip V of Spain looked for ways to unpick the terms of the Treaties of Utrecht, Baden and Rastadt for its own advantage. (The 1717 Treaty of Triple Alliance between France, Great Britain and

Holland to curb Spanish ambitions, was largely the work of Dubois, on d'Orleans' instructions.) Although no open hostilities were in prospect for some time, Villars had plenty to otherwise occupy his time, not least in keeping his young wife under observation as she was openly pursuing an illicit affair with the Comte de Toulouse, one of the late king's illegitimate sons.[40]

Marshal Villars only, and quite reluctantly, took the field as commander again with the outbreak of the war of Polish Succession in 1730, and he was appointed marshal-general by Louis XV three years later, when he was aged nearly 80 and suffering increasingly with poor health. He had the command of the French forces in Italy, but after quarrelling with the King of Sardinia once (Duke Victor-Amadeus of Savoy, who had gained the royal title courtesy of the treaties that brought an end to the war for Spain) he retired from active service, and died in Turin on 17 June 1734, shortly after learning of the sudden death in action of his old friend, Marshal Berwick. Villars' laconic comment, as he still hobbled about with a mangled leg from the Malplaquet wound, was that Berwick always had the luck.

Chapter 10

Marshal Tallard

Undoubtedly best remembered for the catastrophe for French arms and prospects that he presided over on a hot Wednesday afternoon in Bavaria in August 1704, Camille d'Hostun de la Baume, Duc de Tallard, was in fact a diligent and talented soldier, a gifted diplomat, and an urbane, popular and highly cultured man. Born in the Dauphine region on 14 February 1652, the son of Roger Hostun de la Baume, Marquis de la Baune d'Hostun, and his wife Marie (née de Neufville-Villeroi) Camille was granted a commission by Louis XIV at the age of 13, as a cadet in the Gendarmes d'Anglais, and then shortly afterwards was allowed to transfer to the Royal Cravates Regiment of cavalry (originally recruited from Croatia). He served with considerable credit in the Dutch War under the Prince of Condé and was with Marshal Turenne in 1674 in the campaign in Alsace. Tallard quickly earned for himself a good reputation as a reliable young commander, distinguishing himself particularly well under the eye of the marshal-general at the Battle of Sinzheim in the Palatinate in June 1674, where he was amongst those numerous French officers who were wounded in the heavy fighting that raged back and forth across the Elsanx stream.

He fought with great credit subsequently at Seneffe in August that same year, and then in the engagements at Mulhaustein and Urchen. In 1677 Tallard was appointed brigadier (not a general rank at the time) and on 28 December that year, campaigning having wound down for the winter, took the chance to marry Marie-Catherine de

Grolée; the couple in time had two sons, both of whom served as soldiers, and a daughter.

Active during the campaign of the Reunions, Tallard was appointed to the formal command of a brigade of cavalry and was present at the siege of Courtrai in 1683 at the outset of Louis XIV's renewed war with the Spanish. He subsequently serving at the lengthy siege of Luxembourg in 1684, and the following year was promoted to general rank as maréchal de camp. During the opening campaigns of the Nine Years War he took part in the ruthless devastation of the Palatinate, fighting at the siege of Ebersberg where he was again wounded, and at the engagement at Rheinsfeld. In 1692 he crossed the Rhine at Philippsburg with a strong force of cavalry to levy contributions around Heilbrun. Perhaps overly confident and mislead by the lack of any initial response from his opponents, he stayed rather too long and, when suddenly faced with rapidly growing superior numbers, was fortunate to be able to withdraw from contact in fairly decent order. The next year he was made lieutenant-general, and in 1695 became a Chevalier of the Order of the Holy Spirit, an unusual honour for Louis XIV to grant to someone not yet a marshal, and also a Knight of the Order of St Michael. That Tallard was highly regarded in Versailles seems plain, as may be also seen from his activities over the next few years.

Having caught the attention, and become a close confidante, of the king, Tallard was sent in 1697 to the Court of St James in London as the French ambassador, an event so generally welcome that William III sent his own yacht, *The William and Mary*, to facilitate and speed his passage across the Channel; the Earl of Portland was sent to Paris as a reciprocal diplomatic gesture. Tallard was strictly advised by Louis IV not to mention or discuss the vexed question of any possible Jacobite restoration to the throne in London, but he was to actively cultivate good relations with both government ministers and members of the opposition, and other leaders of public opinion. Implicit in all this was the requirement to keep the king and his ministers advised of thought and public opinion in London (amongst those most influential, that is), on a wide range of matters.

Once in post, Tallard's cultivated and courtly manners, witty conversation and wide intellectual powers gained him many friends, most notable amongst them being William III, and his influence was of considerable value in fostering a better semblance, at least, of good relations between Louis XIV and his old Dutch adversary. 'Tallard was convinced of the good faith of King William,' St Simon commented, '[but] he was nowhere near as powerful as we thought.'[1] Uneasily sat the crown on the head of the Dutchman, particularly as his wife, Queen Mary (daughter of James II, still in exile in France), had died of smallpox several years earlier, hence the sensitivity of any mention of Jacobite plans to attempt to return to London. The question was much vexed, as no child of William, by any second marriage, would be eligible to ascend the throne in London; meanwhile, Princess Anne, the late Mary's younger sister, waited in wings, as coincidentally did her father and his supporters in France.

When William III went to Holland, he took Tallard with him, and the two were instrumental in drawing up the partition treaty that would, in other and happier circumstances, have seen the young Prince Joseph-Ferdinand of Bavaria, son of Elector Max-Emmanuel, take the throne in Madrid one day, saving everyone a great deal of trouble and expense. Tallard's achievement in this crucial round of diplomacy was widely acknowledged, for, 'These months of negotiation, in which the future marshal showed himself to be a man of calm nerves and good judgement, established his position in the esteem of the King'.[2]

Peace was near but proved tantalizingly elusive, as the young Bavarian prince suddenly died in Brussels in February 1699. The risk then, obvious to everyone and posed by the question of whether a French prince should occupy the throne, was considerable, and

Louis XIV wrote rather wearily, 'I know how alarmed all Europe would be to see my power raised to a greater height than that of Austria'.[3] Despite such awareness, once the young Duc d'Anjou was established in Madrid, and proclaimed as Philip V (acknowledged at the time by, among others, both William III and the Dutch States-General) the French king with uncharacteristic clumsiness sent his troops in 1701 to occupy the cherished Dutch-held Barrier Towns in the Southern Netherlands, and he then made an emotional declaration that he regarded James II's eldest son, the Chevalier de St George as he was known in France at the time, as the rightful heir to the throne in London. In this maladroit way, considerable offence was given in both London and The Hague, and as a direct result, Tallard was expelled from England as preparations across Europe for the war for the Spanish throne remorselessly gathered pace. This series of gaffes can be seen as a significant, and quite untypical, mistake by the king, as William III and the Dutch States-General had already accepted as a *fait accompli* that the Duc d'Anjou should have the throne in Madrid, and Tallard's expulsion closed a very promising diplomatic avenue that might well, even at such a late stage, have avoided an open conflict that would spread ruin across much of western Europe for 12 years or more.

Working fairly harmoniously with Marshal Boufflers in 1702 to command French forces facing the Dutch, Tallard was then sent to campaign on the middle Rhine. The king in Versailles warned him against the risks of attacking the strongly-held fortress of Breisach as he had proposed, although his instructions on this occasion were untypically imprecise. 'No doubt you have examined the inconveniences that you might encounter of which the only important one is the depth of water in the moats [but] You know the confidence with which I give myself to anything that you think proper for the good of my service.'[4] In the event, the fortifications of Breisach (which was restored to Emperor Leopold at the Treaty of Ryswick in 1697), on the face of things a large fortress but in fact having an inadequate and ill-provisioned garrison, were not as robust as they seemed. 'They were certainly weak on the side facing the Rhine, and they were neglected by the responsible authorities.'[5] The place was invested by Tallard on 18 August, and the siege trenches opened four days later. An appeal for relief had been urgently sent to the Margrave of Baden, but he was unable to come up in time, and with the able assistance of Vauban, the French operations progressed speedily, Despite a spirited sortie led by a Colonel Tanner, which failed to slow the siege very much, Tallard was able to force the submission of the Imperial-held fortress on 8 September 1703, although Louis XIV's eldest grandson, the Duc de Bourgogne who held the nominal command of the army, was to no great surprise given most of the credit. The garrison, which comprised the regiments of Baden, Marsigli and Bayreuth, marched out under good terms the next day, going unmolested to Rheinfelden but having to leave their artillery behind as was customary. Their commanders, who had lacked adequate support throughout, were quickly made scapegoats for the loss, and subsequently suffered a sad and undeserved fate.[6]

Moving on to lay siege to the fortress of Landau in the second week of October, Tallard roundly defeated a relieving Imperial army under the command of the Prince of Hesse-Cassel at the Battle of Speyerbach, fought on 15 November. The armies were not evenly matched as the prince had recently been reinforced and brought forward about 22,000 horse and foot, while Tallard, having to maintain simultaneously a considerable number of troops in the siege lines before Landau, fielded fewer than 18,000 men. Nonetheless, his skilful handling of the French cavalry at a critical moment on the right wing of the army, unlike the effort on the left which was painfully unsuccessful, overwhelmed their Imperial opponents who had to withdraw in considerable confusion with the loss of some 6,000 killed, wounded and prisoners, and twenty-three guns.[7] The Prince of

Hesse-Cassel was amongst those taken captive, although subsequently released on parole, having been held in comfortable confinement for only a short time. Tallard's own losses at a reported 4,000 killed and wounded were certainly not slight, but the success was significant, and as a result the garrison in Landau, despairing of relief, submitted just two days after the action. As a consequence on 14 January 1703, Tallard was made a Marshal of France, in recognition of what had been a very successful and generally well-handled campaign.

When the Duke of Marlborough began his famous march up the Rhine in May 1704, taking with him those troops paid for by Queen Anne's treasury, Tallard was still in command in Alsace, and he received firm instruction from Versailles.

> You and Marshal Villeroi (commanding the French army in Flanders) should come together with a plan to prevent all the forces of the empire uniting with the Dutch and the English and falling upon the Elector of Bavaria, who would be unable to resist them . . . I await your proposals to assist an ally who is so necessary to me, and whose forces, joined to mine, have occupied the attention of all the empire.[8]

At Landau, in early June, Tallard combined forces with Villeroi who had matched the Allied strategic move south to avoid being outflanked. That the French commanders remained in some doubt as to Marlborough's true intentions was clear. 'Tallard was marching towards Landau in order to combine with Villeroi, or to oppose the Duke's passage over the Rhine . . . Tallard [had] the idea that the duke was going to sit down before Landau.'[9] In May, the marshal had already very competently conveyed a huge quantity of stores and materiel through the difficult passes of the Black Forest to help sustain the French and Bavarian armies on the Danube, who were now under the joint command of newly-appointed Marshal Marsin and Elector Max-Emmanuel. Once it was clear that Marlborough's intention really was to move against Bavaria, Louis XIV sent orders that Tallard should take his own troops, some 34,000 strong, to support the campaign there, while Villeroi remained in place to hold firm the line along the Upper Rhine.

Neatly avoiding a blocking force under the command of Prince Eugene of Savoy that was in place and holding the defensive Lines of Stollhofen, Tallard set off on 1 July 1704. Although six days were wasted in an abortive attempt to capture the small and relatively unimportant Imperial-held fortress of Villingen, Tallard managed to keep ahead of Eugene as he hurried in pursuit, vainly hoping at some point to be able to intercept the progress of his opponent. The French march was arduous, as provisions were inadequate and forage along the rough route almost negligible. Scavenging was necessary, and looting and pillaging were rife, so that the Walloon Comte de Merode-Westerloo, one of Tallard's cavalry commanders, recalled that, 'The enraged peasantry eventually killed many of our men before the army was clear of the Black Forest'.[10] On 5 August the marshal reached Ulm, and the next day the planned concentration of French and Bavarian armies on the Danube was successfully achieved, although their numerical inferiority would be apparent once Eugene caught up and joined forces with Marlborough and the Margrave of Baden.

Tallard, however, had instructions that his own army was to operate as a distinct separate formation from that of Marsin, which may not have helped at all with proper coordination of the French forces in the field. The thinking behind this was apparently that it was felt in Versailles that Max-Emmanuel, even now, might switch allegiance at some point, and that Tallard's task would then be to manoeuvre to extricate Marsin's troops out from what would be the dangerously exposed entanglement in Bavaria. Meanwhile, Marlborough and Baden, who had between them successfully but expensively stormed the Schellenberg position a month earlier, were separated from Eugene while he was still on the march. The risk was obvious, as now might have been the opportune moment for Tallard and his colleagues to move swiftly to crush the Allied armies piecemeal while they were divided, but a sense of over-confidence seemed to have settled over the French and Bavarian commanders alike, and for the time being they took no decisive steps. All seemed to be well, as with much of Bavaria having recently been ruined by Marlborough's marauding cavalry, he could now not winter his army on the Danube, and would before long surely have to pull back into central Germany and his supply depots there. The Allied campaign, as a result, would collapse, and the French and Bavarians could it seemed wait for this to take place. Fatally, in doing so, they allowed the initiative in the campaign to pass to, and remain squarely in, the hands of their opponents.

Baden soon went off to lay siege to Ingolstadt further down the Danube, and once free of his cautious influence, on Wednesday 13 August 1704, Marlborough and Eugene surprised the French and Bavarian armies in their newly established encampment on the Plain of Höchstädt. In a bitterly fought action that afternoon and evening, Tallard's cavalry were routed on the right and driven from the field, while his infantry, most of whom were negligently bottled up in Blindheim (Blenheim) village by the Marquis de Clerambault and unable to use the weapons to any good effect, were obliged to surrender at the close of the day. 'It was an entire army merely for the purpose of holding this village, and supporting his right, and of course he had all these troops the less to aid him in the battle which took place.'[11] The marshal was taken prisoner by Hessian dragoons while belatedly attempting to get to Blindheim village and save something from the wreck. He was promptly taken to Marlborough, who greeted him courteously and put him away into his own coach, where the captive could mourn the for his eldest son, François, who had been mortally wounded at his side that day. 'I grieve for Marshal Tallard,' Louis XIV wrote, 'and feel deeply for him at the loss of his son', on learning of the young man's death from his wounds.[12] In the meantime, the beaten French and their Bavarian allies made their sorry way back to the Rhine and comparative security, while the Marquis de Montigny-Languet recalled, that 'We travelled with little bread, having burned a good part of our baggage. We were finally returning with the debris of three armies.'[13]

Tallard afterwards gave as one of the key reasons for this defeat, that the elite Gendarmerie cavalry had unexpectedly been overthrown by British squadrons early in the battle, but this was exacerbated surely by his own physical short-sightedness, added to a growing and ultimately fatal lack of control of the battle as it unfolded. That he had not made any real attempt to correct the folly of de Clerambault in cramming Blindheim village with too many foot soldiers, other than what he attempted in the closing moments of the day, was a telling lapse. Marshal Marsin and the Elector of Bavaria managed to get their own troops off the field, battered but more or less intact, despite the best efforts of a weary Eugene outside Lutzingen village to prevent them from doing so. Tallard wrote of the reasons for the failure of the campaign, and the inherent perils of divided command. 'It is a fine lesson that we should have only one commanding the army, and that is a great misfortune to have to deal with a prince of the humour of M, the Elector of Bavaria.'[14]

'The king received the cruel news of this battle on 21 August, by a courier [sent] from the Maréchal de Villeroi.'[15] The details were as yet far from clear, but that a severe defeat had been suffered seemed plain, 'It puzzled every brain,' St Simon wrote, 'We were not accustomed to misfortune . . . The grief of the king at this ignominy and this loss may be imagined.' Tallard's rather forlorn letter to Louis XIV, written two days after the battle, explaining and attempting to excuse the disaster, ran, in part:

> Sire, It is my misfortune that instead of a victory, I am obliged to acquaint Your Majesty with the loss of a battle, and the defeat

of your army. If the Elector had had more regard to Marshal Marsin's and my advice we should not have come to the extremity of venturing a battle, as I have already written to Monsieur Chamillart. The rules of war required that his Electoral Highness with the succours that Your Majesty had sent to him should act defensively until the departure of so many foreign troops which the Queen of England and the States-General [Holland] had sent into Bavaria. The enemy, knowing that our army marched to pass the Danube they marched also, and the two armies found themselves at six o'clock within half a mile of Höchstädt. The right Wing, which I commanded, extended itself to the Danube, the Marquis de Blainville commanded the infantry which was in the centre of the Wing, having a village [Oberglau] in the front and some hedges that the enemy were possessed of, The centre and the left Wing were commanded by the Elector and Marshal Marsin, extending itself to a wood having likewise a village before them Lutzingen] We were separated from the enemy by a marshy rivulet [the Nebel Bach stream].[16]

Having painstakingly set the scene, Tallard moved on to the main point at issue when attempting to offer an excuse that would stand up to a close examination:

At about eleven o'clock [given as Noon by most accounts] the English cavalry charged that of my Wing which repulsed them with an abundance of bravery, the English returning to the charge attacked the Gendarmerie who behaved themselves very ill, the elector having rallied them, led the up again supported by the rest of the cavalry. His Electoral Highness and I thought the victory on our side, by the happy success of the infantry on the left Wing who had broken through the enemy's right [Eugene's attack was initially thrown back] In the meantime,

> the cavalry of my Wing being charged with fresh troops, was broken and forced to leave the field to the enemy; it was then that I was made prisoner, having no clear way of escaping other than by swimming the Danube.[17]

Tallard only briefly mentioned, almost in passing, the fatal error he had made of allowing so many of his infantry to be uselessly bottled up in the village, with only a far too late effort to get them into position where they could be of any use.

The captive marshal was conducted back to England along with a number of other senior French officers taken that day, and comfortably lodged at first in Chatsworth House in Derbyshire, and then at Newdigate House, Castle Gate, Nottingham. Although treated with great courtesy, as befitted a man of his rank (and fondly remembered by some, from his time as a diplomat at the Court of St James), he was not impressed by the quality of food served, and so he taught his captors how to bake French bread, and introduced celery, found growing wild in the grounds, as a delicacy hitherto unknown on the table in England. With his naturally urbane and polished manners he generally made himself very popular with the local gentry, and was able to hunt in the neighbourhood, when his excursions were always watched with great interest by the locals. He also, reputedly, fathered a child with a local gentlewoman, but details on this point are sketchy. While held in England, Tallard's surviving son, the Marquis de la Baume, was taken prisoner at the Battle of Ramillies in 1706.[18] During his captivity, Tallard was not forgotten or neglected at Versailles, and he was appointed to be governor of the Franche-Comte region *in abstentia*, and apparently this was a sinecure to assist his family while he was detained.

In 1711 Tallard was released and permitted to return to France, accompanied by enormous baggage and a pack of foxhounds that he had acquired. In Versailles he was warmly received by Louis XIV, who appeared to cast no blame or bear any ill-will for the calamity to French arms of the Blenheim battle seven years' earlier. Created Duc d'Hostun in 1714, he was a made a Peer of France in 1715 and appointed to be a member of the regency council that, on the death of the old king, was to oversee France during the infancy of his heir, his great-grandson. The regent, the late king's nephew Philippe Duc d'Orleans, managed to have the will amended to give himself additional powers, and coincidentally to have Tallard removed from the council. Affronted at the snub, and haunted perhaps by the memory of the calamitous events of 1704, Tallard became almost a recluse at his home in the Hòtel de Bretonvilliers in Paris, and at La Planchette, until his recall to court and a place on the regency council in 1717.[19] However, full re-instatement to favour and influence only gradually came about, although in 1723 he was elected to the renowned Académie des Sciences, and the next year was made its president. Tallard was appointed as a minister of state in 1726, but two years' later he died in Paris on 20 March 1728. The old marshal and consummate veteran diplomat was buried in the Church des Dames de Sainte-Elizabeth de Hongrie, and was survived by his youngest son, Marie-Joseph, and only daughter, Catherine-Ferdinande.

Chapter 11

Marshal Vauban

'A man of medium height, rather squat, and with the typical look of a soldier, but at the same time rather boorish and coarse, not to say brutal and fierce',[1] is how the Duc de St Simon, in his characteristically acid way, described the figure that Sebastien le Prestre, Seigneur de Vauban, in time to be made a Marshal of France, cut at the glittering court at Versailles. Well, the pre-eminent military engineer of his day had no intention of becoming an adornment at that assembly, 'a drone' as St Simon was himself once pithily described, being of a far more practical turn of mind. With his expertise in fortification and study of the most judicious methods of the complex techniques required for siege warfare, he could arguably be said to have been, overall, the most effective in the long term of all Louis XIV's marshals. Much of what he learnt, knew and applied relied upon the valuable earlier work of others, Abraham Fabert amongst them, but his further development of these methods was remarkable, as was his work rate. Vauban never had the command of an army in a major action, although he contributed significantly to many of the successes that other marshals enjoyed; accordingly, he cannot be ranked as a great field commander, but his services to the French crown were, all the same, undeniably of the greatest magnitude and widely recognized as such.

Sebastien le Prestre was born in the Morvan district of Burgundy on 1 May 1633, the only son of Urbain le Prestre and his wife Edmée (née Carmignolle), families both akin to being minor provincial gentry rather than anything grander. The father had served the crown as a member of the notoriously ill-disciplined and almost unemployable militia, the *Arrière-Ban*, as had his own father before him, but unblinking service to the crown seemed not to have gone much deeper at the time of the future marshal's birth. The young Sebastien was educated at the Carmelite college at Semure-en-Auxois, where he shone at mathematics and geometry, with an added interest in history and technical drawing. In 1651 he was introduced to the renowned victor of Rocroi, the Duc d'Enghien (Prince of Condé), who, duly impressed with the aspiring young man, agreed to take him into his service. This was an intriguing start to Vauban's career for Condé was, at the time, in open rebellion against the crown, in the series of Fronde civil wars fought largely by over-mighty nobles resentful of what, it was claimed, was burdensome central authority contrary to long-established tradition and practice. Louis XIV had not yet gained his majority, his mother, Anne of Austria, acting as regent for the time being together with the unpopular first minister, Cardinal Jules Mazarin, at a period when France was said to be, 'Dominated by ambitious nobles, whose only object was to get the government into their own hands, and then to share the spoils amongst themselves'.[2]

Taken into active service in the Compagnie d'Arcenay in Condé's own regiment, Vauban was ranked as a cadet (an aspiring officer in effect), and obtaining this coveted post for the young man seems to have largely been due the fact that his uncle, Edmé le Prestre, was marechal de logis in that unit.[3] He first saw action at Clermont en Argonne fighting against loyal royalist forces in 1652, and subsequently worked on repairing the dilapidated fortifications of nearby Verdun, the first of many such endeavours, So assiduously did he undertake the task that in effect and despite his relative inexperience he was left in charge of the work, having clearly shown an aptitude for such a detailed but perhaps unglamorous labour.

Offered the chance to be promoted to ensign after the Frondist siege of Sainte-Menehould on the river Aisne, Vauban refused, as he could not afford the equipment, saddlery and servants necessary to sustain himself as an officer, albeit one of such junior rank. Instead, he was permitted to transfer to the cavalry as a gentlemen trooper. In 1653 he was obliged to submit when the party he was riding with was surprised and overwhelmed by a detachment of cavalry in the king's service. Vauban refused to hand over his sword or his purse, as was demanded, and his captors were so impressed by the young trooper's bold manner that he was permitted to give his parole not to serve again until formally exchanged, and ride away unhindered. When word of this encounter came to Cardinal Mazarin, he promptly offered the young man a place in the royal army, if he would only change sides. This was just too tempting to resist and having metaphorically 'turned his coat' and entered the king's service, amongst the first operations Vauban undertook was to help re-take Sainte-Menehould. Louis XIV, although still a minor and closely guarded, was present to observe the capture of the place, and noted with approval how the young engineer, so recently a rebel against his authority, conducted himself.

Active throughout the remaining months of the Fronde troubles, Vauban served at the engagements at Saint Ghislain, Condé and Landrecies, and during which latter action the notoriously critical Marshal de la Ferté-Sennetière, a very hard man to please, was particularly complimentary at his conduct while under heavy fire. In 1654 he was wounded twice at the siege of Stenay, although on the second occasion this was apparently because he detonated a mine but not taken the trouble to move far enough out of the way; the lesson was no doubt well learned. However, he was well enough to command the subsequent siege operations at Clermont en Argonne, where his extensive mining activity bluffed the Frondist garrison commander into making a rather a premature submission. Later that year, Vauban was at the relief of Arras when Turenne drove the rebels away towards Le Cateau. Meantime, that October the king announced a general amnesty for all involved, so that the civil war would eventually stutter to a tired and rather untidy end. Vauban's reward for his endeavours came in the form of a cash bounty, and a commission in the Régiment de Bourgogne (previously the Regiment de Condé, and du Repentis). All the same, it must be said that Louis XIV struggled always to quite forgive the troublesome senior nobles who had been in rebellion for so long, but was clearly less concerned with the more junior rebels who, in most cases, had simply followed their local nobility into battle; Vauban was just one such, and his devotion and loyalty to his king would prove to be both remarkable and of the utmost value.

The following year, Vauban was active in the operations to bring the war with Spain to a slow conclusion, conducting mining operations at Landrecies under the watchful eye of Marshal Turenne and Marshal de la Ferté, and then at Condé sur Escaut and Saint Ghislain. So well conducted were his activities, that at the surprisingly young age of 22, he was appointed Engineer-in-Ordinary to the king, which while not in itself a rank, was a clear indication of high trust and special responsibilities. His abilities in the often much neglected field of military engineering, which was felt by some to be a rather menial role and hardly fitting a gentleman, were increasingly evident.

Following an unsuccessful siege of Valenciennes in 1656, the French army was effectively bottled up in Condé-sur-Escaut and Saint Ghislain, where Vauban, although wounded, helped with the defence while being carried about on a litter. The next year he was the only survivor of the four engineers with the army under Marshal de la Ferté that laid siege to Montmédy on the river Chiers, the last remaining Spanish-held fortress on the French border. The operation saw heavy French casualties, with a valiant defence by the garrison whose own commander was killed. De la Ferté was sufficiently impressed by Vauban, who had been wounded yet again, to offer him a commission in his own regiment, with another simultaneous commission in the garrison Régiment de Nancy. The offer was promptly accepted, although the marshal should really have got approval from the king first. In this remarkable way, Vauban held commissions in three units (those of Bourgogne, de la Ferté and Nancy), at the same time, and drew the pay accordingly. This was in addition to his appointment as Engineer-in-Ordinary to the king, with the likelihood of further generous bounties from time to time for good service. This state of affairs was not unique, although reading a little oddly today, but was certainly a mark of the reputation he was building, and the high regard in which he was held for his particular abilities as an engineer in the field. Noted for his desire to see for himself how things were going, Vauban repeatedly ran risks, and was once taken prisoner near to Oudenarde on the Scheldt by Spanish troops, while scouting the best places for siege trenches to be dug. He offered his parole, and this was promptly accepted, so that he was duly exchanged before too long and could recommence his duties. 'One must reconnoitre in person' he wrote, 'or have it done by sure, intelligent men.'[4]

On 25 March 1660 Vauban married Jeanne d'Aunay, daughter of the impoverished Baron d'Epiry whose debts Vauban had to partly settle as a part of the marriage agreement. This was all rather to the engineer's shrewd mother's disapproval, and she did not see fit to attend the wedding ceremony. The contract for the betrothal described Vauban at this point as 'Ingenière ordinaire du Roy, Capitaine Lieutenant du Regiment d'infantrie de Companie de la Marechal de la Ferté Servitre, et Capitaine d'une Compagnie de Garinsonne de Nancy',[5] and in time he would be able to purchase for a family home the small country estate and chateau at Bazoches. Not that he enjoyed much leisure to live there for very long at any given time, as the incessant demands of the king and his ministers for war were relentless. Despite his long absences either out on campaign or supervising the building or rebuilding of the fortresses that would keep France secure, Vauban's marriage was apparently a success, and the couple had two daughters, Charlotte and Jeanne-Francoise, and a son who unfortunately died when only two months old. Jeanne was also appointed to be the executor of his will, but he was evidently not above a certain degree of philandering. The ladies involved duly looked to him for support, so that shortly before his death Vauban wrote of the claims of a certain Madame Districh, an Irish émigré [who he clearly did not altogether trust], that she 'Claims to have had a child by me . . . I would not risk the salvation of my soul for it; for that reason, I beg Friand [Vauban's secretary] to give her 2,000 livres. I find the claims difficult to believe, but all the same I make provision for them.'[6]

Wounded at the siege of Douai during the opening phase of the War of Devolution, Vauban was well enough to be with Louis XIV at the memorable capture of the city and fortress of Lille, in the late summer of 1667. The Chevalier de Clerville, by virtue of his seniority as commissary-general of fortifications, had nominal command of the repairing of the siege works, but Vauban did most of the leg-work, and was rewarded with the prestigious appointment as a lieutenant of the Gardes Royal. He soon obtained permission to sell this commission, for 20,000 livres, as he could not afford the cost of the expensive uniforms and accoutrements required. Vauban's plans for the rebuilding of the fortress were approved (unlike those presented by de Clerville, who was in effect snubbed, and went off sulking into semi-retirement), and he was simultaneously appointed to be governor of the Lille citadel, yet another mark of royal approval and favour. The massive and complex rebuilding work was only completed in 1674, not before rumours of theft of stores and mis-use of money had been maliciously raised, with Vauban writing to the Marquis de Louvois, the minister for war, 'Appoint some honest man who will probe everything to the bottom and then report to you on it . . . Knowing my own scrupulous probity and sincere fidelity, I fear neither the king, nor yourself.'[7] The matter, apparently mischief-making by those envious of the engineer's growing reputation, was quietly dropped.

After carrying a tour of inspection of the fortifications in southern France, Vauban oversaw the attack on Rheinburg during the French offensive into on Holland in April 1672. This capture paved the way for the strategically important but impetuous crossing of the lower Rhine at Tollhuis in the second week of June. He was, however, concerned when Louis XIV abruptly refused a Dutch approach to cease hostilities, in return for which several key fortresses would be left in French hands. The engineer had been engaged in surveying the towns recently captured and wrote a detailed memorandum on those worth keeping and those where the defences had better be demolished. However, the king appeared to have lost interest, and Vauban was instructed to return to Lille and complete the rebuilding work there. However, when Louis XIV moved against Maastricht in the summer of 1673, Vauban was summoned once more to take part in the siege. The garrison commander, Major-General Jacques Farieux, was an experienced and capable officer who vigorously thwarted the French siege work at every step. The trenches were opened on the night of 17/18 June, at the personal direction of the king, but really this was just for forms sake, and 'The operations were directed by a siege head [Vauban], who received the orders from the king, and accounted to nobody but him'.[8] Always concerned for the well-being of the soldiers, Vauban deplored attempts by the general officers present to try and push the pace of the siege; 'The loss is always a result of excessive haste, at the cost of our best troops who perish miserably on such occasions'.[9] Despite this, a sharp attack made during the night of 24/25 June was soundly beaten off, during which both James Duke of Monmouth, and John Churchill (later to be the 1st Duke of Marlborough) were engaged at the side of Charles de Batz, Comte d'Artagnan of the Musketeers, who was killed in the attempt.

Vauban's innovative use of narrow parallel trenches (the 'Turkish practice' after its use against the Venetians in Crete) to make several different approaches to the Maastricht defences, attracted the king's notice, as the garrison could never be quite sure where the main French effort would come. 'The way in which the lines were drawn,' he wrote, 'prevented then enemy from attempting anything. The enemy, astonished at seeing us approach him with so many troops and in such a fashion, adopted the plan of attempting nothing since we advanced with so many precautions.'[10] Sharpshooting by the Dutch troops caused many casualties amongst the soldiers labouring in the trenches and Vauban was often much at risk, but Jacques Farieux submitted on 1 July, after mounting a resistance of only 13 days, which was appreciably sooner than had been expected. Good terms were granted, and the garrison were permitted to march out with the honours of war, while Vauban received a purse containing 4,000 livres from Louis XIV for his part in the siege. Impressed at the modest scale of French losses in the seizure of such a key fortress, the Comte d'Aligny wrote 'Monsieur Vauban, in this siege as in so many others, saved many men by his knowledge'.[11]

Vauban's field, his speciality and expertise, was plainly in the complexities of the art of designing and building fortresses proofed as far as possible against the effects of artillery bombardment and subterranean mining on the one hand, and on the other diametrically opposed hand the most expeditious and cost-effective ways of overcoming those same fortresses and defences by means of a well-handled siege. Louis XIV's wars were, initially, offensive/defensive in character and designed to expand his realm and make surer what were hitherto porous and vulnerable frontiers, particularly in the north and east of the country, a region largely devoid of major natural barriers. However, having alerted and alarmed most of the states of western Europe against him and his ambitions, the need to defend what had been achieved became paramount. This inevitably called for the construction of a massively enlarged and extended defensive system, and the work was largely entrusted to Vauban, with his great energy, to undertake and that he did so and so well, can be readily seen.

Concerned at the exposed, irregular and overly extended nature of France's northern borders and the lack of a cohesive defensive strategy in place to address the problem, Vauban wrote to Louvois with advice on the best way to approach this thorny strategic weakness. He urged the development of a chain of mutually supporting fortresses. 'The king ought to give a little thought to squaring off the boundaries of his lands . . . whether it is accomplished by treaty or by a successful campaign, you must continue to preach the need to tidy up the boundaries [borders].'[12] Such an enormous and expensive programme of building would, in time, be undertaken under Vauban's direction, but Louis XIV's campaigns of conquest were not yet quite done with.

Sent to inspect the fortifications at Nancy and Alt-Brisach, Vauban then directed the siege operations against Spanish-held Besançon in the Franche-Comte region, which was successfully concluded in May 1674 after only 19 days. Later that summer, newly promoted to brigadier of infantry (in addition to his other appointments) he was sent in some hurry to take command of the French garrison of Oudenarde on the river Scheldt, which had come under threat from a renewed joint Dutch and Spanish offensive. The fortress held out long enough for Condé to approach with a relieving army, and Vauban was commended for the capable defence he had maintained under some pressure. Ambushed shortly afterwards while on the road to La Bassée, he was lucky to escape with his life, as several of his party were wounded in the affray. Yet again Vauban was warned of the king's displeasure at his exposing himself to such risks, but these were simply an inescapable part of carrying out his duties as he hurried from one fortress to another in pursuit of the instructions that flowed in an almost constant stream from Versailles. As the war ambled on, Condé sur Escaut and Bouchain both fell to Vauban's siege tactics, in the latter case on 11 May 1676 after only a week's token resistance, and Aire-sur-la-Lys submitted soon afterwards. At the end of the year he was in Verdun, suffering from the bitterly cold weather. 'For my part,' he wrote ruefully, 'I will be glad enough to come through it without getting my nose and ears frost-bitten.'[13]

In March 1677 Vauban supervised the siege of Valenciennes, where a surprise attack by Marshal Luxembourg's infantry overwhelmed the rather flimsy defences, and the attention of the French then moved on to Cambrai where the ill-defended town was also soon given up, with the Spanish garrison retiring into the formidable citadel to continue the defence. Louis XIV permitted a premature infantry assault, overriding Vauban's protests at the lack of wisdom in making such an attempt, but Luxembourg's unexpected success at Valenciennes may have influenced the decision to go ahead. This new attack was bloodily repulsed with the loss of 440 French soldiers killed or wounded. The king acknowledged his mistake in allowing the attempt, and a more measured approach undertaken and overseen by Vauban was successful, with only slight losses, so that the garrison submitted on 17 April. The king asked to be introduced to the Spanish governor, so that he could congratulate him on the staunch defence his troops had made of the citadel. Vauban was now promoted marechal de camp, and sent to oversee the siege operations against Saint Ghislain, where the field commander, Louis de Crevante, Marshal d'Humières, was strictly warned, that the valuable engineer was 'Not to be allowed to undertake work in the trenches'.[14] As before, this caution proved impossible to implement in any meaningful way, as Vauban was immune to pressure on the subject.

The Chevalier de Clerville having died, Vauban was promoted to be Inspector-General of Fortifications at the age of 45, and in March 1678 he supervised the siege of Ypres, where the water-logged ground, sodden with winter rain, proved difficult for the digging of the necessary works. Louis XIV was once more present, eager to watch progress, and had to be almost manhandled out of an exposed trench by the alarmed French sappers he was talking to, while apparently oblivious to the fierce musketry coming from the defenders of the fortress. The king accepted this robust and clearly well-meant behaviour with wry good humour. On hearing of this, Vauban wrote to Louvois:

> Whatever care you may take to construct your trenches, there is never any place in them where you are completely safe from all hazards . . . It is not for me to find fault with the actions of my sovereign, but as my conscience obliges me to speak freely on anything that may serve for the conservation of his person, and especially on subjects relating to the craft I profess, it would be even less proper to remain silent . . . His majesty ought never to appear in the trenches.[15]

As it was, Louis XIV would soon give up active campaigning and so Vauban's concerns on the point could be laid to rest. Instructions still flowed from Versailles to field commanders who were almost at their wit's end, at the insistence that the king's engineer was not to be allowed to expose himself to danger.

At the peace that came with the Treaty of Nijmegen in August 1678, France retained many of the fortresses taken in recent years, significantly strengthening her frontier defences. Vauban was tasked with rebuilding, re-siting on occasions, and strengthening these places, and this would prove to be a lengthy and expensive undertaking. Eventually, a double line of fortified towns, the 'Pre-Carré' as it was known, would be established, running from the Channel coast to the difficult country of the Ardennes, Moselle valley and Hünsrück.[16] That the vast outlay from Louis XIV's treasury would pay dividends would be seen in time, but the king occasionally baulked at the cost, even having to ask on one occasion why Vauban thought it necessary to remove an entire hill when rebuilding a certain fortress. All the same, the engineer was keen to avoid over-stretching French resources, and spreading French garrisons too thinly over too much ground. He wrote that, 'I am of the opinion that we should build no further fortifications outside these two lines, on the contrary, I think that in the due course of time it would be best to destroy all fortifications that do not form part of these lines'.[17]

Sent once again to inspect the fortifications in the far-flung south and west of France, and also the fortified ports on the Channel coast, Vauban was kept fully occupied, but with the 1679 campaign of 'Reunions' by which Louis XIV obliged the civic authorities in Alsace, Franche-Comte and Lorraine to acknowledge French sovereignty, or at least implicit overlordship, he was employed to strengthen the defences of Strasbourg and adjacent Kehl on the far bank of the Rhine, and Saarlouis to the south of the Hünsrück. Late in 1680 he was sent to inspect the outpost of Casale in northern Italy, recently acquired from the bankrupt Duke of Mantua, and French-held Pinerolo, before travelling wearily to Provence and then with hardly a pause, hastening back to inspect construction work in the Franche-Comte.

In August 1683 Louis XIV presented impossible terms to the governor of the Spanish Netherlands, and invaded the region the same day, without waiting for a response, so that in November Vauban was at the brief sieges of Courtrai and Dixmuide, where neither garrison put up much of an effort. Early in 1684 Luxembourg was invested by Marshal de Créquy, and on 11 May after a sharp bombardment of the defences, Vauban could express his satisfaction with the way the siege lines, were progressing, although a premature attack three days later was beaten off with heavy losses. At the end of the month, the garrison commander, the Prince de Chimay, asked for terms, and a formal capitulation was made on 3 June, with the garrison being accorded the honours of war. The Treaty of Ratisbon, agreed in mid-August 1684, saw France retain possession of Luxembourg, and general acknowledgement of the gains made under the campaign of the 'Reunions'.

With the resumption of peace, temporary but welcome for all that, Vauban was busily engaged in an engineering project to provide water for the palace at Versailles, by means of the construction of a large aqueduct, which, however, was never completed. He was also tasked to rebuild the defences of Belle-Isle, on the Biscay coast, work that took six years to complete, and in 1687 he was sent to strengthen the defences of Landau facing the Rhine frontier, and at Belfort to the south of the broken country of the Vosges, work which required no less than 13 years' labour to accomplish. A proposal put forward to fortify Paris to a modern standard did not find royal approval, however, as Louis XIV had enough experience of how belligerent the citizens of that city could at times prove themselves, such as during the Fronde civil wars; the long-overdue fortification of Paris would have to wait for the mid-nineteenth century to be accomplished.

With the commencement of what would be known as the Nine Years War in 1688, and France facing a formidable coalition of opposing powers, Vauban, by now a lieutenant-general, was employed at the attempt to recapture the strategically important fortress of Philippsburg on the Rhine. The weather was foul, with the soldiers often knee-deep in mud, and while the Dauphin was present, and in nominal command of the siege, as usual Vauban did the work, so that the garrison capitulated on 28 October, after only a short defence. The French then moved on to seize Mannheim, which they did without difficulty, and to Coblenz in November, after a pointless and expensive bombardment at which Vauban protested. Taken ill that winter with influenza, he remembered that he was being overwhelmed with work. In 1690, although once again not that well, he was sent to inspect construction work being carried out at the defences of Charleroi, Philippeville and Mauberge, before having to return to Lille to recover properly. The following spring he supervised the complex siege operations against Mons where, despite fresh difficulties with flooded ground and a stout defence by the garrison, terms were agreed for a capitulation by the Spanish governor, the Prince de Berghes, on 8 April. For this fresh success, Louis XIV presented Vauban with a handsome gift of 100,000 livres, together with an invitation to attend him at a private supper – a most unusual honour that attracted much envious attention.

The following July, Louvois' lacklustre son, Barbezieux, took over the post of minister for war. Although undeniably demanding and often unreasonable, the older man had been a firm supporter of Vauban and his expensive projects, and he would be missed. At the hard-fought siege of Namur in 1692, Vauban had some 20,000 conscripted labourers working in the trenches, effort that was again hampered by Louis XIV insisting on seeing for himself at close quarters how things were progressing. A chance musket ball fired from the defences struck a gabion right beside the king on one occasion, again causing a great deal of concern although he appeared to be completely unruffled. The Dutch garrison withdrew into the citadel in early June, and bad weather slowed the French operations. An attempt by William III to threaten Mons and draw off the French main army came to nothing, so that a capitulation of the Namur citadel on terms was agreed on 1 July, at a cost to the French of some 5,500 killed and wounded. Vauban was then tasked to go south to Nice, recently taken from the Duke of Savoy, and draw up plans to strengthen the fortifications there. His proposals were, however, thought to be too elaborate and expensive, and had to be watered down to save money. Louis XIV was careful not to offer offence to his gifted engineer, and his letter ran, in part, 'Continue to write to me; do not be disappointed if I do not always adopt your suggestions . . . I assure you that no one could have a higher opinion of, or more esteem and friendship for, another as I have for you.'[18]

The intermittent alliance that Louis XIV had enjoyed (if that is the right term) with Duke Victor-Amadeus of Savoy proved troublesome, and after Savoyard troops had invaded the Dauphine in the summer of 1692, Vauban was sent to supervise the construction of a strengthened barrier for the region. He deplored the forward stance that France maintained in northern Italy, most particularly the exposed fortresses of Casale and Pignerole, which could only be maintained at great expense and wasteful diversion of effort.

'If, instead of chasing butterflies beyond the Alps they [the king and his ministers] had taken care to defend the frontier properly, we should have been secure now.'[19] On 9 May 1693 Vauban was rewarded by being made a member of the newly created Order of St Louis, holding one of the only eight grand crosses of the order. The indication of high esteem from Louis XIV was evident, but he was not yet made a Marshal of France, an omission that many thought odd, when some, whose achievements seemed to be less evident, had been so honoured. In part his provincial, almost humble, background told against him, no matter what his successes in the royal service might have been, but there was also the problem that much of the work he did to such good effect could hardly be put into the hands of a marshal, as it was deemed to be too menial for someone of such elevated rank to undertake. The king was clearly reluctant to lose the services of one so skilled at the art of military engineering, and while Vauban understood this, the relative slowness of his promotion undoubtedly rankled.

After the bitterly-fought battle at Landen in late July, Marshal Luxembourg moved to invest the fortress of Charleroi on the river Sambre, and Vauban was hastily summoned north to supervise the siege works. The garrison commander, the Marquis de Villadarias, put up a robust defence, and the breaching batteries could only begin their work properly in mid-September. Vauban's detailed knowledge of the layout of the city defences was a distinct asset, so that after a stubborn resistance of 32 days the marquis capitulated, having very capably slowed the French campaign to something approaching a crawl as the cold months of autumn came on; he had inflicted some 4,000 casualties on his opponents in the process. The survivors of the garrison were permitted to march out with their colours and small arms and go to Brussels without molestation.

Sent to organize the improve the defences in Brittany, Vauban was accorded the honorary title Lieutenant-General of Marine while he did so. On 18 June 1684 an Allied landing was made at Camaret Bay, which the Breton militia, sent at Vauban's command, handsomely beat off, killing General Thomas Tollemache, the leader of the expedition, in the process. In the meantime, Namur on the river Meuse had been invested by William III, and when the place fell, Vauban was disturbed that so notable a fortress, whose defences he had strengthened, had been obliged to submit after a valiant defence but in relatively modest time, while a French army (under Marshal Villeroi) marched ineffectively to and fro. The engineer took some comfort in the heavy Allied casualties incurred in taking the place, but Namur was undeniably a key fortress, and its loss was a blow. The war was stumbling wearily on now, Savoy had concluded an agreement to reforge its alliance with France, and with Austrian hopes dashed, operations in Italy came to an agreed end. In Flanders, the newly rebuilt fortress of Ath was invested by a French army under Marshal Catinat, fresh from his adventures in Italy, and Vauban was at his side in the siege operations which began in mid-May 1697. During an inspection of the work in the trenches, Vauban was struck by a spent musket ball fired by one of the garrison, and received a nasty bruise to the shoulder, but he typically shrugged the incident off, although the king was displeased when he heard of it. Nonetheless, he typically wrote solicitously to his engineer, 'I am sorry to hear of the wound that you have received, but at the same time I am relieved to know that it is not dangerous, and that there is every hope you will soon be restored to health'.[20] On 4 June, the garrison commander asked for terms, and these were promptly granted, the siege having been conducted in such a prudent way that French casualties were light. Although as usual they had to leave their artillery behind, the garrison were permitted to march out with the honours of war.

With the coming of peace at the Treaty of Ryswick in October 1697, Vauban was tasked by Louis XIV to provide a memorandum setting out the key points in how to maintain the most effective defence of

France with least cost and effort. The engineer had already expressed concern that rather too much had been negotiated away to achieve the recent peace, but his advice, when it came, was that overstretch had to be avoided, and far-flung forward posts (Casale, Pignerole and Kehl quickly came to mind), places difficult to maintain and defend, should be given up or demolished, as they dispersed effort and materially weakened the defence of the heart of France. A prime example of this policy when in practice would be the eventual demolition of Alt-Briesach, standing exposed on the far bank of the Rhine, and its replacement with a brand-new fortress, Neuf-Briesach, on the nearside left bank.

Few expected the peace to last very long, and in November 1700 King Carlos II died in Madrid, and the long War of the Spanish Succession began in earnest soon afterwards. Vauban was not immediately employed, and he had recently written to the king to point out that promotion had long eluded him, hinting heavily that to this was perhaps now well overdue. Although the letter seems to have gone unanswered for a time, sure enough, on 14 January 1703 Vauban was made a Marshal of France, able to be addressed by Louis XIV as 'cousin'. The Duc de St Simon wrote that, 'The king said nothing of this until after dinner, when he suddenly announced his decision'.[21] That Vauban had never commanded an army in battle, the defence of Oudenarde and the affair at Camaret Bay not counting as such, made the promotion all the more notable, although it was undeniably well merited. The newly-elevated Vauban soon accompanied the Duc de Bourgogne, the king's grandson (and eventual intended heir), at the siege of Alt-Briesach, where the Imperial garrison submitted quite quickly.

Failing health was having an effect, and Vauban was again not employed for some time, while a shadow had been cast over him and his reputation on account of his openly expressed and rather radical opinions on more equitable means of taxation. His laudable aim was to lighten the burden on the common people, who he saw as inherently being France's major strength, while the nobility and clergy, by and large, escaped many taxes. Such views were unsurprisingly highly unwelcome in Versailles and the old engineer was suspected of meddling in matters that were not his concern. When he produced a pamphlet on the subject, 'The Dime Royal, or a Project for a Royal Tithe', it was quickly suppressed, and in an indication of his fading influence, the advice he offered towards the conduct of the faltering French siege of Turin in 1706 was pointedly ignored. Nonetheless, in the grim aftermath of the Ramillies defeat in that year, Vauban was given the command of the troops on the Channel coast between Dunkirk and Gravelines, An entrenched camp that he had constructed at Dunkirk was so strong that it was still in use during the Revolutionary Wars 90 years later, but increasing frailty dogged him, and he was at last permitted to retire from active service on 6 November of that year. On 30 March 1707, by now a widower, and largely ignored his king and those at Versailles, Vauban died at his home in Paris, attended only by his son-in-law, Jacques de Mesrigny.

The effectiveness of the defences that Vauban designed and oversaw in construction, was only once put to a real test, in the fraught years between 1708 and 1711, when Marlborough and Eugene, at the height of their considerable powers, proved unable to break cleanly through into the interior of France in any significant way. The principal exception was their notable seizure of Lille, undoubtedly in itself a fine feat of arms that owed much to the demoralization rife in the French ranks, both high and low, after the disgrace of the defeat at Oudenarde. French field armies valiantly played their part in these years of peril, of course, but could surely not have done so long and so well without the bedrock support provided by the fortresses which proved to be the valuable life's-work of the recently deceased Marshal Vauban. The old engineer's influence had faded, partly due to his straying into affairs that were not really thought to be his concern, such as the onerous tax burden imposed on the French population, but despite this late coolness in their relationship, Louis XIV undoubtedly regretted his death, saying on learning the news that, 'I have lost a man very devoted to my person and to my state'.[22]

Chapter 12

Marshal Berwick

James FitzJames (created Duke of Berwick in 1687), was born out of wedlock in Moulins in the Bourbonnais on 21 August 1670, the son of James, Duke of York and his mistress, Arabella Churchill,[1] and he would become one of the most talented and formidable of the field commanders that Louis XIV ever had in his service. As the nephew of both Charles II of England and of John Churchill, 1st Duke of Marlborough, he enjoyed a remarkable family lineage, but his firm allegiance to the Roman Catholic faith meant that he had to pursue his remarkable career in the service of France and of Spain. Not only was it legally not possible for a Roman Catholic to hold a commission in the service of England, Scotland or Ireland, but Berwick's close connection with his father after his exile in 1688 made any such employment by William III unthinkable. Not that Berwick would have sought such a post, as he considered, not without some reason, that the Dutchman had illegally usurped his father's throne. Intriguingly, while he never came to cross swords with Marlborough in the field, uncle and nephew remained on good terms, frequently corresponding with one another, even while actively on campaign.

Educated at colleges in Juilly, du Plessis and Paris, young FitzJames briefly served the Habsburg emperor, Leopold I, under the tutelage of Lieutenant-General Francis Taaffe, and was with Duke Charles V of Lorraine's army at the capture from the Ottomans of Buda (Ofen) in Hungary in 1686.

> Towards the end of July, the trenches were opened, and batteries were erected . . . A breach having been made in the first enclosure the assault was given; but as there were only a few troops ordered to do this attack, and it was rather difficult to enter the breach they were soon repulsed. Few soldiers, indeed, were lost but numbers of volunteers were killed and wounded . . . The batteries were brought nearer, and reinforced with several large pieces of cannon; but yet the breaches were not quite practicable [that is, capable of being entered by a soldier, unaided, with both hands on his musket or matchlock] until the 27th of July.[2]

FitzJames was amongst the foremost of the attacking troops, as were several other English and French volunteers, as an engineer, Jacob Richards, recalled, 'Mr FitzJames was in all the action with Count Taaffe, behaving himself with remarkable gallantry'.[3] Berwick's own account of the final assault some weeks' later, went on:

> The attack began about noon, and lasted six hours, and there never was more courage shown than on this day by both parties. The Christians, notwithstanding the showers of balls, arrows, grenades, stinkpots, and powder chests, and the explosion of twelve mines, or fougades [fougasses] of bombs, still endeavoured to make good their lodgements, but they were on the point of giving way.[4]

A fresh attack under the army commander, Duke Charles, stabilized things, and the strength of the garrison steadily ebbed away with the heavy losses they suffered daily. Eventually 'The breach was carried almost as soon as it was attacked. The [grand] vizier and the garrison commander, Abdi Ali Pasha, were slain in the breach and all who were found in the town were put to the sword.' In fact, although the victorious troops carried out a brutal sack, having taken Buda by storm, it was an exaggeration to say that all the inhabitants were massacred, and the Aga-Vizier of the regular Ottoman Janissary infantry only submitted the citadel on the promise of good terms, which were duly granted and observed. Deplorable as it now seems, it was also customary at the time, and well into the nineteenth century, to permit troops to sack a town that had to be taken by force.

After a brief visit to his father in London, FitzJames was back in Hungary for the next years' campaign and fought at the remarkable victory gained by the Margrave of Baden against the Ottomans at 2nd Mohacs (Berg Hazan) on 12 August 1687, on the same ground of the great defeat of the Hungarian Jagalon princes by Sultan Suleyman the Magnificent in 1526. The young Englishman performed so well in the action that he was made temporary major-general by Emperor Leopold. The following year was appointed to the command of Taaffe's Regiment of Cuirassiers, with the regular rank of major-general, a distinction of which he remained very proud, although he was never to serve the emperor or his family again.

The Duke of York became James II of England on the death of his older brother Charles II in 1687, and this son almost immediately and unsurprisingly received a shower of appointments, being made Duke of Berwick, a Knight of the Garter, Baron of Bosworth, Earl of Tynmouth, Lord-Lieutenant of Hampshire, and governor of Portsmouth, together with the command of the 3rd Troop of Life Guards. With the arrival of William of Orange the very next year, however, Berwick proved unable to hold Portsmouth for the crown, the naval captains in the port apparently refusing to comply with his orders, and James II summoned his son to join him at Rochester in Kent; Colonel Thomas Tollemache (who would one day be mortally wounded in the surf at Camaret Bay) succeeded him as governor of Portsmouth. In January 1689 Berwick accompanied his father into exile in France, and then went to campaign in Ireland, serving in the Jacobite army at the famous but abortive siege of Londonderry, in Donegal and Enniskillen, and fighting with considerable skill at difficult engagements in Newry, Dundalk, Cavan and Belturbet. He commanded the cavalry of the right wing of his father's army at the Battle of the Boyne in July 1690, where his horse was killed and he was ridden over and trampled, barely escaping with his life. Later that summer he conducted the defence of Limerick against the Williamite forces, and in September was made commander of his father's army in Ireland, by that time clearly a flagging and forlorn enterprise. Despite a lack of numbers which prevented him saving Cork and Kinsale from capture, Berwick conducted a prudent and well-handled defence of the line of the River Shannon, and was present at the engagement at Aughrim on 22 July 1691, before leaving Ireland to return to France. Together with the hundreds of Irish who could not reconcile themselves to stay under William III's increasingly burdensome rule, Berwick was reviewed by his father at Vannes, where the nine regiments of foot, two of dragoons and two of horse, all units who would in time earn the name and reputation of the 'Wild Geese' in French service, were reformed, together with two companies of bodyguards.[5]

Serving under Marshal Luxembourg, Berwick distinguished himself at the siege of Mons, and shortly afterwards was at the hard-fought Battle of Steinkirk early in August 1691. Present a few weeks' later at the dashing cavalry action at Leuze, where the Prince of Waldeck's exposed rearguard was almost overwhelmed, he remembered:

> The first line of the enemy did wonders, and our troops were put into confusion, but at last, after a smart resistance, the enemy gave way. Our first line being formed again, partly with the Gendarmerie, we marched against the second line of the enemy [who] took to flight, at the sight of this, their third line turned their backs and fled too. We pursued them no further

> than the rivulet [the Catoir stream], for their whole army was returning, and formed on the other side.[6]

The following year Berwick was appointed to the command of the 1st Troop of Irish Horse Guards in the French service. But for the destruction of the French fleet, beached and burned at Barfleur and La Hogue in May 1692, he would have accompanied James II and his younger brother, Henry FitzJames, on an expedition to resume campaigning in England in a fresh attempt to recover the throne in London. Berwick lamented over the crushing naval defeats, undoubtedly an 'unhappy adventure' that the English seamen were 'More accustomed and handier than our people at this kind of manoeuvre'.[7]

On 29 July that year Berwick fought at Landen, where he was again un-horsed, and too winded to escape was taken prisoner during the hand-to-hand fighting for the villages of Neerwinden and [Over] Landen, A French officer recalled that:

> At last, by the conduct and valour of the Duke of Berwick, the attack made on the village of Landen proved successful, but the Prince of Orange, knowing how important it was to recover that post, sent a detachment of fresh troops, which came to attack the village with great fury. The Duke of Berwick, seeing this, prepared to make a vigorous defence . . . As soon as the enemy made the attack, he rushed upon them, and forced his way to their third line, where, being overpowered by their numbers, he was obliged to yield himself a prisoner [and] brought to the Prince of Orange. Marshal Luxembourg, after he had lost Landen, immediately sent a [the] brigade of Guiche to recover it.[8]

He had been recognized by his uncle, Charles Churchill, the Earl of Marlborough's younger brother, despite earnest attempts to conceal his identity, and was then introduced to William III, who the younger man refused to properly acknowledge; this discourtesy was repaid when the king refused to permit a parole to be granted, as would often be the practice. Nonetheless, Berwick was released soon after the battle in exchange for the wounded Duke of Ormonde and resumed service under Marshal Luxembourg at the siege and capture of Charleroi. In 1695 he was present at the controversial bombardment of Brussels by Villeroi, and was soon afterwards appointed by his father, now living in St Germain, to the command of all his land forces. Berwick also found time to marry, his bride being Honora, Countess of Lucan, the widow of Patrick Sarsfield, who had been killed at Landen, and the couple had one child James FitzJames. Honora's son by Sarsfield, James 2nd Earl of Lucan, was adopted and brought up by Berwick (the youngster died in 1718).

Remarkably, in 1696 Berwick went clandestinely to London, to sound out opinion on the chances for success of a Jacobite restoration, and if it seemed appropriate, to make the necessary arrangements for such an enterprise. He found little enthusiasm amongst potential supporters, and wrote of the exploit, that:

> I had several conversations with some of the principal noblemen, but it was in vain that I made the strongest representations I could think of and urging the necessity of not letting slip so fine an opportunity; they continued firm in their resolution not to rise, till the king [James II] had landed an army. To say the truth, their reasons were good; for it is certain that as soon as the Prince of Orange had discovered their revolt . . . he would have immediately ordered out the fleet and blocked up all the seaports of France; by which means the insurgents would have found themselves obliged to risk a battle with their raw, ill- disciplined troops.[9]

This was a mission of the highest risk, as there were strong rumours of a plot to abduct or even murder William III, and although Berwick would not have approved of such a thing, had he been apprehended, his own liberty and even his life might well have been forfeit. Louis XIV would also not countenance such an action, and, 'The king raised an eyebrow on hearing the rumours. He said he thought the Duke of Berwick may have been in England on his father's business, but was certainly not involved in any such a plot.'[10]

As it was Berwick returned safely to France and promptly resumed campaigning in Flanders, becoming Colonel of the Berwick Regiment, another Irish-raised unit in French service, in 1698. His wife Honora having died in that year, in 1700 he married once more, the bride being Anne Bulkeley, daughter of the Honourable Henry Bulkely, master of James II's household, and despite her having a reputation as being 'a very ill-humoured woman',[11] the union was particularly fruitful, with no fewer than thirteen children (eight sons and five daughters), of whom only eight survived their father.

With the coming of the war for the throne in Madrid in 1701, Berwick served as second in command to Marshal Boufflers in Flanders, acting with great skill against the Dutch commander, Godert Rede van Ginkel, Earl of Athlone, in the opening phases of the 1702 campaign. Naturalized as a Frenchman the following year, he was sent to command the forces operating in Spain in support of the French claimant for the throne, the Duc d'Anjou (Philip V).

> It had been thought necessary to send an army to the frontiers of Portugal to oppose the Archduke [Charles]. A French general was wanted to command this army . . . . But as the Duke of Berwick had never before commanded an army, he [Louis XIV] stipulated that the Marquis de Puységur, known to be a skilful officer, should go with him and assist him with his councils and advice.[12]

With just eight regiments of French cavalry and eighteen battalions of foot under command, Berwick was received formally as captain-general of Spain in Madrid on 15 February 1704, and promptly took firm steps to halt the initially promising campaign being waged on behalf of the Austrian claimant, Archduke Charles. This was Berwick's first opportunity to act as army commander, although he had the valuable assistance of the equally gifted Marquis de Puységur. While lacking any great advantage in numbers, he seized several minor fortresses held by the British and Dutch and their newly declared Portuguese allies, but a lack of forage and remounts, and the blazing heat of high summer, soon brought matters to an effective standstill. Berwick showed his ruthless side at the capture of Castello de Vide, when he demanded an immediate submission by the governor, otherwise he declared he would sack the town. 'We found means to intimidate the governor, by assuring him that, if he defended himself, we would put all the men to the sword, while the women would necessarily be exposed to the brutality of the soldiers.' This may all have been a bluff, but it was effective, and the garrison quickly submitted. 'Thus ended this first campaign, the success of which ought to have been more considerable.'[13] Nonetheless, Berwick was appointed to the Order of the Golden Fleece by Philip V that November and returned to France early the following year. Some at the court in Madrid had not always appreciated his direct manner, however, and one observer described him as 'A great dry devil of an Englishman, who always goes his own way'.[14]

Berwick's undoubted talents were not left idle, and he was soon sent to command the French troops deployed against rebellious Huguenot Camisards in the Languedoc region, where his severe measures effectively put an end to the insurrection. His methods attracted some critical comment, particularly after he had four of the rebel leaders executed, rather than showing leniency, but he was unabashed:

> I know that attempts have been made, in many countries, to blacken our proceedings against these people; but I can protest as a man of honour, that there are no sorts of crimes of which the

> Camisards had not been guilty; to rebellion, sacrilege, murder, theft and licentiousness, the most unheard of cruelties . . . It is surprising that the English and the Dutch, who encouraged this rebellion, underhand, should not have sent them chiefs [commanders] more capable of conducting this affair, or at least should have given them better advice.[15]

Rebellion is rarely a pretty affair, particularly where religion is involved, and there was little doubt that a significant degree of savage conduct, reprisal and counter-reprisal, was conducted in this sorry conflict.

Having firmly settled matters in the Languedoc, in October 1705 Berwick was sent on to attack Savoyard-held Nice. 'The city was one of the strongest in Europe,' he wrote, 'I was furnished with a very indifferent army, and had I not prevailed upon M. de Vauvre, Intendant of the Marine in Toulon, who was appointed to be my intendant for this siege, I know not how I could have succeeded.'[16] The town fell readily enough, but the stout-hearted garrison in the citadel, under the able command of the Marquis de Carail, bravely held out. 'The besieged made several sallies [sorties], but they were always repulsed with loss.'[17] The artillery exchanges were ferocious, and Berwick recalled that:

> The enemy answered with fifty pieces of cannon to our seventy, and our sixteen mortars; the artillery was fired by both sides as fast as musketry, and the noise and smoke was such, that we could neither see nor hear each other. That day, we had the Marquis de Filey, and a brigadier of engineers both killed by the same shot.[18]

The Marquis de Carail only submitted early the following January, largely due to declining morale amongst his rapidly dwindling garrison and did so even though a relieving force under Duke Victor-Amadeus was approaching fast and was hardly more than nine miles away.

> About 4.00 o'clock in the afternoon the Duke of Berwick being at the batteries, heard the besieged beat the chamade [offer to negotiate a surrender], whereupon he ordered the firing to be discontinued. Hostages were exchanged and the articles of capitulation were drawn up. These articles were very honourable for the Marquis of Carail and his garrison.[19]

Had de Carail only held out a little longer, Berwick would certainly have had to abandon the siege, his guns and equipment, and withdraw in some haste. As it was 'on the 6th January the Marquis de Carail went out of Nice by the breach, at the head of his garrison, with arms, baggage, and unusually was permitted to retain six pieces of cannon, and two mortars. The garrison which [had] consisted of one thousand four hundred men, was now reduced to 550 men and 80 officers.'[20] The success in securing Nice was widely acknowledged as having been a masterful display of Berwick's tactical expertise and determination, when able to deploy only limited numbers, and moreover an operation conducted in biting wintry weather.

Warmly received at Versailles after the victorious campaign in the south, Berwick was created a Marshal of France on 15 February 1706, and promptly sent back to Spain, reaching Madrid on 12 March. Fending off an Allied offensive with great skill, the newly-created marshal managed to recover Madrid, which had briefly been lost, and the key city of Carthagena. Worsening cold weather having then necessarily closed active campaigning, he took the field again in the following spring. Berwick was confronted by opponents who sought to force the issue before he could be joined by Philippe, Duc d'Orleans, who had been reported to have been sent by Louis XIV with additional troops to bolster the French effort in Spain. The

Marquis de Langallerie recalled that, 'The allied generals, confident in the courage and ardour of their soldiers, resolved to attack the Duke of Berwick before he received reinforcements headed by the Duc d'Orleans'.[21] The encounter at Almansa on 25 April 1707 was fiercely fought over two hours in the afternoon, and resulted in a decisive victory for Berwick and the Chevalier d'Asfeld.[22] The marshal reported that:

> The battle began on the right; our cavalry charged the left of the enemy with so much bravery, that they were broken; but the infantry of the enemy fired so briskly upon our people that they were obliged to give way, our cavalry however rallied again, and re-charged that of the enemy . . . The enemy's left wing was entirely routed.[23]

Berwick's casualties, at some 5,000 killed and wounded, were not by any means light, but the Allied loss, including prisoners, amounted to over 7,000, and their main field army was broken beyond ready repair. His opponent, the Earl of Galway, recalled the ferocious nature of the fighting that day, and wrote: 'We gave them battle, and were defeated, both our wings being broken and routed. Our foot was hounded by the enemy's horse, so that none could get off.'[24] The hasty withdrawal of the Portuguese cavalry early in the battle was but one of the factors which hampered the earl that day, for he had been outnumbered from the outset, and clearly outfought on the field. The Prussian King Frederick the Great, later in the century, believed Almansa was the most impressive victory of the age.[25]

Berwick went on to capture Valencia on 6 May, and in the process almost the whole of that province together with Aragon was secured for the French claimant, and in grateful recognition of the achievement Berwick was appointed a Grandee of the 1st Class and Duke of Liria and Jérica. The success of the campaign was of such magnitude that the Allied effort in Spain, on behalf of Archduke Charles, never really recovered, despite occasional tantalizing false dawns.

Berwick, accompanied now by the Duc d'Orleans, had taken the city of Valencia without much difficulty, but then became embroiled in argument that some Allied soldiers, taken prisoner but allowed good terms, were returned to their units by slow, difficult and roundabout routes. 'We had a right to send them by what way we pleased, nothing to the contrary having been stipulated in the capitulations.'[26] That some of the paroled soldiers had reportedly joined Spanish irregulars in harassing the French lines of supply no doubt hardened Berwick's attitude. The town of Xàtiva was taken later in the month, and in retribution for its resistance, was put to the torch with the inhabitants banished into Castile, with a warning not to return. Berwick wrote that this was done 'To impress terror, and by a severe example to prevent similar obstinacy [elsewhere]'.[27] Orleans went on to recapture Saragossa, and on 14 October, despite increasingly foul weather, the town of Lerida was stormed and sacked, but the citadel held out until 11 November, when the governor, Prince Henry of Hesse-Darmstadt, offered to capitulate. He was permitted to do so on good terms for himself and the surviving remnants of his garrison. In further recognition of his string of successes, two weeks later Berwick was appointed by Louis XIV to be the honorary Governor of the Limousine region.

Summoned back to Versailles in mid-March 1708, Berwick's departure was regretted by Philip V. 'The king and his queen cannot imagine why one should take from them a general whom they had asked for, who is necessary to them, whom the Spaniards like, and who has made himself fully acquainted with everything concerning the war in this country.'[28] Delayed en-route, despite the urgency of the summons he had received, Berwick missed the chance, perhaps fortunately, to accompany his half-brother, James (the Chevalier de St George, otherwise known to history as the Old Pretender), in an attempt at a landing in Scotland, with the backing of French troops under the command of Charles Goyon, Comte de Matignon, recently appointed as a Marshal of France. The affair came to nothing, in large part due to mismanagement, together with a marked lack of overt enthusiasm in Scotland to support such a landing, at least until French troops were on the ground as clear evidence of Louis XIV's determination to openly support the Jacobite cause. The ships allotted to the task, commanded by Admiral Forbin, were almost corned by a squadron of the Royal Navy, and then caught in a gale that eventually drove the whole expedition ingloriously back to port. That Berwick doubted the wisdom of the enterprise from the outset, when the details became known to him, may be seen in a lengthy memorandum he submitted to Louis XIV on the matter. His comments were rather cool, and perhaps not quite what the king was hoping to hear.

> I cannot say anything about the problem of transport for that is a naval matter which I do not understand, so I will confine myself to giving my views on the number of troops, on their place of embarkation, and on the means of supplying them . . . Only from Spain can Your Majesty draw troops, and that for two reasons. The first is the need your majesty has of those in Flanders to prevent the enemy from invading your kingdom, and the second is the ease with which they can arrive at the place of embarkation without arousing the least suspicion.[29]

For the 1708 campaign season, Berwick was put in joint command of the French troops on the Rhine and in the Moselle valley, working with Elector Max-Emanuel in facing the Imperial forces led by Prince Eugene of Savoy and George, the elector of Hanover; he arrived in Strasbourg in mid-May. The Allied plan for that summer, lacking subtlety and almost an open secret, was for George to hold the line of the main river while Eugene marched swiftly northwards to join the

Duke of Marlborough in Flanders, and there having combined forces to force a battle on the Duc de Vendôme before he could in turn be reinforced by Berwick. In the event, Eugene was delayed in gathering his full strength, and meanwhile Vendôme sprang into action and seized the key towns of Ghent and Bruges. With the armies of both Berwick and Eugene on the road and heading towards Flanders, the prince rode on ahead, and at his urging Marlborough forced battle on Vendôme and the Duc de Bourgogne close to Allied-held Oudenarde on 11 July 1708, inflicting on them a heavy defeat. The next day, Berwick arrived at Sart le Buissière on the river Sambre, having made good time over difficult country and bad roads. He was dismayed to find that morale amongst the French troops everywhere was dismally low, with almost no attention being given to do anything other than hurriedly garrison scattered and poorly-supported fortresses. Berwick immediately despatched his advanced guard of cavalry to cover Mons, while directing his infantry and trains to Valenciennes as they arrived from the Moselle.

Vendôme and Bourgogne with their battered army lay north of the Ghent-Bruges canal, and no effort was being made to seriously interfere with the increasingly evident move by the Allies to invest and lay siege to Lille. When Berwick's footsore troops arrived from the march, they would effectively constitute the only protection for France that was active and in the field.

> I went post to Tournai, to have the nearer view of the situation of things. There I found a great number of straggling parties of the army . . . Upon a review of them, the whole number at Tournai, Lille, and Ypres, amounted to upwards of nine thousand men, the enemy had made as many prisoners. As it would be some days before my infantry could come up, and the frontier was entirely destitute of troops, I divided these parties among the three places mentioned . . . Monsieur de Vendóme,

> in order to outnumber the enemy, had carried all to the field, scarcely leaving enough behind to guard the gates. I cannot absolutely blame him for this, yet, since 1706, it had always been found that the loss of one battle was followed by that of all Flanders, for want of garrisons.[30]

Louis XIV pressed his commanders to save the city, but Berwick was cautious, acutely aware of the lack of confidence in the French troops after such a humiliating defeat as Oudenarde, and how catastrophic another failure in open battle would prove. Acknowledging that the Allied capture of Lille would be a heavy blow, he nonetheless advised those in Versailles that the effects of the loss of the French field army would be even greater. He even suggested that the place could be recovered at some future point, at no great cost, but the king was not so certain, writing, 'I assure you that it will be easier to save the town under present conditions, than to lay siege to it in enemy hands'.[31] In what continued to be a depressing and dismal campaign, with a marked lack of harmony between Berwick, Bourgogne and Vendôme, all the un-coordinated French efforts predictably failed to prevent the fall of the city and citadel, where the valiant defence of the garrison under the command of Boufflers held out until the second week in December.

Sent back to cover Alsace before the capitulation of the Lille garrison, Berwick went on to take command of the French forces in the Dauphine region in 1709, carrying out a highly effective defensive strategy with shockingly slim resources, the prolonged war effort having drained strength away from all but the critical front in Flanders and northern France. Before undertaking this new assignment, Berwick received a letter from his uncle, the Duke of Marlborough, suggesting that as the omens for a negotiated peace settlement were good, given the general war weariness on all sides, he was willing to use his best endeavours to facilitate the onset of negotiations to bring matters to a close, to mutual satisfaction:

> I received a private letter from the Duke of Marlborough, signifying that the present occasion was a very favourable one, to set on foot a negotiation for peace; that the proposal must be made to the deputies of the States-General [Holland], to Prince Eugene and to him . . . Nothing could be more advantageous than this advice of the Duke of Marlborough; it opened to us an honourable way of putting an end to a burdensome war.[32]

The approach was first outlined to the Duc de Bourgogne, and to minister for war Michel de Chamillart, but the king promptly drew the erroneous conclusion that the state of the Allied armies must be poorer than thought, if such a suggestion had been made in earnest. So, the chance was let to go by, but this may after all have been no more than an illusion, and rather predictably the war trundled on. In any case, Marlborough in taking this initiative, had plainly exceeded his authority, and made aware of this, he soon anxiously asked that the letter be returned to him for burning.

Matters were not at all promising on Berwick's arrival in the Dauphine. 'My first attention was to examine the state of the magazines, and I found that far from having a sufficiency for the whole campaign, there was not enough for the daily subsistence of the troops till the end of May . . . the want of money was another great difficulty.'[33] Using Briançon as the central pivot of his defensive scheme, Berwick deftly kept the Savoyard and Imperial forces facing him at bay. While doing so he was able to send some 10,000 troops to campaign elsewhere on France's threatened borders, and his arrangements were so effective to be able to write to Louis XIV at the close of the year that, 'Your Majesty may rest assured the enemy will affect nothing against this frontier'.[34] While matters proceeded apace in the Low Countries, where Marlborough and Eugene strove to break through the French fortress belt, and in Spain where Vendôme's efforts were proving highly successful, Berwick adeptly continued to keep the Dauphine frontier calm and secure.

Created Duc de Fitz-James in the French peerage in 1710, Berwick arranged to settle the title, when he died, on his second son, as the eldest boy, the Duc de Liria (Earl of Tynmouth), would inherit the substantial Spanish estates already granted to Berwick by a grateful Philip V. Four years' later, despite ill-health, as the war for the throne of Spain stumbled to an untidy end, he left Versailles in June 1714 to take command of the French and Spanish forces operating against the Catalans in and around Barcelona, doggedly maintaining their allegiance to Emperor Charles, the Austrian claimant in the dispute (who in any case had taken the Imperial throne on the death of his older brother, Joseph, in 1712). Berwick arrived at Perpignan on 30 June, and learned that he had been appointed Generalissimo of the Spanish army by Philip V. Berwick proceeded with some reluctance, as he felt that the uncompromising attitude of the king and his minsters in Madrid had left the Catalans, all but abandoned now by their erstwhile allies, with little option but to continue to resist.

> If the ministers and the generals of the king of Spain had been more moderate in their language, Barcelona would have capitulated immediately after the departure of the Imperialists [in 1713], but as they talked of nothing else publicly but of sackings and executions, the people became furious and desperate.[35]

Berwick arrived before Barcelona on 7 July, and despite troublesome Catalan forces under the able Marqués de Peral threatening the flanks and rear of the besieging French and Spanish troops, a firm blockade was established and the breaching batteries, eighty heavy guns and mortars, could get to work on demolishing the city's defences.

Progress was slow and expensive, and Berwick recalled that, 'It was very difficult to find out how one could make oneself master of the town. . . . I armed myself with patience against all the discourses of the officers of the army, who grew very much tired with the length of the siege.'[36] A generous offer to accept a negotiated submission was refused by the Catalan garrison, but despite a valiant and hard-fought defence, particularly at the bastion of San Pedro, which was taken, lost and re-taken no fewer than eleven times.[37] Barcelona capitulated in the second week of September 1714. Berwick refused a request to grant good terms to the defeated garrison, as he had been obliged in the end to mount a major and costly assault. 'I answered that it was now too late; that we were already masters of the city, and had it in our power to put everything to the sword, and I should not therefore listen to any proposals on this part, except as submitting at discretion to his Most Catholic Majesty, and of imploring his mercy.'[38]

However, there was to be no sack of the place, as 'I promised them their lives would be safe, and even that there be no plunder'.[39] Time would show that this was a hollow promise, one that he could not keep, although in the meantime the discipline in his army held up very well. No lasting guarantee could be given that Philip V would not enact stringent measures against the Catalans for having held out against him for so long. Berwick returned to Madrid on 28 October, to a warm welcome from the king, with his son, Tynmouth, receiving the prestigious Order of the Golden Fleece and formally acknowledged as the heir to the ducal estates of Xerica and Liria. His stepson, the 2nd Earl of Lucan, received an appointment as captain to the Spanish Guards.

On 26 November 1714 Berwick arrived back at Versailles, and with the recent death of Queen Anne in London, hopes for what some rather whimsically felt to be a long overdue Jacobite restoration were revived. Berwick even felt confident enough to write that, 'The majority of the English nation is so well affected that we may venture to say five out of six are for the king [James Stuart, his half-brother]'.[40] Whether this was really so may be disputed, and a great deal of wishful thinking was being displayed, but in any event the accession to the throne in London by Elector George of Hanover was swiftly accomplished, with much chatter but little informed comment or effective resistance. Little could be achieved by James' supporters without the deployment of armed forces in substantial numbers, and an ailing Louis XIV would not supply them for what had every appearance of a fool's errand. An odd proposal to use Swedish troops in the venture rather inevitably came to nothing as King Charles XII was still actively involved in his interminable quarrels with Russia and much of northern Germany, most notably perhaps with Hanover.

The 'Pretender', James, suggested that his half-brother accompany him to Scotland as his captain-general, to assist the Earl of Mar in an attempted 'Rising', but Berwick refused as that would mean effectively deserting the French service to which he had declared allegiance and was now entirely devoting his energies. The resulting strain between the two half-brothers was plain, and a rather world-weary Berwick wrote with some bitterness that: 'We ought always to wish him well, and even render him service, but it is out of principles of honour, and we are not obliged to abandon all our establishments, and leave our children to starve, for his projects or fancy.'[41] Time would erase the simmering resentment over the whole affair, and the two would eventually be partly reconciled, although James Stuart never quite forget what he saw as Berwick's desertion of his cause, at a critical, and perhaps briefly promising, moment.

Louis XIV having died in the summer of 1715, Berwick was appointed by the regent, the Duc d'Orleans, in April the following year to take up the command in the Guyenne, although he declined a simultaneous appointment to also command in the Languedoc. An initial difficulty was that he would be under the *de facto* authority of the Duc du Maine, one of the late king's illegitimate sons, and this had to be resolved as it was not acceptable to Berwick. Amongst his private concerns at this time was the rather wayward career of his stepson, who had without notifying his stepfather given up his service to Philip V in Madrid and was now looking to make his fortune elsewhere. Berwick wrote on 17 April 1717: 'I know nothing of what Lord Lucan designs to do; it may very well be that he has had a mind to go as a volunteer to Hungary, as many others [but] he is not in a condition to find money for such a journey.'[42] Had it been otherwise, Lucan might well have fought under Prince Eugene at both the Peterwardein victory, and the capture of Belgrade from the Ottomans the following year. Peace, of a fragile kind, had come to western Europe, welcome to most indeed, but inevitably many soldiers now lacked employment, and hoped to make their fortunes with the blade elsewhere. Lucan's actions, therefore, were not all that surprising.

When hostilities between Spain and France broke out in January 1719, with the coming of the War of the Quadruple Alliance, Berwick's 20,000-strong army, in a brief and very well-handled campaign in that summer and autumn, took the key towns of Fonterrabia, San Sebastien and Urgel, before unseasonal bad weather intervened. That Philip V and his second wife, Elizabeth (née Farnese), had overstepped their powers was evident, and their dangerous ambitions had to be firmly dealt with. Surprisingly the Basque provinces grandees indicated that they would willingly accept French overlordship, if their ancient rights were guaranteed, but Berwick was not interested in such things, being beyond the scope of the orders he had been given. He also had trouble with his wayward commander of cavalry, the Prince de Conti, who was pithily described as 'Haughty and impetuous, suspicious, and a great drunkard'.[43] 'That Berwick's son, James-Francis, Duke of Liria, was at the time prominently employed in the Spanish service was not allowed to complicate matters, and he wrote with sound fatherly advice: 'Always obey the king [Philip V] and his ministers, and avoid all intrigue. I am doing the same.'[44] The following year Berwick was appointed to serve as a member of the council of regency led by the Duc d'Orleans, while still holding the command of French forces in much of the south of the country, and in June 1724[45] he was amongst a number made Chevalier of the Order of St Esprit by the young Louis XV, and became governor of Strasbourg in 1730. In those idle moments left to him, he became avidly interested in gardening, and devoted more and more time to the management of his estates and compiling his lengthy memoirs.

With the outbreak of hostilities in the War of the Polish Succession in 1730, Berwick was given the command of the French forces on the middle Rhine, and deftly seized the Imperial-held fortress of Kehl, across the river from Strasbourg. He was, however, disappointed to find that the preparations for new operations had been inadequate, particularly with regard to the proper supply of horses, and made his views known plainly to Versailles. He would never see this lack remedied, for suddenly, and in highly dramatic fashion, his end came swiftly early in the morning on 12 June 1734 while at the siege of Philippsburg. Berwick was neatly decapitated by a stray round-shot, while standing in an exposed sapping position that he had been warned was particularly risky. 'The sap was advanced but not the trenches . . . In vain did they represent to him the danger to which he exposed himself, considering the great fire of the besieged . . . he was killed by a cannonball.'[46] In fact, whether the deadly projectile came from an Imperial or a French battery was never really known for sure, and if the latter, was a notable instance certainly of blue-on-blue casualties. 'The death of this illustrious general, whom France will forever rank among her great commanders, was not only lamented by all the officers and soldiers, but by the whole kingdom . . . He resembled Marshal Turenne, even in the manner of his death.'[47]

Marshal Villars, campaigning in Italy and hobbling about still with his painfully mangled leg from the Malplaquet wound, envied his old friend this sudden release from earthly woes, remarking that he had always been lucky: 'Cette homme a toujour été heureux.'[48] In his will, James FitzJames, Duke of Berwick, English-born but akin to being a French hero, asked to be buried when his time came next to his first-born son, James, who had died in 1721, in the English Benedictine Convent in Paris, but it is not certain that his wishes were ever carried out.

Appendix 1

The Marshals of France during the Reign of King Louis XIV

(Date of appointment given in brackets. Those Marshals featured in this book are in bold.)

Nicolas de l'Hopital, Duc de Vitry (1617) d.1644
Honore d'Albert d'Ailly, Duc de Chaulnes (1620) d.1649
Jacques Nompar de Caumont, Duc de la Force (1621) d.1652
François, Marquis de Bassompierre (1622) d.1646
Gaspar de Coligny, Duc de Chatillon (1622) d.1646
François Annibal, Duc d'Estrees (1626) d.1670
Timoleon d'Epinay de St-Luc (1627) d.1644
Urbain de Maille, Marquis de Breze (1633) d.1650
Charles de Shomberg, Duc de Halluin (1637) d.1656
Charles de la Porte, Marquis de Meilleraye (1639) d.1664
Antoine, Duc de Grammont (1641) d.1678
Jean-Baptiste, Comte de Guabriant (1642) d.1643
Philippe de la Motte, Duc de Cardona, (1642) d.1657
François, Comte de Rosnay, (1643) d.1660
Henri de la Tour d'Auvergne, Vicomte de Turenne (1643), Marshal-General (1660) d.1675
Jean, Comte de Gassion (1643) d.1647
Caesar, Duc de Choiseul (1645) d.1675
Josias, Comte de Rantzau (1645) d.1650
Nicolas de Neufville, Duc de Villeroi (1646) d.1685

Antoine, Duc d'Aumont (1651) d.1669
Jacques d'Etampes, Marquis de la Ferté-Imberty (1651) d.1663
Henri, Duc de la Ferté-Sennetiere (1651) d.1681
Charles de Mouchy, Marquis d'Hocquincourt (1651) d.1658
Jacques Rouxel, Comte de Grancey, (1651) d.1680
Armand de Caumont, Duc de la Force (1652) d.1672
Philippe de Clerambault, Comte de la Palluau (1652) d.1665
Caesar d'Albret, Comte de Miossens (1653) d.1676
Louis de Foucault, Comte de le Daugnon (1653) d.1659
Jean de Schulemberg, Comte de Montejeu (1658) d.1671
Abraham de Fabert, Marquis de Esternay (1658) d.1662
Jacques de Mauvisière, Marquis de Castelnau (1658) d.1658
Bernardin Gigault, Marquis de Bellefonds (1668) d.1694
François de Créquy, Marquis de Marines (1668) d.1687
Louis de Crevant, Duc d'Humières (1668) d.1694
Godefroy d'Estrades, Comte de Estrades (1675) d.1686
Philippe de Montau-Benac, Duc de Navailles (1675) d.1684
Frederic Armand, Duc de Schomberg (1675) d.1690
Jacques Henri de Dufort, Duc de Duras (1675) d.1704
François d'Aubusson, Duc de la Feuillade (1675) d.1691
Louis Victor de Rochechouart, Duc de Montmart, Marshal de Vivonne (1675) d.1688
François Henri de Montmorency, Duc de Luxembourg (1675) d.1695
Henri Louis d'Aloigny, Marquis de Rochefort (1675) d.1676
Guy de Durfort, Duc de Lorges (1676) d.1702
Jean, Comte d'Estrees (1681) d.1707
Claude de Choiseul, Marquis de Francières (1693) d.1711
Jean Armand de Joyeuse, Marquis de Grandpre (1693) d.1710
François de Boufflers, Duc de Boufflers (1693) d.1711
Louis-François de Neufville, Duc de Villeroi (1693) d.1730
Anne-Hilarion de Costentin, Comte de Tourville (1693) d.1701

Anne-Jules, Duc de Noailles (1693) d.1708
Nicolas Catinat (1693) d.1712
Louis-Joseph de Bourbon, Duc de Vendôme (1695) d.1712
Claude-Louis-Hector, Duc de Villars (1702) Marshal-General (1733) d.1734
Noel Bouton, Marquis de Chamilly (1703) d.1715
Victor Marie- Duc d'Estrees (1703) d.1737
François Louis Rousselet, Marquis de Chatenau-Renault (1703) d.1716
Sebastien le Prestre, Marquis de Vauban (1703) d.1707
Conrad, Marquis de Rozen (1703) d.1715
Nicolas Chalon de Ble, Marquis de Huxelles (1703) d.1730
René de Froulay, Comte de Tessé (1703) d.1725
Camille d'Hostun, Duc de Tallard (1703) d.1728
Nicolas Auguste de la Beaune, Marquis de Montrevel (1703) d.1716
Henri, Duc d'Harcourt (1703) d.1718
Ferdinand, Comte de Marsin (1703) d.1706
Alberico Cybo-Malaspina, Duc de Massa (1703) d.1715
James FitzJames, Duke of Berwick (1706) d.1734
Charles Auguste Goyon, Comte de Matignon (1708) d.1729
Jacques de Bazin, Marquis de Bezons (1709) d.1733
Pierre de Montesquiou, Comte d'Artagnan (1709) d.1725

Appendix 2

The Holy Roman Empire

Reference with often be found in the text to the 'Empire', to 'Imperial troops', the 'Imperial court' and so forth, so it may be helpful to explain simply (for what is a rather complex subject) what the Holy Roman Empire was comprised of in the late seventeenth and early eighteenth centuries.

The Holy Roman Empire, as it stood at the accession of King Louis XIV in 1667, was in effect a relic of the early mediaeval regime, created with papal approval, under Emperor Charlemagne, but which had progressively become largely a body of Germanic states who maintained a theoretical historic link to the 'old' Roman empire. By long tradition, the role of emperor was held by a member of the Austrian branch of the House of Habsburg, whose court lay in Vienna in Austria, but the Holy Roman Empire is not to be confused with the quite separate Austrian empire, which was growing in the east as the power and influence of the Ottomans lessened, particularly after the defeat of the sultan's army at Zenta in Hungary in 1697.

The Empire was divided into ten 'circles' for administrative convenience, and these circles comprised Austria, Bavaria, Swabia, Franconia, the Upper Rhine, the Lower Rhine, Burgundy, Westphalia, Lower Saxony and Upper Saxony. Within these circles, the individual rulers had almost complete control of their own affairs, although tacitly acknowledging the over-arching authority of the emperor in Vienna. There was inevitably, a degree of friction between the self-confident German nobles and the Imperial court in Vienna, whose best interests did not always seem to align that well. States such as

Brandenburg (Prussia), Saxony and Bavaria often considered their own interests as not being those of the empire as seen from Vienna. Still, that the Holy Roman Empire saw at least a part of its historic mission to hold back burgeoning French ambitions along the course of the river Rhine, provided a measure of reassurance that was not to be lightly cast away. That Vienna also resisted, with varying degrees of success, the Ottomans in the east, was an additional factor, although this sometimes appeared to the German states to be of passing interest only and more of a concern for Austria alone.

> The emperor could neither wage war, make alliances, nor conclude peace on behalf of the empire without their consent. They were not bound to provide him with an army, nor with any significant amount of money [but] the princes were free to contract alliances as they saw fit, provided that these were not contrary to the interests of the empire as a whole.

The elective process for the supreme role of Holy Roman Emperor was in the hands of the principal rulers (the electors) in the empire, and these comprised an electoral college, made up of the Prince-Archbishops of Cologne, Mainz and Trier, the King of Bohemia (a Habsburg), the Count Palatine, the Elector of Bavaria, the Duke of Saxony, and the Elector of Brandenburg. The Elector of Hanover would join this body in time, in exchange for a large bribe to Vienna.

The emperor's eldest son customarily held the courtesy title of King of the Romans, and his accession to the Imperial throne, on the death of the incumbent, was a forgone event, with the electors, in effect, nodding him through. The jealously-protected rights and privileges of the electors would have to be re-confirmed on each occasion, all the same. Archduke Joseph had this privilege but his younger brother, Charles, not having been made King of the Romans, did not.

Notes

Preface

1. Cronin, V., *Louis XIV*, 1964, p. 134.
2. Ibid., p. 117.
3. Trevelyan, M., *William III and the Defence of Holland*, 1930, p. 147.
4. Baxter, D., *Servants of the Sword, French Intendants of the Army, 1630-1670*, 1976, p. 206. The power that these civilian functionaries wielded, by virtue of their administrative skills and acumen, together with the backing provided by Louis XIV's astute ministers for war, was remarkable.
5. Lynn, J., *The Wars of Louis XIV, 1667-1714*, 1999, p. 133.
6. Baxter, D. *Servants of the Sword*, p. 169.
7. Ibid., p. 207.
8. Wolf, J., *Louis XIV*, 1968, p. 481.
9. Cronin, p. 164.

Introduction: The Sun King's Wars

1. The neatly contrived legal 'cover' for Louis XIV's invasion of the Spanish (Southern) Netherlands was that, under a long-standing but largely defunct custom in Flanders, a child of a first parent should inherit before any child of a second parent did so. Accordingly, as Marie-Thérèse was the daughter of King Philip IV's first wife, it was held that she should take precedence over the claim of her half-brother, Carlos, who was the son of the late Spanish king's second wife. Louis XIV could add to that the rather thin argument of the non-payment by her father of the enormous dowry. See Ashley, M., *Louis XIV and the Greatness of France*, 1946, p. 58 for interesting comments on this complex argument.
2. Ibid., p. 82.
3. Louis XIV proposed that the island of Walcheren be given to England in return for overt support for his war against the Dutch. See Ashley, p. 83, for details on this rather curious suggestion.
4. Petrie, C., *Louis XIV*, 1938. p. 172.
5. Ibid., p. 175.
6. Wolf, p. 222.
7. Ibid., p. 203.
8. The young John Churchill, who would in time become the 1st Duke of Marlborough, served at the French siege of Maastricht with one of the English regiments lent by King

Charles II (for a large consideration) to Louis XIV in his war with the Dutch. Churchill fought alongside James, Duke of Monmouth, who he would defeat at the Battle of Sedgemoor in 1685 during the duke's ill-fated rebellion against his uncle, James II. Louis XIV was impressed by Churchill's conduct during the siege, and offered him a commission in the French army, but this was refused, as it would entail him having to convert to Catholicism, which he was unwilling to do.

9. The German states, the margravates, duchies, archbishoprics, principalities and so on, were constituent parts of the Holy Roman Empire, owing titular allegiance to the emperor in Vienna, by long tradition always a Habsburg. Emperor Leopold I saw himself as the protector of those states, even though many of their leaders had happily accepted offers of French gold to stay out of the war with the Dutch (gold that was seldom forthcoming in practice), and when Turenne moved into German territory to engage the Elector of Brandenburg, great offence as taken throughout the empire.
10. Petrie, *Louis XIV*, p. 134.
11. Wolf, p. 260.
12. Ibid., p. 261.
13. Ashley, pp. 127–8. Despite the revocation of the Edict of Nantes, a number of recalcitrant Protestant groups remained in France.
14. Wolf, p. 452.
15. Ashley, p. 151.
16. The causes of the War of the Spanish Succession were complex but the point at question was simple – who should succeed King Carlos II when he was in his grave. The initial 'easy answer' to a tricky problem settled on a young Bavarian prince because when the Spanish Infanta Maria-Theresa married Louis XIV she renounced any pretensions for herself or her children to the throne in Madrid. Emperor Leopold however, had married the queen's younger sister, and she had made no such renunciation. Their one daughter was in time married to the Elector of Bavaria. So, the son of that last union, the young Prince Joseph-Ferdinand of Bavaria, seemed like a valid and fairly neutral choice, and as such broadly acceptable to all. When he died suddenly in Brussels, where his father, Elector Max-Emmanuel, was the Governor-General, there were immediate, but unproven, suspicions that poison had been in play. However, Louis XIV had little relish for the trouble and expense of renewed war in order just to place a French prince of the throne in Madrid, as he had a treasury in a sorry state, and the likelihood is that Joseph-Ferdinand died of natural causes after all.
17. Churchill, W., *Marlborough, His Life & Times*, 1947, Book I, p. 556.
18. Falkner, J., *Marlborough's Wars, Eye-Witness Accounts*, 2005, pp. 102–03. See also, Wace, A., *The Hampshire Regiment*, 1968, p. 75. for a fuller and highly entertaining account of Tom Kitcher's exploits with the bayonet at Ramillies.
19. Despite the encumbrances attending an army on campaign in the late seventeenth century, Marshal de Créquy was noted for his ability to move fast and hit hard.
20. Wolf, p. 651.
21. The soldiers of the day were almost all men who had grown up on the land, before enlistment, and would often, when not otherwise busily employed on military duties, help local farmers with tending crops and herds, and particularly in autumn once the year's campaigning was done, to bring in the harvest in return for a good meal and a draught of ale or cider.

22. Cronin, p. 134.
23. During the War of the Spanish Succession, with French resources stretched, soldiers were drafted (chosen by lot) from the militia into regular service, but this was technically illegal, as the militia was intended for local defence duties only. Much resentment was caused by this illicit practice, and it was widely evaded.

Chapter 1: Marshal Turenne

1. Ramsay, C., *The History of Henri de la Tour d'Auvergne, Viscount de Turenne*, 1740, p. 3.
2. Ibid., p. 9.
3. The fortress of Bois le Duc ('Boiled Duck' to British soldiers in the Great War) was known in the seventeenth century as 'The Maid of Brabant', as it had formerly never been taken by a hostile army.
4. Weygand, P., *Turenne*, 1930, p. 25.
5. Ibid., p. 26.
6. Ibid., p. 28.
7. Prince Thomas, a scion of a junior branch of the Carignan family, was the paternal grandfather of the renowned Imperial commander, the French-born Prince Eugene of Savoy.
8. Wedgwood, C., *The Thirty Years War*, 1938, p. 465.
9. Weygand, *Turenne*, p. 40.
10. Ibid., p. 42.
11. Ibid., p. 44.
12. Ibid., p. 45.
13. Archduke Leopold became Holy Roman Emperor in 1657. His sons, Joseph (1705) and Charles (1712) eventually succeeded him on the Imperial throne in Vienna.
14. Weygand, *Turenne*, p. 49.
15. Ibid., p. 61.
16. Cronin, p. 106.
17. Weygand, *Turenne*, p. 105.
18. Wolf, p. 148
19. Ibid., p. 117.
20. Ibid., p. 154.
21. Ibid., p. 157.
22. Ibid., p. 189.
23. Lynn, *The Wars of Louis XIV, 1667-1714*, p. 23.
24. Weygand, *Turenne*, pp. 200–02.
25. Ibid.
26. Ibid., p. 207.
27. Lynn, *The Wars of Louis XIV, 1667-1714*, p. 129.
28. Ibid., p. 131.
29. Ibid., p. 133.
30. It was widely thought that the bright red cloak worn by the Marquis de St Hilaire had attracted the attention of the Imperial gunners. St Hilaire, also gravely wounded in the incident, only narrowly escaped with his life. The marquis refused to be tended to until it had become evident that Turenne could not be saved.
31. Wolf, p. 244.

32. Cronin, p. 202.
33. Wolf, p. 79.

Chapter 2: Marshal de Fabert

1. Hooper, G., *Marshal Abraham Fabert, His Life and Times*, 1892, p. 64.
2. Ibid., p. 90.
3. La Valette was also known as the Soldier-Cardinal, with a solid reputation as a vigorous campaigner. He was, nonetheless, often at odds with Cardinal Richelieu.
4. Hooper, p. 225.
5. Mazarin's charming nieces all married well, although a degree of scandal lingered over them. One was the mother of Marshal Vendôme, and another was the mother of the famous Imperial commander Prince Eugene of Savoy. See Fraser, A., *Love and Louis XIV*, 2006, for interesting comments on this.
6. The other marshals created by Louis XIV at this time were Castelnau (who was actually lying stricken with a mortal wound sustained at Dunkirk), and Montejeu.
7. Hooper, p. 221.
8. Ibid., p. 241.
9. Ibid., p. 250.
10. Ibid., p. 264.
11. That Fabert's three daughters married so well (and apparently so often), indicates very nicely the degree to which he had risen in a highly competitive society, where rank and breeding meant so much.

Chapter 3: Marshal de Créquy

1. The Battle of Tornavento, in northern Italy, which took place on 22 June 1636, was a particularly hard-fought affair between two armies, French and their Savoyard allies and their Spanish/Italian opponents under the command of the Marques de Leganez, which were of roughly equal size. Both commanders entrenched their troops, and the day was expensive but in effect a tactical draw, with neither side gaining a sure advantage. The Spanish army commander skilfully slipped away unmolested after darkness fell. Accounts of the casualties suffered vary but are generally felt to have been about 3,500 killed and wounded in both armies.
2. François de Créquy would be killed at the Battle of Luzzara in northern Italy in 1702, fighting under the command of the Duc de Vendôme, while his younger brother, Nicolas, had died of a fever during the assault on Tournai in 1696 (some reports say he was killed while serving in the siege works themselves).
3. Baxter, D., *Servants of the Sword*, p. 206.
4. The *Arrière-Ban* was a militia formed from noble families for service at times of urgent need. They were notoriously ill-disciplined, poorly trained and insubordinate. and their use lapsed soon afterwards. See Lynn, *The Wars of Louis XIV*, p. 133.
5. Wolf, pp. 250–1.
6. Ibid. Louvois went on, 'The day passed with several slight skirmishes The Marshal d'Humières returned to join the army with his detachment; Marshal de Créquy returned in the evening to his camp before Bouchain. Monsieur went there the next day.'

7. Lynn, *The Wars of Louis XIV*, p. 146.
8. Wolf, p. 252.
9. Lynn, *The Wars of Louis XIV*, p. 151.
10. Ibid., p. 154.
11. Baxter, *Servants of the Sword*, p. 207.
12. Wolf, pp. 412–13.
13. Falkner, J., *Marshal Vauban and the Defence of Louis XIV's France*, 2012, p. 100. The Prince of Chimay's Spanish/Walloon garrison in Luxembourg were many of them raw and only partly trained, but they nonetheless put up a good fight. See also Rennoldson, C. (ed.), *Renaissance Military Texts, Warfare in the Age of Louis XIV*, 2005, p. 3, for interesting additional comments on this siege.

Chapter 4: Marshal Luxembourg

1. Trevelyan, M., *William III and the Defence of Holland, 1672-1674*, 1930, p. 304.
2. Ibid., p. 209.
3. Ibid., p. 316.
4. Ibid., p. 322.
5. Ibid., p. 325.
6. Ibid., p. 329.
7. Wolf, p. 256.
8. Lynn, *The Wars of Louis XIV 1667-1714*, p. 68.
9. Ibid.
10. Wolf, p. 265.
11. Mitford, N., *The Sun King*, 1966, p. 89.
12. Chandler, D., *The Art of Warfare in the Age of Marlborough*, 1976, p. 52.
13. Wolf, p. 458
14. Chandler, *The Art of Warfare in the Age of Marlborough*, p. 53.
15. Wolf, p. 471. Louis XIV was concerned in particular, at the considerable additional expense of re-equipping his troops with flintlock muskets. He was also quite reluctant to phase out the use of the pike, although it was well known that Austria, under pressure from the Ottomans in the East, had done so in the 1680s.
16. Ibid.
17. St John, B. (ed.), *The Memoirs of the Duke of St Simon*, Vol 1, 1876, p. 53. See also Chandler, *The Art of Warfare in the Age of Marlborough*, p. 202, for additional details.
18. St John, Vol. 1, p. 53.
19. The doughty Dutch Field Deputy, Sicco van Goslinga, visited the battlefield of Landen in 1707, and found it still littered with the bones of many of the fallen.
20. Wolf, p. 474
21. Langallerie, M., *The Memoires of the Marquis de Langallerie*, 1710, p. 34
22. Some reports (St John, Vol. 1, p. 34), say 16 September rather than the 12th.
23. Wolf, p. 474
24. St John, Vol. 1, p. 43.
25. Ashley, p. 157.
26. Wolf, p. 651.
27. St John, Vol. 1, p. 56.

Chapter 5: Marshal Catinat

1. Plantavit de la Pause, G., *Memoirs of the Duc de Villars*, 1830, p. 215.
2. The 'Parlement' in Paris was a powerful and quasi-independent law court, whose increasingly assertive members were often at odds with the crown.
3. The Chevaux-Légers were not, despite their title, true light cavalry, but just those who did not wear armour, other than a helmet.
4. De Broglie, E., *Catinat, l'Homme et la Vie, 1637-1712*, 1902, pp. 9–10. Some accounts have it that the young Catinat enlisted in the Gardes Françaises, but de Broglie is firm that this was a subsequent appointment from the king, after the elder brother had been killed before Lille.
5. A 'hornwork' was a powerful position pushed forward of the main defences of a city or fortress.
6. De Broglie, p. 12.
7. The price Louis XIV paid for the fortress of Casale was 1 million livres (100,000 pistoles), plus the payment of an annual subsidy to the Duke of Mantua.
8. Lynn, *The Wars of Louis XIV, 1667-1714*, p. 181.
9. De Broglie, p. 47.
10. Ibid., p. 49.
11. Paoletti, C., *William III's Italian Ally*, 2019, pp. 90–2.
12. De Broglie, pp. 86–7.
13. Ibid., p. 87.
14. Ibid., pp. 89–90.
15. Savoy-Piedmont was always in a precarious position, lodged as it was between the threat of the French King in expansionist mood to the west, and the Austrians, with their aspirations to secure much of northern Italy, to the east. That Duke Victor-Amadeus II, in particular, would ally himself alternately to Versailles and then Vienna, illustrates the necessity, as it was seen in Turin, of the need to secure a balance of influence, and a measure of protection, when faced with crushing odds.
16. De Broglie, p. 106.
17. Ibid.
18. Ibid., p. 108.
19. Ibid., pp. 135–6.
20. Ibid., p. 115.
21. Catinat was unsure how to respond to the numerous letters of congratulation he received on being made a marshal. Some thought his tone too brusque and aloof, while others, mostly other marshals it should be said, thought his tone too humble for one of such elevated rank.
22. Wolf, p. 475.
23. De Broglie, p. 154.
24. Ibid.
25. Lynn, *The Wars of Louis XIV, 1667-1714*, p. 27.
26. De Broglie, p. 173.
27. Lazard, P., *Vauban, 1633-1707*, 1934, p. 273.
28. De Broglie, pp. 197–8.
29. St John, Vol 1, p. 191.

30. Ibid.
31. De Broglie, p. 196. The march made by Prince Eugene to turn the flank of the French position at Castiglioni was a remarkable feat, made over mountainous country and in poor weather. The prince also ignored protests from neutral Venice that he had, in part, crossed their territory to close with Catinat. Eugene was also apparently aware that Catinat had strict orders not to violate Venetian territory, and so would be hindered from observing, or attempting to block, his approach march.
32. Shoberl, F. (tr.), *Memoirs of Prince Eugene of Savoy*, 1811, p. 37.
33. Wolf, p. 516.
34. De Broglie, p. 202.
35. St John, Vol 1, p. 192.
36. De Broglie, p. 217.
37. St John, Vol 1, p. 192.
38. De Broglie, p. 220.
39. St John, Vol 1, p. 192.
40. Falkner, J., *The War of the Spanish Succession, 1701-1714*, 2015, p. 18. See also Shoberl, p. 65.
41. Falkner, p. 260.
42. St John, Vol 1, p. 244.
43. Ibid., p. 245.
44. De Broglie, p. 288.
45. Treasure, G., *Seventeenth Century France*, 1967, p. 272.
45. St John, Vol. 2, p. 231.
47. Falkner, J., *Prince Eugene of Savoy*, 2022, p. 33.

Chapter 6: Marshal Boufflers

1. Louis XIV pressed Boufflers to mount an attack on Ostend, but he was reluctant, and the king eventually gave way. 'I am convinced that you have as much desire as I have to do something advantageous to the state and glorious to yourself . . . that is why I praise above all your wisdom. I take great pleasure in giving command of my armies to men enough in control of themselves to prefer the good of the state to my advantage or their fame . . . I am well satisfied with you and the sincerity with which you have spoken, continue to do the same.' See Wolf, p. 469.
2. St John, Vol. 1, p. 7.
3. Ibid.
4. Chandler, *The Art of Warfare in the Age of Marlborough*, p. 100.
5. General John Cutts was nicknamed 'the Salamander' for his liking of being in the hottest fire.
6. Lynn, *The Wars of Louis XIV, 1667-1714*, p. 250. Lynn says some 18,000–20,000 were killed or wounded. David Chandler largely agrees, putting the toll at 18,000, see *The Art of Warfare in the Age of Marlborough*, p. 308.
7. Clark, G., *The Later Stuarts*, 1934, p. 173.
8. Chandler, *The Art of Warfare in the Age of Marlborough*, p. 270.
9. Childs, J., *The Nine Years War*, 1991, p. 40.
10. Wolf, p. 483.
11. Cronin, p. 257.

12. Langallerie, p. 53. See also, Mitford, N., *The Sun King*, 1966, p. 177.
13. St John, Vol. 1, p.127.
14. Chandler, *The Art of Warfare in the Age of Marlborough*, p. 107.
15. St John, Vol. 2. p. 130.
16. Wolf, p. 606.
17. Chandler, *The Art of Warfare in the Age of Marlborough*, p. 232.
18. Lynn, *The Wars of Louis XIV, 1667-1714*, p. 280.
19. Chandler, D (ed.), *Military Memoirs, Captain Robert Parker and the Comte de Merode-Westerloo*, 1968, p. 153.
20. St John, Vol. 2, p. 36.
21. Ibid., pp. 40–1.
22. Petrie, C., *The Marshal Duke of Berwick*, 1953, pp. 232–3.
23. St John, Vol. 2, p. 50.
24. Ibid., p. 109.
25. Wolf, p. 568.
26. Norton, L., *First Lady of Versailles*, 1978, p. 314.
27. St John, Vol. 2, p. 111.
28. Ibid., p. 166.

Chapter 7: Marshal Villeroi

1. The Duc de Gesvres, on one occasion, picked an argument with Villeroi over their respective humble family origins, 'Gesvres annoyed the Marechal de Villeroi', as the Duc de St Simon recalled, 'What did our fathers spring from? From tradesmen, yours was the son of a dealer in fish in the markets, and mine was a peddler, or perhaps worse. The king had to step in and put an end to the resulting unseemly quarrel which was [becoming] the talk of the court'. St John, Vol. 1, p. 150.
2. Wolf, pp. 481–2.
3. St John, Vol. 2, p. 69.
4. Ibid., p. 71.
5. Wolf, p. 655.
6. Ibid., p. 516.
7. Chandler, D., *The Art of Warfare in the Age of Marlborough*, p. 100.
8. McKay, D., *Prince Eugene of Savoy*, 1977, p. 60.
9. Wolf, pp. 517–18.
10. Ibid.
11. St John, Vol. 2, p. 193.
12. Ibid., p. 195.
13. Ibid.
14. Ibid., pp. 195–6.
15. St John, Vol. 2, p. 198.
16. Some reports have it that the detention lasted six months. See Lynn, *The Wars of Louis XIV, 1667-1714*, p. 280.
17. Ibid.
18. Wolf, p. 656.
19. Churchill, Vol I, p. 655.

20. Chandler, D (ed.), *Military Memoirs*, p. 26.
21. The caution shown by the French King in 1705, writing to Villeroi not to attempt an open battle with its attendant risks – 'The situation in Flanders requires great precautions on your part to avoid having a combat forced on you' – had quite changed by the following spring. See Wolf, p. 540.
22. Ibid., pp. 541–3.
23. St John, Vol. 1, p. 319.
24. Ibid., p. 338.
25. Wolf, p. 554.
26. St John, Vol. 1, p. 339.
27. Wolf, p. 657.
28. St John, Vol. 1, p. 341.
29. Ibid., Vol. 3, p. 348.
30. Ibid., p. 361.
31. Ibid., p. 357.

Chapter 8: Marshal Vendôme

1. Mitford, p. 87.
2. Norton, *First Lady at Versailles*, p. 280.
3. Norton, L. (ed.), *St Simon at Versailles*, 1980, p. 100.
4. Mitford, p. 77.
5. St John, Vol. 1, pp. 138–9. The Duc de St Simon, in his very entertaining account of the court and circle of Louis XIV, expressed his dislike and disapproval of Vendôme and his conduct in strident terms. He perhaps overstated things, his prejudice getting better of his judgement: the marshal was certainly a brawler, but not uncouth all the same, although his personal habits were not of the most refined. The Comte de Merode-Westerloo famously refused to go to his quarters again, having once found Vendôme sitting on his commode while issuing orders to his officers. See Chandler, *Military Memoirs*, for a fuller account of the occasion. Louis XIV, while highly fastidious, tolerated him and his ways on account of his royal lineage, added to his undoubted prowess as an army commander, who enjoyed wide popularity both with the troops and the public generally.
6. Colonel De La Colonie incorrectly gives the date of the capitulation as 18 July. See Horsley W. (tr & ed.), *Chronicles of an Old Campaigner*, 1904, p. 51,
7. St John, Vol. 1, p. 321.
8. Wolf, p. 529.
9. Ibid.
10. Chartrand, R., *Louis XIV's Army*, 1988, p. 13.
11. St Simon, who was not at all impartial, remembered the Grand Prior, Philippe de Vendôme, to be a 'liar, swindler and thief; a rogue to the marrow of his bones'. See St John, Vol. 1, p. 322.
12. Ibid., p. 335.
13. Ibid.
14. Langallerie, p. 292.
15. Philippe Duc d'Orleans, nephew to Louis XIV, wounded in the hand at the siege of Turin in 1706, would become the Regent of France on the old king's death in 1715, and during the minority of his infant great-grandson, the young Louis XV.

16. Lynn, *The Wars of Louis XIV, 1667-1714*, p. 309.
17. Norton, *First Lady at Versailles*, p. 257.
18. Ibid.
19. Norton (ed.), *St Simon at Versailles*, pp. 100–01.
20. Petrie, *The Marshal Duke of Berwick*, p. 227.
21. St John, Vol. 2, p. 26.
22. Ibid., p. 31.
23. Mitford, p. 218.
24. Norton, *First Lady at Versailles*, pp. 270–1.
25. Ibid., p. 278.
26. Ibid., p. 281.
27. Ibid., p. 271.
28. St John, Vol. 2, p. 37.
29. Wolf, pp. 556–7.
30. St John, Vol. 2, p. 69.
31. Norton (ed.), *St Simon at Versailles*, p. 134.
32. St John, Vol. 2, p. 149.
33. Ibid., p. 150.
34. Ibid., p. 157.
35. Lynn, *The Wars of Louis XIV, 1667-1714*, p. 340.
36. Ibid., p. 341.
37. St John, Vol. 2, p. 157.
38. Ibid., pp. 237–8.
39. Ibid. Philippe, the Grand Prior, like his older brother, had no children either, and so, accordingly, the line stretching all the way back to King Henry IV and his mistress died out.

Chapter 9: Marshal Villars

1. De la Pause, G., *The Memoirs of the Duc de Villars*, 1735, p. 191.
2. Ibid., p. 193.
3. Ibid., p. 207.
4. Ibid., p. 208.
5. Ibid., p. 212.
6. Ibid., p. 218.
7. Ibid., pp. 221–2.
8. Ibid., p. 212.
9. Ibid., p. 233.
10. Ibid., p. 247.
11. Ibid., p. 249.
12. Ibid., p. 263.
13. Ibid., p. 272.
14. Ibid., pp. 377–8.
15. Sturgill, C., *Marshal Villars in the War of the Spanish Succession*, 1965, p. 22.
16. T'Hopf, B. (ed.), *The Marlborough-Hiensius Correspondence, 1702-1711*, 1951, p. 55.
17. Marshal Villars was understandably concerned at reports of the indiscreet behaviour of his lively young wife at court, while he was away on campaign.

18. Wolf, p. 528.
19. Ibid., p. 532.
20. Ashley, p. 191.
21. Lynn, *The Wars of Louis XIV, 1667-1714*, pp. 297–8.
22. Langallerie, pp. 264–5.
23. St John, Vol. 1, p. 319.
24. One of the earlier battles of the Franco-Prussian War was fought at Wissembourg in 1870.
25. The Margrave of Baden still suffered from the musket-ball wound to his foot received at the Schellenberg battle in early July 1704. This refused to heal properly and led indirectly to his death in 1708.
26. St John, Vol. 1, p. 382.
27. Lynn, *The Wars of Louis XIV, 1667-1714*, p. 57.
28. Ibid., p. 329
29. Ibid., p. 330.
30. Amongst the more unreasonable demands made of Louis IV by the Allies was a requirement that he use his own on troops to remove his grandson from the throne in Madrid, if the young man refused to go. A number of key French fortresses were, in the meantime, to be handed over as surety that the French king would do what was demanded of him. It was perhaps inevitable that this would be refused by Louis XIV, but the Allies were too blind to see it. The king discussed the conditions demanded by the Allies, at the only formal Council of War called throughout his long reign. See Norton, *First Lady at Versailles*, p. 312.
31. Sautai, M., *La Bataille de Malplaquet*, 1910, p. 35.
32. Accounts of the casualties suffered at the Battle of Malplaquet in 1709 vary widely, but what is not in doubt is the those in the Allied army led by Eugene and Marlborough were significantly higher than those in the French army. The day, however, was not a victory for the French, as Villars fought to save Mons, and in that endeavour he failed. French surgeons provided an iron brace to support Villars' mangled knee joint, but he found it cumbersome and only used it for a short time.
33. T'Hof, pp. 463–4.
34. Wolf, p. 569.
35. Ibid.
36. Ibid., p. 572. Sturgill, unlike Wolf, has it that the fortress of Douai was given up without express permission from Louis XIV, see *Villars in the War of the Spanish Succession*, 1969, p. 103.
37. Cronin, pp. 332–3.
38. Lynn, *The Wars of Louis XIV, 1667-1714*, p. 354.
39. Sturgill, p. 148.
40. The Comte de Toulouse proved to be an able naval commander, and badly mauled the Allied fleet at the Battle of Malaga, shortly after the capture of Gibraltar by the Allies in 1704.

Chapter 10: Marshal Tallard

1. Mitford, p. 189.
2. Wolf, p. 497.
3. Petrie, *Louis XIV*, p. 275.

4. Wolf, p. 531.
5. Stoye, J., *Marsigli's Europe, 1689-1730*, 1994, p. 229.
6. The unfortunate Imperial commander in Breisach, Baron Philippe d'Arco, was executed by the public headsman on 18 February 1704, for having given up the indefensible fortress too lightly, when his totally impracticable orders had been to resist to the utmost. His deputy, Count Luigi Marsigli, with whom he was not on the best terms, was pardoned, although dismissed from the emperor's service. See Stoye, p. 248.
7. David Chandler says that Tallard had some 8,000 troops, but this must in all likelihood be an error given the reported number of casualties suffered by the French. See Chandler, *The Art of Warfare in the Age of Marlborough*, p. 302.
8. Wolf, p. 534. Tallard's reported short-sightedness apparently played a significant part in his inability to grip the battle as the Duke of Marlborough's attack mounted in intensity. In particular, his inexplicable failure to rectify the Marquis de Clerambault's error in packing too many infantrymen into Blindheim village, where they could not effectively operate to any degree, may be attributed to this physical limitation. In addition, the unexpected repulse of the elite Gendarmerie squadrons early in the battle appears to have unsettled the composure of the marshal at a critical moment.
9. Trevelyan, G., *Select Documents for Queen Anne's Reign*, 1929, p. 100.
10. Lynn, *The Wars of Louis XIV 1667-1714*, p. 290
11. St John, Vol. 1, pp. 295–6.
12. Churchill, book 1, p. 893.
13. Lynn, *The Wars of Louis XIV, 1667-1714*, p. 283.
14. Langallerie, pp. 247–8. See also Trevelyan, p. 120 for interesting comments by the Marquis de Montigny-Languet, on the parched state of the Nebel stream during the battle.
15. St John, Vol. 1, pp. 289–91.
16. Coxe had it that the young man was mortally wounded at Ramillies in 1706, see Coxe, W., *Memoirs of the Duke of Marlborough*, 1848, Vol I , p. 417, 'A son of Marshal Tallard, who was mortally wounded'. The Earl of Orkney, the commander of the British infantry at Ramillies, however, wrote on 24 May 1706 that 'We had two very young gentlemen prisoners with us . . . Both of them of great quality – a nephew of Marshal Luxembourg and Marshal Tallard's only son'. No mention is made of the young Tallard being wounded or injured. See Trevelyan, p. 41. Lediard also refers to him only being taken prisoner, see Lediard, T., *Memoirs of the Duke of Marlborough*, 1736, vol II., p. 22.
17. The grand Hotel de Bretonvilliers, once the Paris home of Marshal Tallard, was demolished in the 1840s.

Chapter 11: Marshal Vauban

1. Halevy, D., *Vauban, Builder of Fortresses*, 1924, p. 117.
2. Hebbert, F., and Rothrock, G., *Soldier of France, Sebastien le Prestre de Vauban*, 1990, p. 18.
3. Vauban, although he had served as a cadet when young, and presumably had benefited from the experience, was sceptical of the real value of such appointments. The post of Marechal de Logis was akin to that of Company Quartermaster.
4. Hebbert & Rothrock, p. 96.

5. Blomfield, R., *Sebastien le Prestre de Vauban, 1633-1707*, 1938, p. 11.
6. Halevy., pp. 68–9.
7. Ibid., p. 35.
8. Ibid., p. 41.
9. Hebbert and Rothrock, p. 65.
10. Halevy, p. 41.
11. Lynn, *The Wars of Louis XIV, 1664-1714*, p. 120. Vauban's innovative use of parallel trenches to disguise the main intended point of an attack, quite a novelty in western Europe at the time (although commonly practised by highly-skilled Ottoman engineers), was of significant benefit at the siege of Maastricht. Louis XIV took a particular interest in the newly-introduced practice, having first noticed Abraham Fabert's use of it.
12. Hebbert & Rothrock, p. 41.
13. Ibid., p. 54.
14. Halevy, p. 52.
15. Hebbert & Rothrock, pp. 96–7.
16. Thc 'Pre-Carré' (enclosed field) constructed and improved at Vauban's, direction, comprised the fortresses of a first line- Dunkirk, Bergues, Furnes, Knocke, Ypres, Menin, Lille, Tournai, Conde-sur-Escaut, Valenciennes, Le Quesnoy, Mauberge, Phillipeville and Givert with a supporting second line – Gravelines, St Omer, Aire-sur-la Lys, St Venant, Bethune, Arras, Douai, Bouchain, Cambrai, Landrecies, Avesnes, Marlenbourg, Rocroi, Mézières, Sedan and Stenay.
17. Kekewitch, M (ed.), *Princes and Peoples, France and the British Isles, 1620-1714*, 1994, p. 239.
18. Petrie, *Louis XIV*, p. 151.
19. Halevy, p. 40.
20. Petrie, *Louis XIV*, p. 252.
21. Halevy, p. 195.
22. Blomfield, p. 188; see also Lazard, P., *Vauban, 1633-1707*, 1934, p. 94.

Chapter 12: Marshal Berwick

1. Arabella Churchill, the older sister of John Churchill (one day to be the 1st Duke of Marlborough), was a lady in waiting at the court of Charles II of England when she became the mistress of the king's younger brother James, Duke of York (King James II in due course).
2. Petrie, C., *The Marshal Duke of Berwick*, 1953, pp. 28–9.
3. Ibid.
4. Aubrey, P., *The Defeat of James Stuart's Armada, 1692*, 1979, p. 79. See also, McLoughlin, M., *The Wild Geese, the Irish brigades in the service of France and Spain*, 1980, p. 5.
5. Petrie, *The Marshal Duke of Berwick*, pp. 93–4.
6. Aubrey, pp. 119–20.
7. Plantavit De La Pause, p. 333.
8. Petrie, *The Marshal Duke of Berwick*, pp. 102–03.
9. Mitford, p. 183.
10. Petrie, *The Marshal Duke of Berwick*, p. 116.

11. St John, B., vol 1, p. 270.
12. Petrie, *The Marshal Duke of Berwick*, pp. 171–2.
13. Ibid., p. 176.
14. Ibid., p. 182.
15. Ibid., p. 184.
16. Ibid., p. 186.
17. Ibid., p. 187.
18. Plantavit de la Pause, p. 102.
19. Ibid., p. 103.
20. Langallerie, p. 333.
21. Ibid.
22. The Chevalier d'Asfeld, Claude François Bidal, became a Marshal of France in 1734.
23. Petrie, *The Marshal Duke of Berwick*, p. 211.
24. Churchill, Book Two, pp. 223–4.
25. Kamen, H., *Philip V of Spain, the King who Reigned Twice*, 2001, p. 59.
26. Petrie, *The Marshal Duke of Berwick*, p. 217
27. Kamen, p. 67.
28. Ibid., p. 60.
29. Petrie, *The Marshal Duke of Berwick*, p. 222.
30. Ibid., p. 229.
31. Norton, *First Lady at Versailles*, p. 287.
32. Petrie, p. 232.
33. Ibid., pp. 217–18.
34. Ibid., p. 239.
35. Kamen, p. 88.
36. Petrie, *The Marshal Duke of Berwick*, pp. 254–5.
37. Plantavit de la Pause, p. 154.
38. Petrie, *The Marshal Duke of Berwick*, p. 256.
39. Falkner, The War of the Spanish Succession, p. 210.
40. Petrie, *The Marshal Duke of Berwick*, p. 301.
41. Ibid., p. 308.
42. Ibid., p. 317.
43. Pavitt, O., *The Man Who Would be King, Philippe Duc d'Orleans*, 1997, p. 243.
44. Petrie, *The Marshal Duke of Berwick*, p. 321.
45. Plantavit de la Pause has it that this took place in 1725, see p. 156.
46. Ibid., p. 164.
47. Ibid.
48. Petrie, *The Marshal Duke of Berwick*, p. 334.

Bibliography

Allen, M., *Armies and Enemies of Louis XIV, 1688-1714*, 2019.
André, L., *Michel le Tellier, et l'organization de l'armee monarchique*, 1906.
Anon., *Catinat, Marechal de France, Seigneur de Saint Gratien*, 1988 (reprint).
Ashley, M., *Louis XIV and the Greatness of France*, 1964.
Aubrey, P., *The Defeat of James Stuart's Armada, 1692*, 1979.
Baxter, D., *Servants of the Sword, French Intendants of the Army, 1630-1670*, 1976.
Baxter, S., *William III and the Defence of European Liberty, 1650-1792*, 1966.
Belhomme, V., *L'Armée Française en 1690*, 1895.
Berenger, J., *Turenne*, 1987.
Blomfield, R., *Sebastien le Prestre de Vauban, 1633-1707*, 1938.
Chandler, D. (ed.), *Military Memoirs, Captain Robert Parker and the Comte de Merode-Westerloo*, 1968.
__________, *The Art of Warfare in the Age of Marlborough*, 1976.
Chartrand, R., *Louis XIV's Army*, 1988.
Childs, J., *Armies and Warfare in Europe, 1648-1789*, 1982.
__________, *The Nine Years War, and the British Army*, 1991.
Churchill, W., *Marlborough, His Life and Times*, two-book reprint edition, 1947.
Clark, G., *The Later Stuarts*, 1934.
Corvisier, A., *L'Armêe Française de la fin de XVII siècle*, reprint, 1964.
__________, *Les Generaux de Louis XIV et leur origine sociale* (essay), 1959.
__________, *Louvois*, 1983.
Coxe, W., *Memoirs of the Duke of Marlborough* (3 vols) 1847.
Créquy, C., *Memoires pour servir a la vie de Nicholas de Catinat, Marshal of France*, 1775.
Cronin, V., *Louis XIV*, 1964.
De Broglie, E., *Catinat, l'Homme et la Vie, 1637-1712*, 1902.
Doolin, P., *The Fronde*, 1935.
Duffy, C., *The Military Experience in the Age of Reason*, 1987.
Ekberg, C., *The Failure of Louis XIV's Dutch War*, 1979.
El Hage, F., *Vendôme*, 2016 (French History, vol 32).
Falkner, J., *Great and Glorious Days, Marlborough's Battles*, 2002.
__________, *Marlborough's Wars, Eye-Witness Accounts*, 2005.
__________, *Marshal Vauban, and the Defence of Louis XIV's France*, 2012.
__________, *The War of the Spanish Succession, 1701-1714*, 2015.
__________, *Prince Eugene of Savoy*, 2022.
Federn, C., *Cardinal Mazarin*, 1922.
Fitz Patrick, W., *The Great Condé and the Fronde*, 1873.

Francis, D., *The First Peninsula War*, 1974.
Fraser, A., *Love and Louis XIV*, 2006.
Godley, E., *The Great Condé*, 1915.
Halevy, D., *Vauban, Builder of Fortresses*, 1924.
Hatton, R., *Louis XIV and His World*, 1972.
Hebbert, F. and Rothrock, G., *Soldier of France, Sebastien le Prestre de Vauban*, 1990.
Hooper, G., *Marshal Abraham Fabert, His Life and Times*, 1892.
Kamen, H., *The War of the Succession in Spain, 1700-1715*, 1969.
__________, *Philip V of Spain, the King who Reigned Twice*, 2001.
Kosmann, E., *La Fronde*, 1954.
Langallerie, M., *Memoires of the Marquis de Langallerie*, 1710.
Laparelle, J., *Marshal Turenne*, 1907.
Lazard, P., *Vauban, 1633-1707*, 1934.
Lediard, T., *Memoirs of the Duke of Marlborough*, 1736 (3 vols).
Legrand-Girarde, E, *Turenne en Alsace*, 2018 reprint.
Lepage, J-D., *Vauban and the French Military under Louis XIV*, 2009.
Lynn, J., *Giant of the Grand Siècle, the French Army, 1610-1715*, 1996.
__________, *The Wars of Louis XIV, 1664-1714*, 1999.
McCloughlin, M., *The Wild Geese, the Irish Brigades in the service of France and Spain*, 1980.
McKay, D., *Prince Eugene of Savoy*, 1977.
Mitford, N., *The Sun King*, 1966.
Money, D (ed.), *1708, Oudenarde and Lille*, 2008.
Murray, G (ed.), *Letters and Despatches of the Duke of Marlborough*, 1845 (5 vols).
Norton, L., *First Lady of Versailles*, 1978.
__________ (ed.), *St Simon at Versailles*, 1980.
Plantavit de la Pause, G., *The Memoirs of the Duc de Villars, Marshal-General of France*, 1730.
__________, *The Life of James Fitz-James, Duke of Berwick*, 1738.
Paoletti, C., *William III's Italian Ally*, 2019.
Parnell, A., *The War of the Succession in Spain*, 1888.
Pavitt, O., *The Man who would be King, Philippe Duc d'Orleans*, 1997.
Petrie, C., *Louis XIV*, 1938.
__________, *The Marshal, Duke of Berwick*, 1953.
Ramsay, C., *The History of Henri de la Tour d'Auvergne, Viscount de Turenne*, 1740.
Rey, M., *Campagne de Marechal de Tallard en Allemagne, 1704*, 1763.
Rousset, C., *Histoire de Louvois*, 1864 (4 vols).
Rowlands, G., *Louis XIV, Vittorio-Amadeo II, and French military failure in Italy*, 2000.
__________, *The Dynastic State and the Army under Louis XIV*, 2002.
Rule, J., *Louis XIV and the Craft of Kingship*, 1974.
Sautai, M., *Les Manoeuvres de Denain*, 1905.
__________, *La Bataille de Malplaquet*, 1910.
Segur, de, P., *Le Tapissier de Notre-Dame, les Dernière années du maréchal de Luxembourg*, 1903.
Shoberl, F. (tr.), *Memoirs of Prince Eugene of Savoy*, 1811.
Sonnino, P., *Louis XIV and the Origins of the Dutch War*, 1988.

St John, B. (tr. and ed.), *Memoirs of the Duke of St Simon*, 1876 (3 vols).
Stoye, J., *Marsigli's Europe, 1680-1730*, 1994.
Sturgill, C., *Marshal Villars and the War of the Spanish Succession*, 1965.
T'Hopf, B. (ed.), *The Marlborough-Hiensius Correspondence, 1702-1711*, 1951.
Tournoux, P., *Defense des Frontiers*, 1960.
Treasure, G., *Seventeenth Century France*, 1967.
Trevelyan, G., *Select Documents for Queen Anne's Reign*, 1929.
Trevelyan, M., *William III and the Defence of Holland, 1672-1674*, 1930.
Tuetey, L., *Les Officiers sous l'ancien regime*, 1908.
Vauban, S. (ed. Rothrock, G.), *A Manual of Siegecraft and Fortification*, 1969
Vaughan, D., 'Campaigns in the Dauphiny Alps', *English Historical Review*, 1913.
Vogue, de, C. (ed.), *Memoires du Marechal de Villars*, 1895 (5 vols).
Wauters, E., *La Bataille de Steenkerque, Dimanche, 3 Août 1692*, 2018.
Wedgwood, C., *The Thirty Years War*, 1938.
Weygand, M., *Turenne, Marshal of France*, 1930.
__________, *Histoire de l'Armee Français*, 1938.
Wilson, C., *The Duke of Berwick*, 2018 (reprint).
Wolf, J., *Louis XIV*, 1968.
Wykes, A., *The Royal Hampshire Regiment*, 1968.
Ziegler, F., *Villars; Le centurion de Louis XIV*, 1996.

Index